Pete Gordon

Peter · Gordon

fusion

a culinary journey

Peter • Gordon
fusion
a culinary journey

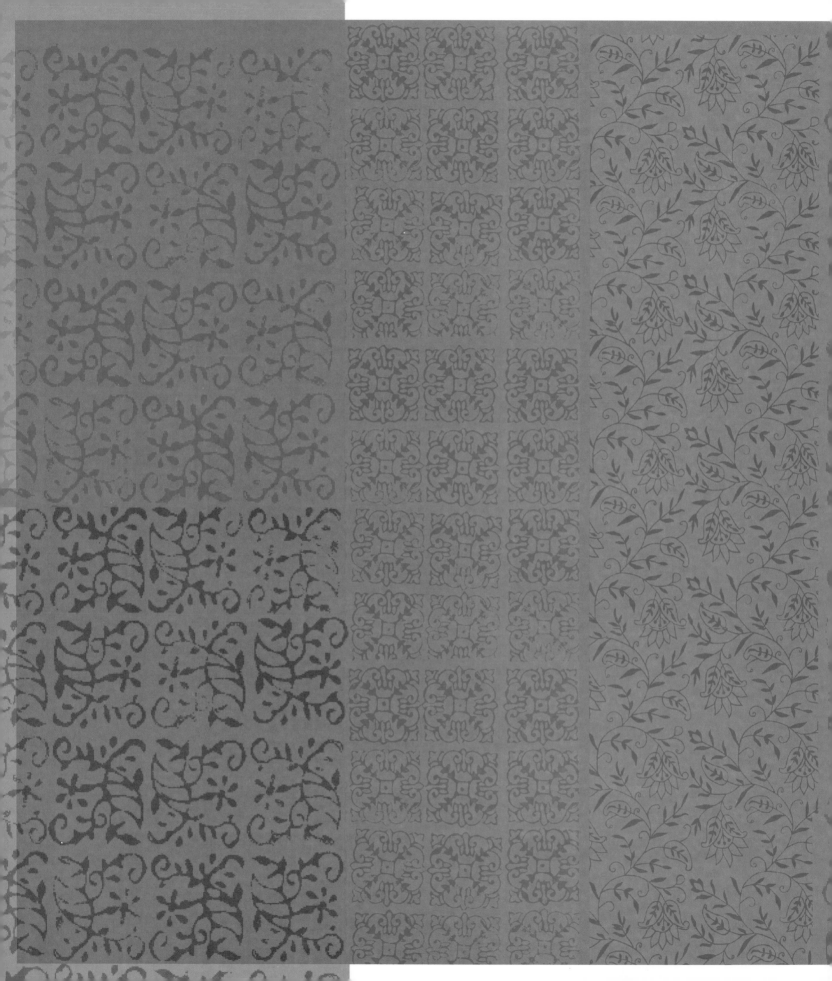

contents

Fusion cuisine: What is it?

The style of food I love cooking, the food that is my life's passion and which, ultimately, I find the most exciting and rewarding of all, is Fusion cuisine.

Fusion cuisine takes as its starting point the belief that any ingredient, from any region of the world, has the potential to be cooked and eaten with any other ingredient from any other part of the world – so long as the result is lip-smackingly delicious. This belief informs everything I do. It's a style of cooking that has enormous potential to continuously surprise and evolve.

It all started for me way back in the late '60s in Wanganui, New Zealand, the town I was born in. In those days, New Zealand's presence was not particularly noticeable on the global culinary radar. In fact, it might be said that many Europeans arriving in New Zealand were somewhat dismayed with what they found there. The ingredients were top quality, due to the endless acreage of grass fields and pollutant-free oceans and rivers, but modern-day basics like a good espresso, avocados, olive oil and fine dining were not in abundance. In fact, they were barely part of the national consciousness. I can remember Dad's mum Molly Gordon, my Gran, once sending us a packet of pine nuts that she'd found on one of her travels; when I tried them I almost spat them out – they were unsalted and untoasted and were nothing like the peanuts I was more familiar with. What was Gran thinking when she bought them, I wondered.

As a young boy, one strangely obsessed with the food pages from women's magazines and TV shows like Graham Kerr's *The Galloping Gourmet* (New Zealand's foremost culinary star to grace the screen around the world), I had two ways I liked to spend my pocket money. I'd either head to Parnell's garden shop on Victoria Avenue to buy plants for the garden at home, or to the big supermarket nearby to buy 'exotic' ingredients. I can remember when this supermarket had a European cheese promotion and I saved and saved in order to be able to buy some. I must have been around 12 at the time, and when I'd saved enough cash I went in and discovered exotic tins and red wax-wrapped shapes, all of which were *cheese* – I thought I'd gone to Culinary Heaven. In those days cheese was always bought as a large half-kilogram chunk, cut from an even larger slab, and it was either eaten grilled on toast or cut into cubes, put onto toothpicks, and stuck in an apple as part of a buffet. I have moved on, you'll be pleased to know, but as a young kid from a small New Zealand town, with no gastronomic tradition supporting me, this is what I thought good food was all about.

Moving to Melbourne, Australia, in 1981, aged 18, I discovered an alternative culinary universe – and the music of Grace Jones. Here was a city inhabited by people from all over the world: from Italy, Greece, Vietnam, Poland, France, Korea, Spain, Africa and America – every country I'd ever read about. I was so amazed at meeting people who didn't speak English and who didn't count mashed potatoes as part of their diet. What these people had in common was an obsession with their own national cuisines, eating things I'd simply never heard of, from *kim chee* through to *andouillette* and cous cous.

I completed a four-year cookery apprenticeship, attending William Angliss College every Friday for three of those years, and, although I wasn't aware of it at the time, this is where my Fusion cuisine philosophy was initiated.

I'd eat at numerous restaurants, which were surprisingly affordable even on apprenticeship wages, and would usually discover a new ingredient or technique that would just blow me away. I can still remember eating silken tofu for the first time at Kuni's restaurant off Bourke Street. It was the most amazing thing I'd ever tasted. Served simply, cut into a large cube, sitting in a beautiful *raku*-fired pottery bowl with an ice cube and cold water, it was topped with finely grated daikon (*mooli* radish) and served with *tamari* (wheat-free soy sauce) on the side. Simple, subtle, beautiful. I fell in love with tofu at that instant, even though I'd been eating the more readily available spongy tofu for years.

I went to college and begged that they teach us about this amazing ingredient but was quickly told that I was at college to learn about cooking – not how to serve raw fish and bean curd which was how my teachers viewed Japanese food. I was gutted. And this is pretty much how my apprenticeship years went. I'd taste an aromatic Thai coconut fish curry at a Brunswick Street restaurant and ask my lecturers to teach me the intricacies of Thai cuisine, but would be told that wasn't really a classic cuisine either. College, in those days, focussed instead on Europe, Escoffier, thirty things to do with eggs and ice carving!

So, I'd head off to strange-smelling food stores, where I couldn't understand anything spoken by the staff or written on the packaging, and buy things that either looked or smelled intriguing. Home I'd go with my new purchase and see what I could do with it. I didn't buy cookbooks in those days, so I never followed classical, ethnic recipes which might have led me along a more traditional path. Instead, when it was my turn to cook something for my flatmates, I'd simply open the cupboard and create something from the ever-growing range of ingredients I'd gathered. Maybe a pumpkin soup seasoned with Japanese miso and Thai galangal, topped with a little braised Chinese pak choy and Turkish feta. Or a braised beef shin stew with Chinese wood fungus, Japanese seaweed and dried Italian porcini mushrooms, served with Moroccan harissa-spiced mashed sweet potatoes and green beans tossed with Chinese fermented yellow soy beans(!). It was during this time I realised that ingredients from different countries *could* be served in harmony, and I wondered why we were always taught at college to only respect tradition.

One person who did encourage me, apart from my hungry flatmates and family, was my last employer in Melbourne, Tony Rogalsky. Tony helped nurture my enquiring mind and taste buds. He'd let me experiment with staff dinners when I first started cooking for him, and as I became a more senior chef at his restaurant, Rogalsky's, he'd allow small hints of what I was doing to appear on the menu. I can remember playing around with my own Indian curry spice mix, using about 18 spices, which seemed incredibly exotic. He also encouraged my pickled vegetable and pickled fruit obsession, and many other parts of my evolving Fusion repertoire.

However, to some less experienced and possibly nervous cooks, and to a reasonably large number of restaurant chefs and critics, Fusion represents not only a momentary fad to be derided and insulted, but also a threat, a threat to traditional culinary values. Apparently, it's not worthwhile. It's a jumble of ingredients put together seemingly with little skill, with, at best, a childish and unrefined playfulness; at worst, a juvenile arrogance and wanton disregard for tradition. If I'm being honest, unfortunately this can sometimes be the case. For myself, however, and for the many adventurous and open-minded supporters of Fusion cuisine, it allows a unique freedom to use the world's extraordinary, myriad ingredients from far-flung regions, in delicious combinations – whether they be potatoes (originally from Peru), vanilla beans (Mexico), *nam pla* (Thai fish sauce), broccoli (Italy), tamarind (tropical Africa), raspberries (Scotland!), soy (Asia) or Argan oil (Morocco). This list is, obviously, endless.

Historically, and I'm talking ancient times here, ingredients were mostly local and regional due to the difficulties of transporting them and keeping them in a fresh and edible state once they were on the move. The transportation of dried spices was the one major exception, and the fairly common contemporary use of these, and the perception that they are part of our everyday traditional cooking repertoire, derive from the evolution of the legendary Silk Road. This road was, in fact, around 9000 kilometres of many interconnected 'paths', some of which were on land, others operating by river and sea. These paths allowed the transportation, exchange and trade of many items, some of which were food, by merchants, monks, traders and nomads. Various civilisations dating back to the Han Dynasty (which itself is credited with expanding the already existing trade routes in the first place around 100 BC) began to have contact with other civilisations from Mesopotamia, Persia, Egypt, Rome, India and Mediterranean Europe. This has meant that many of today's national cuisines have developed as a direct result of this extraordinary

absorption and reinvention of foreign influences – historical Fusion.

Pomegranate molasses is a relatively new import into Europe from Asia, unlike, for example, dried saffron, ground ginger or cardamom, which, although 'exotic' originally, have now been commonplace for centuries. These spices have been considered a 'traditional' ingredient in dishes dating back hundreds of years, and when used today in a recipe of whatever provenance, let's say English gingerbread, the dish is still considered a 'classic'. Even if we were to add dried dates to our cake, it would manage to remain traditional as our grandmothers always had dried dates in their pantries – well Molly Gordon did anyway – and dates seem for many to be part of the classical repertoire of ingredients. However, the moment we dare to add, say, lovely sweet and sour pomegranate molasses (one of many recent interlopers to have infiltrated the Western culinary consciousness), our English ginger loaf apparently becomes something quite different, what some critics might term a messed-about Fusion version of a classic. Not so. Dates and pomegranates have been grown and harvested in the same areas of the world for centuries. Therefore it seems it is in their application, the modernity of their inclusion in so-called classical fare, rather than their geographical provenance, which makes all the difference. I must point out that Worcestershire sauce, a very traditional British condiment, has tamarind in it which originated in Tropical Africa. Yet, we don't consider this sauce a Fusion concept. Why not? Because, put simply, time breeds familiarity. Historical Fusion is acceptable. To its critics, modern Fusion isn't.

While chefs in the Western world have happily been using dried herbs and spices from around the globe for centuries, incorporating them into their national cuisine, they haven't historically been able to source fresh, exotic fish, meat, fruit and vegetables. In recent years though, travel, freight and refrigeration have improved immensely, and so the melting pot of various cuisines has been made even richer and more dense now that modern societies are able to sample fresh ingredients from many exotic locations. In London we take for granted the ability to source green papaya and the delicious fruit, mangosteen, from South-East Asia. Fresh wild salmon and grouse get flown down to us at the start of their seasons, and white Italian truffles are freighted over to the USA with much fanfare. I have to say the best book I have read on the subject of food and travel is *Moveable Feasts* by Sarah Murray, and I'd recommend you read it. It's informative and fascinating.

But food is also a political force, one that has helped to shape history in many unexpected ways. One example is a small, sub-tropical evergreen bush, a member of the camellia family from China. Tea. The growing British demand and desire for tea (which led to the 1839–1860 Opium Wars in China) has had huge historical repercussions. Similarly, the belief that nutmeg would ward off, or even cure the plague, led, in a very roundabout way, to the claiming of Manhattan for the British (read the wonderful *Nathaniel's Nutmeg* by Giles Milton). Even in recent history, there are tales of ocean 'battles' over various fish species that were once plentiful off the British coast, the Pacific and in South-East Asia, between large factory-ships and smaller day-boats. Economic and political sanctions were the outcome.

So, who is to say that we must never experiment with so-called classical dishes? I realise that once a recipe has been altered it is no longer the classic it once was,

but why not try using Vietnamese fish sauce to season a traditional Lancashire meat stew in place of salt, and adding a little tamarind to counteract the inherent sweetness of the meat and vegetables? The dish may well benefit from this cross-cultural play. It will definitely change its character, but surely if it tastes good, or even if it tastes intriguingly different, that can be seen as a positive thing. After all, the classic version still remains for generations to enjoy; and the refreshed version can equally be appreciated with absolutely no harm done to the old in the pursuit of the new.

Without historical Fusion, the Italians wouldn't be able to serve classical polenta or risotto at their tables, as obviously corn and maize are from the New World – the Americas as it was once called – and rice hails from tropical and sub-tropical southern Asia. Thai cuisine would have neither chillies nor peanuts as these ingredients also hail from the New World – and there would be no coriander tossed over their luscious coconut curries as this aromatic herb started life in south-west Asia, north-west Africa and the Mediterranean. Ratatouille would be absent from the repertoire of French cuisine as the tomatoes required for this classic dish originated in the New World and its aubergines in India. And the British have Peru to thank for their national vegetable, the potato, and China to thank for their tea. In New Zealand we think of feijoa and tamarillo as being national fruits – but they are, in fact, both from South America. And where would a pavlova be in Australia or New Zealand without a slathering of fresh passionfruit pulp (South American) or some sliced kiwifruit (Chinese)? If you were to trace the individual sources of all of the classic ingredients from each classical cuisine, I promise you'd be amazed at the vast and incredible range of their countries of origin.

Without this extraordinary historical Fusion of ingredients, many cuisines would be so much less intense and flavoursome. And it's with this in mind that contemporary Fusion cuisine promotes the introduction of foreign ingredients into our everyday lives here and now, to enrich and stimulate us. Fusion cuisine refuses to adhere to politically or geographically drawn borders created generations ago by men in robes or suits, which forbid that you must ever mix, for example, Herb A from the North with Protein B from a region in the South. Food doesn't obey borders and checkpoints. It's on the move and always has been. To force it to conform to political boundaries smacks just a little of culinary fascism.

Modern Fusion cuisine allows you the possibility to create perhaps the most stimulating, gorgeous meal you'll ever experience. Yes, it can be fun and yes, it can be playful, but never forget, it is as challenging as any other cuisine, requiring thought, commonsense and a good palate to achieve it.

Fusion is, therefore, simply one of many cuisines, happily sitting amongst them like a benevolent magpie, borrowing highlights from them all, and in the process creating new highlights of its own. This is surely something worth doing.

New Zealand is, of course, where my culinary journey starts.

I tend to have an image of myself as a contemporary, cross-cultural mix of ancient Scottish whaler (John Stenton Workman, born 1817 in Edinburgh) and a Maori 'princess' of Ngati Kahungunu origin ('Ellen' Rewhaunga [Kokoroiti], born Te Kopi, 1820) – which is actually the truth. I was born in a seaside river town called Wanganui in 1963. My parents Bruce and Betty (or Timmy as she's always been known) already had three daughters born within four years, so when I joined the family, creative and inventive food wasn't something that Mum could focus on. She had to slave over the stove for hours every day just to keep us fed - like many women of her time. Food was very much a practical, must-do task, simply keeping everyone alive and growing. Mum's style of cuisine in those days would best be described as informal: simple fare, well cooked, using limited ingredients. On the other hand, my paternal grandmother, Molly Gordon, treated dinner time as a formal occasion when Grandpa Will would inform her, and us, when we were staying at their house in Cavendish Square, Wellington, of his day's comings and goings. Dessert would always be served from a wooden trolley which she'd wheel in after we'd cleared the mains. The same trolley came to represent afternoon tea for me, and my siblings, as Gran would load it with all sorts of seemingly fancy things such as caramel shortbread (made with boiled condensed milk), Vegemite toasts (made from leftover white bread that she'd bake smothered in butter and Vegemite until crunchy), melting moments and yo-yos (typical New Zealand biscuits), oat slices and the like. Gran would also make strange, unfamiliar things such as lemon

sago pudding and fly cemetery (cold bread and butter pudding layered with sultanas which represented the departed flies). We ate jellies at almost every meal, jellies that she'd set in her reliable thin metal moulds (one of which I used for my pomegranate panna cotta on page 236).

In Wanganui, food and eating was somewhat more practical. My sisters and I were each allocated a small vegetable patch in the back yard and we'd battle trying to outdo each other's crop production. We also each had a dedicated apple tree. We'd grow corn, beans, tomatoes, pumpkin, potatoes, apple cucumbers and regular cucumbers. We had a fantastic passionfruit vine that grew along the garage wall, producing hundreds of fruit each summer. My very first memory of cooking anything at all comes from this time, when I would have been about four years old, helping Mum make an apple pie on the bench of our kitchen, the apples from our own trees. However, also around this time, things changed drastically at home when my parents divorced. Amongst many changes, my youngest sister Tracey and I went to live with our Gran, Molly, for a while in Wellington, whilst Vicki and Donna moved up to Auckland with Mum. Molly's mother, Great Grandma Shout, was living with her as well, so the house was filled with three out of four of the family's generations of living relatives. Tracey and I were in awe of Grandma Shout as she seemed very powerful, very old and very scary in equal measures - in fact, it was her grandfather, John Workman, a part-time whaler amongst many things, who was one of the first wave of Pakeha (white) settlers in New Zealand.

Gran used to take us to Seatoun beach to collect seaweed from the foreshore. We'd tie it in bundles behind her old Wolseley car and drag it back to her compost heap, the stones falling out along the way, where she'd ferment it to make a wonderful liquid fertiliser. She'd also let us help her roll out pastry for tarts, shape biscuits, stir chutneys, peel vegetables and help serve dinner. Gran used food as a way to keep us busy, as much as to keep us fed, and when I look back at this time, I realise that this is probably when it first occurred to me that the preparation, cooking and eating of food was in many ways a social event, not only a way to fill your stomach.

Much in the family continued to change over the following year. Tracey began primary school and I, kindergarten, and we no doubt ate our way through numerous roast, boiled, grilled and braised animals – as well as the odd cake. Gran would make a shoulder of mutton last forever, first by slowly roasting it for a main meal, then by cooking the leftovers with barley to make a hearty soup, and finally by making stock from the bones for a light consommé-type broth – although consommé was certainly never a word we would have used. Gran had lived through a Depression and had learnt to be thrifty, and her gold-mining forebears had even been known to boil up river stones with water and manuka (a native tree) to provide a daily meal. Gran grew pumpkins in an unusual way too, trailing the runners up onto the branches of the huge macrocarpa trees that bordered her property so that when she needed to pick one, she'd just cut it down from the tree. The trees themselves looked like they had Halloween lanterns in them.

Eventually the four siblings were reunited and we all went to live with Dad back in Wanganui – and continued our gardening. By now, we had a pet sheep, named Lamb Chops after the TV show hosted by Sharee Lewis. She was a fantastic addition to the household because although we weren't living in the countryside, we had a farmyard pet which gave us a bit of kudos amongst our school friends. The only annoying thing about her, though, was that she'd leave droppings all over the backyard that we'd have to take turns at cleaning up. I guess, ultimately, we became a bit bored with Lamb Chops. One day we came home from school and she was gone, but we thought nothing

of it. A few weeks later, having a Sunday roast dinner, Dad informed us that we were eating our previously beloved pet sheep. Vicki literally spat the food out and ran screaming from the table to become vegetarian for a while. That was when we learnt the connection between life and death, food and function, pets and practicalities.

At this time a Cockney woman called Rosemary had moved in along with her children, Cindy and Dean, to help Dad look after us and the house. I continued to cook cakes, fudge and biscuits and the like, from recipes I'd cut out of women's magazines and the ever-popular and indispensable *Edmond's Cookbook*, and I knew that one day I'd become a chef. I knew without a doubt that that was what I'd do with my life: travelling lots, cooking all around the globe and experiencing wonderful times. I'd wear a big, tall, white chef hat and make soufflés and hollandaise sauce and cook for royalty at banquets. When I was seven, I was helping Dad cook dinner one night, more likely getting in the way as much as anything else, whilst Rose was bathing Cindy and Dean and my sisters were watching the TV show *Julia*. I went out to check how everything was cooking and climbed up onto the slightly wobbly stool. The unthinkable happened and I fell off, grabbing something to steady my fall – which, unfortunately, was the deep-fryer itself along with its contents. I tipped a good 3 litres of boiling beef dripping (rendered ourselves from carcasses Dad and his mates would break down in the garage), and the family's fish and chips on top of me and ruined that night's dinner. I spent quite a lot of time over the next few years in hospital, eventually having a skin-graft, but I have to say I have never been put off cooking, and I have a macabre love of deep-fried foods.

Whilst I was in hospital my father married Rose and eventually our Wanganui family was joined by my brother Craig. Around the same time, Vicki and Donna moved up to Auckland to live permanently with Mum and her new husband, and we soon welcomed a baby brother, Shaun, into the family. At this point, aged eight, I found I had gone from having three siblings to seven, which was fantastic. Living with Dad and Rose in Wanganui meant that Tracey and I got to do lots of outdoor things such as helping Dad and his mates with their summer fishing off Castlecliff beach; digging for *toheroa* (really large flat oval clam-type shellfish) on lower west coast beaches of the North Island, and crayfishing and paua-gathering at Ngawi on the bottom of the North Island where we'd stay in an old woolshed, also used to store bales of agar seaweed destined for Japan. Dad always owned a dinghy or a boat of some sort and we'd have fishing rods, set-nets and flounder nets with us whenever we went camping as Dad loved the fact we could contribute to the daily meal. He's a bit of a hunter-gatherer and an awesome father. One Christmas day Dad, brother Dean, a neighbour from Wanganui and I were off the northern tip of the Coromandel Peninsula, fishing a few kilometres offshore in our tiny 3-metre aluminium dinghy. *Jaws*, the movie, had come out that summer. As we sat in the dinghy not long after sunrise with our lines overboard hoping to catch our lunch, two enormous grey fins appeared side by side about 500 metres behind us. We gave a united, fear-filled groan and Dad told me to pull the anchor in as he headed inshore – our tiny horsepower Seagull outboard-motor opened to full throttle. The fins appeared again, having turned towards us and now only about 300 metres away. Suddenly, from my white lips, the theme tune from *Jaws* issued forth. I simply couldn't stop myself. Dad realised I hadn't pulled in the anchor and quickly did so, explaining that to a hungry shark the spinning trailing anchor would look like a fleeing tuna and its next meal. Dad and I were talking about this incident recently and to this day he has no idea what the beasts were but he was as terrified as we were.

Aged 15, I applied to become an apprentice chef with Air New Zealand. I loved this time in my youth as I got to fly down to Wellington, the capital, and stay with my cousin Lynnette – an inspirational foodie to me – she even used olive oil to dress her salads, which was unheard of at the time. After several interviews, I was eventually turned down, which was a huge blow as I'd thought it would be a great way to learn to cook and travel at the same time. So, I thought long and hard about my future, aged all of 16, and decided that what I now wanted to do above all things was to become a winemaker and own my own vineyard. I have no idea why I thought this was such a great idea as my family didn't really drink wine at all. My glamorous, wonderful Mum only drank sweetish Muller Thürgau

and Moselle from a cask in those days and New Zealand wasn't really producing world-renowned wines as it does now. However, I began my studies for a Bachelor in Horticultural Science at Massey University in Palmerston North in 1981, aged 17. After three months I realised that this probably wasn't quite right either. If I were to become a great winemaker I decided that I should really head to Australia and study at one of the prestigious wine colleges there. My mother had offered to shout me a holiday trip to Australia for my 18th birthday and so I decided I should use the ticket to get me there and then get a job cooking in one of the outback mines(!) to save enough money to get me through college. I decided that I would work for my father for four months at his engineering workshop to save some money before heading to Oz. Synchronising my departure with Di and Charles's marriage, I flew to Melbourne a week after the huge event to begin *my* next big adventure.

In 1986, I returned to New Zealand to set up the kitchen of a Wellington restaurant called The Sugar Club. The owners Ashley and Vivian had a site, but no chef, and no idea what the food concept would be, and I was in London wanting to head back to New Zealand to see my father who wasn't well. It was in the kitchen at The Sugar Club that I first began mixing and fusing ingredients in a really planned, organised way – dishes to be sold to the dining public. Previously, I'd simply mixed up whatever was in the cupboard at home as a way to create a meal wherever I was living at the time. We were the first restaurant in town to mix Asian and Western ingredients together which appealed enormously to the regulars who realised that this was the start of something new and exciting. We made all our own bread as well as goat's cheese, ice creams and parfaits, chutneys and preserves. We dried our own tomatoes before sun-dried tomatoes took over most restaurants' menus. I had a truly wonderful time creating and experimenting with a new-found freedom, and this is also where Michael McGrath, my partner for over 20 years, and I first met. In 1989, Michael and I headed to London and another culinary chapter began.

Between 1995 and 2005 I returned to New Zealand at least once a year, often cooking at culinary events and the like. One such event I cooked at several times was the Seresin Vineyard Waterfall Bay Dinners, which the world-renowned film director of photography and vineyard owner Michael Seresin organises. Michael is one of those many New Zealanders, like myself, who have made their living and career primarily outside New Zealand, but who, like so many ex-pats, love their homeland with a passion. In many ways we've both probably contributed more to New Zealand's reputation by being based offshore than if we'd been living there full time, although Michael now spends much more of the year at his fantastic vineyard in Marlborough and his amazing home in the Marlborough Sounds.

My next major New Zealand culinary adventure began in 2005 when I was asked to be consultant executive chef to a new restaurant in a five-star hotel in Auckland, the SKYCITY Grand Hotel. The restaurant is called dine by Peter Gordon, not something that slips off the tongue easily, but fairly descriptive of what it is. Eighteen months later, I helped set up Bellota, a wonderful contemporary (not really Fusion as such) Spanish tapas bar which is also part of the SKYCITY group, and also very successful. In the kitchens at dine and Bellota, my chefs have also learned to appreciate the creative possibilities and excitement that new ingredients bring, which is what really excites and drives me. Ironically, I have also been a consultant chef to Air New Zealand for over 13 years now. I think having travelled and had so many food-led adventures all over the globe, I'm probably able to contribute a great deal more to the passengers' culinary experience than I would have previously, if I had completed my apprenticeship with them. In 2006, Michael McGrath and I also joined forces with Auckland businessman Steve Cozens, and award-winning New Zealand winemaker Michelle Richardson, when we set up Waitaki Braids Vineyard in North Otago. So, although I never managed an apprenticeship with Air New Zealand, and I never really even began studying oenology, I have, in fact, achieved both of those goals in my life.

I've also witnessed the amazing creation and nurturing of a vibrant food culture in New Zealand, one that in the short space of 25 years has gone from a meat and three vegetables mentality, to one where people are loyal to their favourite local olive oil or saffron producer. They have their preferred grape varietals and salad greens. New vegetables in differing forms keep hitting the supermarket shelves and farmers' markets have appeared all around the country. In Wanganui, they are even growing olives, which I would never have thought possible, and the olive oil coming from these trees is truly exceptional. You can find these at the bustling Wanganui Farmers' Market on the banks of the Whanganui River. Look out too for Annette Main's famous bread – called Peter Gordon's kumara bread! Our lamb and farmed venison have been highly rated around the world for many years but we now also breed Wagyu beef in several areas, the best coming from the Firstlight herds in Hawke's Bay – meltingly rich with really deep textured flesh and tasty fat. Kate White and her husband Pete Irving are producing wonderful organic honey in Kurow, just down the road from our vineyard, and their organic beeswax is being used offshore by one of the world's most ethical pharmaceutical companies. Wasabi is now grown in several places around the country – needing pure water as it does, New Zealand is a natural habitat. Our indigenous herbs kawa kawa and horopito are used in numerous ways from flavouring muffins, dressings, rubs and marinades, to the cooking of food in a hangi – an earth oven that Maori introduced from the Pacific. In fact, I created and cooked a gourmet hangi at Turangawaewae marae, home of the Maori King, in May 2009. Hangi food is moist and succulent and the spectacle of hangi is something all visitors should experience. Our wines are world class, with our winemakers travelling around the globe, consulting to vineyards in South America, Europe and the USA, with many European winemakers now coming to New Zealand to see how we do it and taking some of our know-how back to the old countries.

All in all, contemporary New Zealand is a brilliant place to have a great foodie experience. Our produce is world class, the clarity of flavour second to none and our producers, farmers, restaurateurs, fishermen and winemakers are keen to show the world that this group of Pacific islands, with just over four million people, is well up to speed when it comes to producing mouth-watering food and flavoursome wines.

one.
canapés,
tapas
& nibbles

Kumara, spinach & feta tortilla with sumac & yoghurt

There are really two tortillas in the culinary world. The Mexican corn- or flour-based wrap, and the Spanish potato, onion and egg omelette. To make it a little more confusing, the Italians have their frittata which in many ways is just like the Spanish tortilla, although you'll find it made with the addition of spinach, cheese and other ingredients. For the sake of this chapter, as tapas make up quite a few of the recipes, I've called this a tortilla in honour of Spain – albeit a non-traditional Fusion version. Kumara are a sweet potato indigenous to New Zealand, but you can simply replace them here with regular sweet potatoes or even baking potatoes. Sumac is produced by grinding up a red berry, most of which are sourced from the Middle East. It has an astringent and sour taste to it and is traditionally sprinkled over tomatoes, salads, grilled fish and flat breads.

Makes 1 tortilla – which could be cut into 4 as a light lunch, or cut into 20 tapa-sized pieces

300 g kumara, scrubbed
80 ml olive oil
1 red onion, peeled and thinly sliced
3 large eggs
80 g feta, diced
50 g raw spinach, coarsely shredded
60 g thick yoghurt
1 clove garlic, peeled and finely chopped
1 Tbsp sumac

Preheat oven to 180 °C. Cut the kumara roughly into 1-cm dice and toss with a quarter of the olive oil and some salt and pepper. Lay on a baking tray lined with parchment and roast until cooked.

Meanwhile, sauté the onion in half the remaining oil until caramelised, stirring often.

Break the eggs into a bowl and mix in the onion and kumara while still a little warm, then add the feta and spinach and season lightly, depending on how salty your feta is.

Heat up a 20-cm frying-pan until it's quite hot and then add all but 1 Tablespoon of the remaining oil. Once that gets hot, add the mixture slowly and leave it for 10 seconds. Then, using a spatula, begin to bring the cooked outer edges into the centre and move the runny centre to the outside. This allows the tortilla to cook more evenly, and stops it overcooking which will make it a little dry. After a minute, flatten the top with a spatula, turn the heat to medium–low and place a lid on the pan. Cook the tortilla for 2 minutes, at which point the outer edges will be set and golden. Place under a grill, or in the oven, until the middle and the top have set.

Leave to sit in the pan for 2 minutes, then gently shake it from side to side to loosen the tortilla before carefully inverting the pan onto a plate and tipping the tortilla out. Leave it to cool.

Mix the remaining Tablespoon of olive oil into the yoghurt along with the garlic.

To serve: Cut the tortilla into bite-sized chunks and dollop on the yoghurt and then sprinkle with the sumac.

Goat's cheese fritters stuffed with Thai basil, with sherry vinegar, palm sugar syrup & almonds

These delicious fritters are based on an incredibly simple but completely moreish tapa which has been on my menu at Bellota, the tapas bar I created in 2006 in Auckland, New Zealand, since the day we opened. At Bellota, we simply roll goat's cheese into balls and deep-fry them, but here they're made even more special by stuffing them with Thai basil, although if you're stuck for this particular herb then stuff them with a mixture of basil and coriander instead. They're very popular and we sell them by the truckload. The sherry vinegar and palm sugar combo makes for a great dip and even though they're already crunchy from the panko crumbs, the addition of almonds is the finishing touch.

For 4 per (1 per person) as a tapas or make them smaller and get 6–8

200 g goat's cheese – something like a French chèvre or Spanish Monte Enebro
a small handful of Thai basil leaves
2 Tbsp grated or chopped pale palm sugar
10 ml (2 tsp) sherry vinegar
3 Tbsp flour
1 small egg, beaten
½ cup panko (Japanese breadcrumbs)
vegetable oil for deep-frying
10 toasted almonds, roughly chopped

Bring the cheese to room temperature and divide into four equal pieces.

Reserve a few Thai basil leaves for garnish, then pound the rest into a rough paste using a mortar and pestle, or shred them.

One at a time, using your hands, form the goat's cheese into a ball. Poke a finger into the centre and spoon, pipe or poke a quarter of the basil paste into the hole. Fold the cheese back over the hole and form back into a ball. Do the same with the remainder, then place the balls in the fridge to firm up for 10 minutes.

Place the palm sugar, sherry vinegar and 2 teaspoons of water in a small pan and slowly bring to the boil, making sure the sugar dissolves. Simmer for a few minutes, until the syrup thickens a bit, then take off the heat.

Roll the balls in the flour then coat in the beaten egg. Roll them in the breadcrumbs making sure you press the crumbs on firmly. Place back in the fridge for at least 30 minutes to again firm up.

In a pot large enough to hold them all in one layer, bring 5 cm of the vegetable oil to 180 °C. Add the reserved Thai basil leaves and fry until they stop sizzling then remove with a slotted spoon onto kitchen paper. Lower the balls into the hot oil off the back of a slotted spoon and cook for 2 minutes or so, at which point they'll be a lovely golden colour. On the off-chance that they pop open while frying – which can sometimes happen – just remove them and finish them in a hot oven. This is simply the moisture from the cheese escaping. Once they're cooked, remove them from the oil and lay on kitchen paper for a few minutes to cool down.

To serve: Simply serve them on a plate with the dipping sauce in a small bowl and the almonds and deep-fried basil leaves scattered on top.

An egg poached in black vinegar, truffle oil, chilli & spring onions on Parmesan mashed potato

This tapa really is quite fun, and definitely quirky. The pairing of the black spiced vinegar and truffle oil is wonderful, and when you combine that with the chilli and the Parmesan mash it's even better. Many years ago, I ate a poached egg at the chef's table in the kitchen at Arzak restaurant in San Sebastian and it made me wonder for ages how they'd managed to flavour a poached egg whilst also cooking it perfectly. Juan Mari Arzak and his daughter Elena were both on that night, and I suppose I could have asked them, but I didn't. What I came up with is a more home-handyman approach – wrapping it in plastic wrap along with the flavourings, and then poaching the 'package'. Black vinegar is a spiced and sweetened vinegar from China which is utterly delicious. There are many differing styles – but find one that contains most of the following: rice vinegar, glutinous rice, sugar, salt, spices and orange peel. Yum. And if you can't find it, I give a good cheat's recipe below.

For 4

Cheat's black vinegar

50 ml rice vinegar (or balsamic vinegar)
10 ml (2 tsp) soy sauce
10 g Muscovado or demerara sugar
3 strips orange rind – fresh or dried
2 cloves

Bring everything to a simmer, cook for 2 minutes, then leave to infuse for an hour before passing through a fine sieve.

1 large potato, 300 g, peeled and sliced
30 g grated Parmesan, plus a few shavings to garnish
30 ml (2 Tbsp) extra virgin olive oil
20 ml (4 tsp) black vinegar
5 ml (1 tsp) white truffle-flavoured oil
½ red chilli, thinly sliced
1 spring onion, thinly sliced
4 eggs

Place the potato into a pot, cover with cold water and add a teaspoon of salt. Bring to the boil and cook until done, then drain and mash with the Parmesan and all but 1 teaspoon of the olive oil. Keep warm, although this can be reheated.

Unroll 40 cm of plastic wrap then fold it to create a double-thickness piece 20-cm long without any air bubbles in it. Make four of these. Line four tea cups with these sheets and divide 2 teaspoons of the vinegar amongst them. Divide the truffle oil amongst them as well, then scatter half the chilli in and half the spring onion. Crack an egg into each cup and scatter with the remaining chilli and most of the spring onion.

Pull the plastic wrap edges together, then, making sure you squeeze out any excess air, create what would best be described as a huge tear-drop with the egg in the centre. Put a rubber band or kitchen tie around the top to seal each bag.

Bring a 2-litre pot of water to the boil then gently drop the egg bags in the water. Bring back to the boil, then turn the heat down to a rapid simmer and cook the eggs for 8 minutes at which point the yolks will still be runny but the whites set. Carefully remove the egg bags from the water and lay on a tray.

To serve: Divide the mash amongst four small warmed plates. Carefully unwrap the eggs, it may be helpful to snip them open with a pair of scissors. Place each egg and its cooking 'juices' on the mash, drizzle with the reserved black vinegar then scatter over the remaining spring onion and Parmesan shavings and eat piping hot.

A deep-fried egg with lime chilli dressing, garam masala & crispy shallots

I've had a version of this dish on the menu at the Tapa Room since the day we opened in August 2001. However, what I like about this one in particular is the addition of garam masala, a spice mix from India. I've eaten deep-fried eggs similar to this in South-East Asia (without the garam masala), but have also read about a Moroccan/Egyptian version, *Baid Mutajjan*, in a cookbook by one of my favourite authors, Claudia Roden – *A New Book of Middle Eastern Food*. In this version, the eggs are hard-boiled before frying them and then serving them as an accompaniment to a main meal.

For 4

4 eggs

2 juicy limes

10 g (1 Tbsp) grated pale palm sugar (if it's a soft sugar just measure it out)

½ bird's eye chilli, thinly sliced (more or less to taste) or any other red chilli

1 tsp fish sauce

a small thumb of ginger, peeled then finely julienned or chopped

vegetable oil for deep-frying the eggs

1 Tbsp garam masala (recipe follows)

a small handful of fresh coriander leaves

1 spring onion, finely sliced

1 Tbsp crispy shallots (buy these from Asian food stores or make them yourself - see following page)

Bring a pot of water to the boil then carefully lower the eggs in on a slotted spoon and bring back to the boil. For a medium-sized egg, boil 4½ minutes. Take the eggs from the boiling water and place in a bowl, then take to the sink and run cold water over them for 2 minutes to cool them down. Leave the eggs in the water for a few more minutes, then peel them. Once peeled, place back in the bowl of water – this stops them collapsing on themselves if their yolks are still quite soft.

Meanwhile, finely grate the zest from half of one of the limes into a bowl. Add the palm sugar and chilli and mash it together. Squeeze the juice from the limes over this mixture, you need 40–50 ml, and mix until the sugar has dissolved. Stir in the fish sauce and ginger and leave for a few minutes.

Heat 6 cm of vegetable oil to 180 °C. I find it best to deep-fry the eggs in a medium-sized deep pan as the eggs can splatter a bit. Carefully remove the eggs from their bath and lay on kitchen paper, then roll them around a little to remove excess water. Carefully lower them into the oil and move them around a little to colour them evenly. They're ready when they turn a dark golden brown. Remove them from the oil, place on fresh kitchen paper briefly to absorb excess oil, then roll on a plate scattered with the garam masala.

To serve: Place the eggs on 4 individual plates and scatter with the coriander and spring onion. Drizzle on the lime chilli dressing and finish with the crispy shallots.

There's one thing that's certain about garam masala (literally 'hot spices') – every North Indian and Pakistani food lover will tell you that their recipe is the best of all, handed down by generation after generation of wonderful family cooks. At least that's what my friends say. There really is no definitive recipe, but here is mine, based on many experiments, various mood swings and a little eavesdropping. As with all spice mixtures, make this in small batches as and when you need it as spices deteriorate once you grind them.

For ⅓ cup

Garam masala

8-cm cinnamon quill, snapped into smaller pieces
2 Tbsp green cardamom seeds (not the pods)
1 Tbsp black peppercorns
1 Tbsp black cumin seeds
1 Tbsp coriander seeds
2 tsp whole cloves
1 tsp freshly grated nutmeg
1 tsp fennel seeds

Mix everything together in a small bowl then place half of it into an electric spice or coffee grinder. Grind on full speed for 20 seconds, tip into a clean jar, then grind the rest, add to the first batch and shake well. I keep my mixture in an airtight jar in the fridge.

Crispy shallots

To make crispy shallots, simply peel red Thai shallots, or small regular shallots and rinse in a colander under gently running cold water for 10 minutes. Pat dry between kitchen paper then deep-fry in small batches in clean oil at 160 °C. Drain on kitchen paper and store in an airtight container.

A deep-fried courgette flower stuffed with walnuts, garlic & bread, drizzled with honey

In Turkey, there is a wonderful classic sauce, more like a chunky pesto in texture, called *tarator*. It contains nuts, stale bread soaked in water which is then squeezed out, garlic, oil and sometimes vinegar or lemon juice. Everything is pounded together and it seems to be served with anything from fish through to cucumber salad and boiled cauliflower. Whenever I think of courgette flowers I always think of Italy – although obviously they call courgettes 'zucchini'. I've eaten them in Italy many times, usually stuffed with a filling based on ricotta, but this is more up my street – especially when they're drizzled with a lovely floral but light honey.

For 8

2 slices of 2-day-old sourdough or country bread – it must be a little stale and firm

3 cloves garlic, peeled

2 generous pinches of dried chilli flakes, or try Spanish pimenton (smoked paprika)

1 Tbsp fresh tarragon leaves off the stem

2 spring onions, sliced

100 g goat's cheese – something like a French chèvre or a Spanish Monte Enebro – keep it chilled until needed

50 g walnuts, lightly toasted

8 courgette flowers – the blossoms must be plump, if they've collapsed they'll be very hard to stuff

120 g flour

2 tsp baking powder

1 tsp sugar

½ tsp salt

220 ml beer (use a light lager)

vegetable oil for deep-frying

80 ml runny honey for drizzling over the cooked blossoms

Remove the crusts from the bread and discard then cut the bread roughly into chunks. Place in a food processor with the garlic, chilli, tarragon and spring onions. Pulse blitz it until you have coarse breadcrumbs. Cut the goat's cheese into chunks and add this and the walnuts to the bread, and pulse blitz it again. Do not purée the mixture – if it looks like
it's going to do that, then you're going to have to break it up between your fingers – this is why the bread needs to be a little stale.

Divide the stuffing equally into eight lumps, then roll each into a squat sausage shape about 5 cm long. Leaving the blossoms lying on a board, pull opposing petals open until you can see into the blossom. Gently but forcefully poke the stuffing into the cavity until it's pressed hard against the top of the baby courgette, then gently wrap the petals back around the stuffing, giving the flower a gentle squeeze in the palm of your hand to remove any extra air. Stuff the remaining blossoms the same way then place on a tray in the fridge while you make the batter.

To make the batter, sieve the flour, baking powder, sugar and salt together into a wide bowl, then whisk in the beer to form a smooth, lump-free batter and put to one side for 5 minutes.

You need to deep-fry the flowers in a pan or a wok wide enough that they can lay straight. Heat up at least 8 cm of vegetable oil to 180 °C. Dip the flowers into the batter one at a time, rolling them in it to coat evenly and thoroughly. Carefully lower the first flower into the hot oil and once it's been sizzling for 20 seconds, batter another flower and lower it into the hot oil. Once the first one looks golden, gently roll it over onto its other side so it cooks evenly. Each flower should take around 1½–2 minutes to cook. As soon as one is ready, very carefully lift it out of the hot oil using two slotted spoons or tongs and lay it on kitchen paper. Once it's out, roll the other one still in the oil over, then batter and cook the next one. If you're feeling confident you can cook three or four at once.

To serve: One per person is the perfect amount for tapas, just drizzle with the honey while still hot and eat straight away.

Not long after we opened The Providores restaurant in 2001, we were approached by a renowned Scottish whisky company to launch their new creation – a whisky matured in Scotland in Cuban rum casks. The whisky is truly wonderful: mellow, rich, spicy and flavoursome. However, what I needed to do was to come up with some canapé ideas that would show a fusion of the two cultures. This is when I created this canapé, uniting famous cold-smoked Scottish salmon with cassava chips. Cassava, also known as *yuca*, tapioca or manioc, is a really important source of carbohydrate for many people around the world. In Cuba, it's called *yuca* which, incidentally, is also the term given to Cuban yuppies living in Florida – Young Upwardly-mobile Cuban Americans. It originates in South America, but is mainly grown these days in Africa, as well as China and South-East Asia. Anyway, this really simple canapé works so well because the cassava chips are crisp and moist if cooked properly, the salmon is rich and the crème fraîche works as a foil for the chilli sauce. When preparing cassava it's important that you discard any discoloured pieces, and any pieces that have a slightly soapy smell to them. When boiling it make sure you don't cover the pot with a lid, but cook it to the point where it looks slightly overcooked – you may need to pull pieces out of the boiling water as they're ready. Undercooked cassava will not go flaky when deep-fried – rather it will be dry and chewy.

For 24 canapés

Cassava chips with smoked salmon, sweet chilli sauce & crème fraîche

1 cassava root – around 25-30-cm long

80 g caster sugar

50 ml white wine vinegar, rice vinegar or cider vinegar

2 moderately hot red chillies, stem removed, finely chopped

2 cloves garlic, peeled and chopped

1 thumb of ginger, peeled and finely chopped

vegetable oil for deep-frying

200 g smoked salmon, thinly sliced

100 g crème fraîche

Peel the cassava. The easiest way is to cut the ends off and discard them, then cut it into three pieces of even length. Using a small sharp knife peel the skin off – although a good potato peeler will work with a bit of effort. The skin is very woody and covered with a thin layer of wax which helps preserve it when transporting by ship. Once you've peeled all three pieces, cut them lengthways roughly into quarters and place in a large pot covered generously with cold water and add a Tablespoon of salt. Bring to the boil then cook until a sharp knife goes through the flesh reasonably easily. The different pieces will likely be ready at differing times, so you can remove them with a pair of tongs or a slotted spoon as they're done. Place on a tray to cool down – don't put them under running water – they'll be quite tender.

Once they're cooled enough to handle, pull the woody vein out from the centre and cut each piece lengthways in half to give you 24 wedge-shaped chips.

While the cassava is cooking, bring the sugar and vinegar to the boil and cook for 2 minutes. Add the chillies, garlic and ginger and rapidly simmer until the sauce thickens. Take from the heat and leave to cool. This will keep in the fridge for 2 weeks if covered.

Heat 5 cm of vegetable oil to 180 °C. Add 6–8 cassava chips to the hot oil and fry until golden and crispy, gently moving them around from time to time, then drain and place on kitchen paper while you cook the rest.

Lay the sliced salmon on a board and cut into strips – you'll need 24. Drizzle a little of the chilli sauce onto each one and as the cassava chips are cooked, wrap them tightly in the salmon.

To serve: Stack the salmon-wrapped chips on top of each other and serve with a bowl of crème fraîche that you've stirred some of the chilli sauce into.

Steamed crab, shiitake, corn & coconut custard pots with wasabi tobikko

These custards are a lovely way to serve crab – although you can also make this with sliced steamed prawns, scallops, oysters and even a vegetarian version using steamed pumpkin. You'll need a steamer deep enough to hold your serving dishes easily – I always use bamboo steamers which are easy to get hold of in most Chinese supermarkets and cookware shops. The crunchy texture that the sweetcorn gives contrasts perfectly with the creamy custard, and the wasabi *tobikko* used as the final garnish gives even more textural excitement. If you can't get hold of this wonderful Japanese ingredient, made from flying fish eggs (although usually dyed with artificial colouring!), then you can use any of the fish roes on the market mixed with a little watered-down wasabi paste. Even the best sustainable caviar works well in this recipe. These are best eaten hot from the steamer, but they can also be made up to six hours in advance and eaten cold. I give a recipe for dashi on page 66, but if you don't have the time or ingredients to make this, then use a light fish, vegetable or chicken stock and add an extra Tablespoon of light soy sauce to the mixture.

For 8

6 shiitake mushrooms, stems discarded, the caps thinly sliced
½ a fresh corn cob, the kernels sliced off
100 g white crab meat (from the legs)
1 spring onion, thinly sliced
80 g brown crab meat (from the body – very tasty)
½ tsp finely chopped or grated peeled ginger
4 medium eggs
100 ml dashi (see page 66)
400 ml coconut milk
2 Tbsp wasabi tobikko

Set your steamer basket or baskets above boiling water, and have at hand the dishes you're going to serve it in. Glasses work well so you can see everything, or use ceramic ramekins.

Divide the shiitake, corn kernels, white crab meat and the spring onion amongst eight heat-proof glasses or ramekins.

In a bowl, whisk together the brown crab meat, ginger, 1 teaspoon flaky salt (less fine salt, if using) and the eggs for 10 seconds. Whisk in the dashi for a few seconds, then lastly the coconut milk. Make sure it's mixed well, then ladle or pour it into each glass or ramekin.

Place in the steamer and cook for 12–15 minutes with the lid tightly on until cooked. To test if they're cooked, poke a skewer or thin knife into the centre of two of them, it should come out clean, although a little moist. If it still looks like uncooked egg, then you'll need to keep cooking until ready.

To serve: Carefully remove the steamer from the boiling water and leave for 5 minutes. Then give the dishes a wipe – be careful as they'll be a little wet and possibly slippery. Spoon on the wasabi tobikko and eat straight away.

This dish is an extreme deliberate example of Fusion cuisine. A classic Japanese 'dish' of raw fish is paired with a classic French sauce – beurre blanc – but one that has in turn been flavoured with wasabi and *yuzu* juice – two classic Japanese ingredients. To top it off, I've added one of my personal 'classic' garnishes – soy tapioca. This tapioca gives a wonderful flavour, but it's also a visual play on salmon eggs or caviar. All up this dish is a perfect tapa – colours that are gorgeous, the flavours subtle and the whole thing really playful. I used fresh grated wasabi for this – which I'm aware isn't that easy to get hold of. Wasabi paste, from a tube or made by mixing the powder with water, will be fine – but it's probably worth noting that most of what we call wasabi is a mixture of horseradish or mustard powder mixed with green food colouring. There just doesn't seem to be enough real wasabi to supply all the world's Japanese restaurants. Yuzu is another hard-to-get-hold-of item – you can simply use lime juice instead. Yuzu has a flavour like a cross between tangerine and grapefruit. Any fresh fish will work for this dish, even raw scallops or oysters – I used salmon fillet. It's quite hard to make just enough soy tapioca for eight portions, so you'll have plenty left over – serve the extra on the side. You'll need to make the tapioca at least 6 hours in advance – it takes that long for it to absorb its marinade.

For 8

Sashimi with soy tapioca & wasabi yuzu beurre blanc

50 g (4 Tbsp) tapioca 'pearls'
150 ml Japanese soy sauce
100 ml mirin
15 ml (1 Tbsp) yuzu juice or lime juice
400 g best quality fish fillet, skin and bones removed
30 ml (2 Tbsp) cream
a few pinches of very finely grated yuzu or lime zest
80 g unsalted butter, cut into 1-cm chunks or thereabouts, take from the fridge 10 minutes before making the sauce
1 heaped tsp wasabi paste (more or less, to taste)
cress or sprouts to garnish

Bring 1 litre of water to the boil and stir in the tapioca. Keep on a gentle boil, stirring occasionally, and after 5 minutes add 200 ml cold water. This seems to help the tapioca cook more quickly. Bring back to a gentle boil and again add a cup of cold water. Bring back to the boil. At this point the tapioca should almost be cooked – by which I mean the centre of most of the pearls will be translucent. They don't all cook at the same speed, but so long as most are translucent that's fine. If they're not ready then cook until they are. Drain through a fine sieve and rinse gently with cold water for 10 seconds then place in a bowl. Stir in the soy and mirin and half the yuzu or lime juice. The tapioca will slowly absorb the liquids, so give it a stir from time to time, keeping it in the fridge. This will need to be made at least 8 hours in advance. If when you come to serve this it's stuck together, then loosen it up a little, either with some extra soy, mirin or water to taste.

When you're almost ready to serve the dish, slice the fish into either 16 or 24 even-sized pieces and place on a tray covered with a not-too-damp cloth while you make the beurre blanc.

In a small pan, bring the cream and yuzu zest to a boil, simmer for 10 seconds making sure it doesn't boil dry, then turn the heat down low. Whisk in the butter, a few pieces at a time, making sure they've almost completely emulsified before adding the next. Once you've added half the butter, whisk in the remaining yuzu or lime juice and the wasabi paste, then continue whisking in the remaining butter little by little. Taste for seasoning, adding a little more juice, salt or wasabi as needed. Keep the pan a little warm, but the sauce may split if heated too much.

To serve: It's important that the plates are warm, or else this buttery sauce can go a little firm. Spoon some sauce onto your plates, then lay 2–3 slices of fish on top. Spoon on some of the tapioca and then garnish with the cress or sprouts. Eat immediately.

I love this mixture of rich duck and aromatic lime leaf – they really seem to be made for each other. I grow my own kaffir limes – even though I live on the top floor of an Edwardian block in inner London. We were bought the tree years ago by Irish friends as appreciation for a dinner we'd cooked, and it's thrived ever since, even producing actual limes. Friends can't quite believe it. My sister Tracey has a large kaffir lime tree growing in her garden – but then she lives in Northern New South Wales in Australia so you might expect that. A lime leaf is actually two leaves joined together – a larger one that is attached to the branch, and a smaller one at the other end. If you're unable to find fresh lime leaves, then you can use frozen ones for this. Dried ones just don't seem to work. Lemon leaves also work a treat – it's the oil in the leaf that adds flavour to the fritter. If you simply can't get lime leaves, then you're going to have to add some grated lime zest to the mixture and simply grill or fry them like little burgers. Beetroot pesto is an old favourite – I created it in 1995 and it finds its way onto all sorts of dishes, but here its added richness, with gorgeous colour, seems a fitting garnish to the fritters. This will make a lot of pesto – so try serving it with grilled pork or lamb chops, or tossed through pasta with duck livers and spinach. If you want to save time, use a pre-made Thai curry paste in the mixture rather than adding chilli, garlic and ginger.

For 12 fritters

Lime leaf-wrapped duck fritters with beetroot pesto

1 medium-sized beetroot
13 lime leaves (doubles as described on left)
1 red chilli, finely chopped (more or less, to taste)
½ thumb of ginger, peeled and finely chopped
5 cloves garlic, peeled
400 g duck breast meat (avoid excessive fat), sliced
15 ml (1 Tbsp) Thai fish sauce
30 g pine nuts, lightly toasted
30 g Parmesan, grated
5 ml (1 tsp) toasted sesame oil
30 ml (2 Tbsp) olive oil
a very small handful of Thai (or regular) basil leaves
a very small amount of coriander leaves
vegetable oil for frying the fritters

Preheat oven to 180 °C. Wrap the beetroot in foil and bake until you can poke a thin knife or skewer through it easily – around 50 minutes. Take from the oven and leave to cool for 10 minutes, then unwrap and peel it by rubbing the skin off with your fingers, or a small knife. It pays to wear gloves as it will stain your fingers badly. Cut into chunks and leave to cool.

While the beetroot's cooking, make the fritter mix. Finely shred one of the lime leaves, using scissors if that's easier. Place in a small food processor along with the chilli, ginger and four of the garlic cloves and blitz to a rough paste. Add the duck meat, fish sauce and ½ teaspoon salt then blitz again to a coarse 'mince'. Divide the mince into 12 even-sized balls, and holding a twin-set of lime leaf in one hand, sit a duck pattie on top of the larger leaf. Fold the smaller leaf over and gently press it into the meat. Place on a tray lined with plastic wrap and prepare the remaining patties. Cover and place in the fridge for at least an hour to firm up.

Place the cooled beetroot in a small food processor along with the remaining clove of garlic, the pine nuts, Parmesan, sesame and olive oils and the Thai basil and coriander leaves. Blitz to a paste, then season with salt and pepper.

Heat 1.5 cm of vegetable oil to 180 °C in a deep-sided frying-pan (to avoid it splattering too much). Carefully lower in the fritters, not overcrowding the pan, and cook for one minute. Turn them over and cook for another 30–45 seconds. Once cooked take them from the cooking oil and place on kitchen paper to drain.

To serve: Dollop a little pesto onto each fritter and eat while hot. Give the leaf a wee chew too – it's quite delicious, if quite inedible.

Lamb, mint & cucumber rolls with hazelnut dukkah & yoghurt

In 2007, I cooked in a huge inflatable white rugby ball capable of holding almost 200 people, very close to the Eiffel Tower in Paris. I was there as part of Tourism New Zealand's marketing campaign to promote New Zealand as the host nation for the 2011 Rugby World Cup. Years earlier I had created menus for the All Blacks' tour of Britain, which we unfortunately didn't win. I think I must be jinxed – as we also didn't win in 2007. However, what I think I did do quite well was introduce a New Zealand theme to the food served in the ball. This is one of the dishes I created and one which proved very popular. I've also made it using rare roast duck breast, sliced like the lamb in this recipe, topped with a dried chilli and peanut sort of dukkah. Dukkah is a great mixture to dip warm bread you've doused with olive oil into, as well as a great sprinkle to serve over fish and salads. It originates in Egypt and can be made with a variety of nuts and spices, and sometimes chickpeas.

For 8

400 g lamb loin (or use the flesh from racks of lamb), trimmed of any sinew or fat

15 ml (1 Tbsp) olive oil

1 long cucumber

30 g hazelnuts, toasted and peeled

1 tsp sesame seeds, toasted

1 tsp cumin seeds, toasted

½ tsp coarsely ground black pepper

½ tsp dried oregano

½ tsp dried rubbed mint

½ tsp dried chilli flakes or smoked paprika

12 mint leaves, shredded

100 g thick yoghurt

Heat up a pan that has a tight-fitting lid. Rub the lamb with the oil, season liberally, then place in the pan. Cook for a minute with the lid on, then roll it 90°, cook another minute and continue to cook this way, with the lid on between each roll, until you've cooked it pink (medium–rare). This will take around 5–6 minutes in total depending on the thickness of the meat. Alternatively, roast it in the oven or barbecue it. Take from the pan, leave to cool, then place in the fridge for at least an hour to chill down and firm up.

Top and tail the cucumber. Using a potato peeler or mandolin, peel thin strips from the cucumber, making sure each strip has the skin still attached. You want eight strips in total. Toss the strips with ¼ teaspoon salt then leave to 'cure' for 30 minutes in a covered bowl.

While the cucumber is curing make the dukkah. Crush the nuts coarsely, using a pestle and mortar or a small food processor, and mix with the remaining dry ingredients (which you can pound briefly to release their oils too). Mix in 1 teaspoon flaky salt (or less of fine salt) and it's ready – keep it stored in an airtight container for up to 3 weeks.

Rinse the cucumber gently in a bowl of cold water, then pat each strip dry with a kitchen cloth. Lay them out on a bench side by side.

Slice the lamb lengthways as thin as you can, into eight strips, discarding the outer edges which will be overcooked and firm. It's easier to do this when the lamb is straight from the fridge. Lay these on a bench too, then sprinkle with the shredded mint leaves and a little of the dukkah. One by one, roll each lamb strip up tightly, then roll the cucumber tightly around the meat – see the photo opposite.

To serve: Dollop on the yoghurt, then dip into the dukkah. Serve extra dukkah and yoghurt on the side.

Prawn, ginger & goji berry dolmas

Dolmas are available in cafés and restaurants throughout Turkey and there are many types found throughout the former Ottoman empire, from Albania to Iraq and Iran. Stuffed vegetables appear in many cuisines, I've eaten lovely stuffed peppers in Italy, stuffed tomatoes in Provence and stuffed kumara and baby pumpkin in New Zealand. However, it was the Ottomans who are credited with wrapping stuffing in leaves, specifically vine leaves. I've eaten such in Greece and Turkey and they make a great snack on a hot day. They can be filled with vegetarian or meat-based fillings, and usually the veggie ones are served cold. However, I decided that I wanted to bring the Ottoman creation in line with other great rice-based cuisines so I've given it an Asian twist by adding prawns, ginger and fish sauce from South-East Asia, and goji berries which tend to be grown in Tibet and Mongolia in place of the more usual currants. It was only recently that I realised that what I'd known as wolfberries, bought cheaply from Chinese food stores for many years, were in fact the supposed super-food now called goji berries. The result is a really tasty rice-dish canapé, the ginger, prawn stock and mint giving it a lovely flavour. Eat cold as a snack, or pass around at a party.

Makes around 24–30

8 medium-sized raw prawns, in their shells

5 ml (1 tsp) sesame oil

2 spring onions, cut into 8

1 white onion, peeled and diced or sliced

1 thumb of ginger, peeled and finely chopped

2 cloves garlic, peeled and chopped

30 g pine nuts, lightly toasted

50 ml olive oil

20 g goji berries

150 g long-grain rice (or use risotto rice)

10 ml (2 tsp) fish sauce

a small handful of mint leaves, shredded

24–30 preserved vine leaves (plus another 12 for cooking)

1 whole lemon and 60 ml lemon juice

50 ml anise-flavoured liqueur such as Ouzo or Pastis

Peel the prawns and remove the heads if they have them. Heat up a pot over moderate–high heat and when it's ready add the prawn shells and the oil and fry until all the shells have turned red. Add the spring onions and 500 ml water and bring to the boil – it will splutter a bit when you first add it. Turn to a simmer, put a lid on, and cook for 15 minutes – this is the stock you use to flavour the rice. Strain it once it's ready.

Sauté the onion, ginger, garlic and pine nuts in half the olive oil to soften, but don't colour them. Stir in the goji berries and the rice then add 450 ml of the prawn stock and the fish sauce. Bring to the boil, then place a lid on and turn to a simmer and cook for 12 minutes. Turn the heat off and leave to sit for 10 minutes, then give it a gentle mix and taste for seasoning. Let the mixture cool down. Cut the prawn tail meat into slices ½ cm thick and stir them in along with the mint. Remove the vine leaves from their jar or sachet and gently squeeze out any excess moisture. If they taste too much of brine, rinse them individually in warm running water. Lay a leaf on a board, vein side facing up, with the pointy tip of the leaf facing away from you.

Take a Tablespoon of the filling and place in the centre of the leaf near the stem edge. Fold this end up and over the filling, then fold both sides towards the middle and roll up like a small cigar. Place on a tray while you roll the remaining dolmas. You can either cook dolmas in a wide pan with a tight-fitting lid, or in the oven in a covered casserole. Lay the 12 remaining vine leaves on the bottom of the pan or the casserole to prevent the dolmas sticking to the dish. Place the dolmas on top, packing them in fairly tight. Slice the lemon and tuck it between the dolmas, then drizzle over the anise liqueur and the remaining olive oil. Put the lid on and either bake at 160 °C for 18 minutes, or cook in a pan over a low heat for 13 minutes. Once cool they're ready to eat.

Ox heart skewers with guindilla chilli, mango & radish salsa

An ox heart is not something that the faint-hearted should prepare. They are a huge muscle, and when one thinks about it, it seems somewhat odd to be cutting one up – well, that's how I feel about it anyway. Interestingly, considering how much work the heart does, it isn't that tough a muscle, although a little marinating will help keep it tasty. Once diced up, people will think it's simply rump steak or the like. At Bellota restaurant in New Zealand our first head chef, Argentinean Mariano Ramon, cooked ox heart kebabs and these went down really well with our Auckland punters – so this dish is created in his honour. As an ox heart is so huge, and one heart will make many skewers, see if your butcher can sell you just half a one! Or, feed the rest to the cat. The pickled chillies in the photo are Spanish *guindilla* chillies – but head to your local speciality food shop and you'll find something suitable there.

For 20

½ an ox heart, trimmed of all sinew and fat
2 cloves garlic, chopped
2 tsp pimenton picante (spicy smoked paprika)
2 tsp freshly ground cumin
150 ml red wine
80 ml olive oil
1 mango
4 radishes
2 spring onions, sliced
2 pickled green chillies, sliced (plus extra for serving with the kebabs)
several stalks of coriander with leaves still attached, shredded
a few flat parsley leaves, shredded
30 ml (2 Tbsp) lemon juice

Cut the heart into 2-cm dice. Rub with the garlic, pimenton, cumin and 2 teaspoons of flaky salt then leave for 5 minutes. Pour over the wine and 20 ml of the olive oil, mix it all together then place in a covered container in the fridge and leave for at least 18 hours – and up to 36 if you like. It's important that you mix it all up twice during this time to make sure the marinade is infusing the heat evenly.

When it's ready, drain the marinade from the heart and discard it. Thread the meat onto skewers and bring to room temperature.

Make the salsa. Peel the mango, remove the flesh from the stone, then cut the flesh into small dice and place in a bowl. Slice the radishes and add these to the mango, along with the spring onions, the sliced pickled chillies, coriander, parsley and lemon juice. Mix it together and taste for seasoning, then mix in half the remaining olive oil.

Brush the remaining olive oil over the ox heart skewers then grill over a moderate–high heat, turning them as they colour. If you cook the heart too much it will become quite dry and tough.

Serve straight from the grill topped with the salsa and with a few spare chillies to the side.

Steamed truffled prawn, tofu & edamame dumpling with ponzu

I really love the experience of eating dim sum, partly because of the variety of tastes, aromas and textures but also the spectacle of the meal itself – sweet, sour, salty, spicy and bitter dishes come out in chaotic order. If you're in a dim sum restaurant pretty much anywhere in the world these days, you'll probably have steaming trolleys pushed up to your table from which you'll make your selection from small bamboo steamer baskets of steamed, deep-fried and, occasionally, grilled little dishes. A taro fritter here, a chicken's foot there, some turnip cake, perhaps. In 2005, I was lucky enough to travel to Guangdong in China to film an episode for a TV show called *Planet Food*. It was an amazing experience and I have to say that one of the highlights was being force-fed by the alleged top dim sum chef in all of China, Ms Chen Xiao Hong. She ran an incredibly tight ship in her kitchen at Guangzhou Restaurant and I hope that if she were ever to make this recipe she'd approve! I had a few edamame left over so added them to the basket along with the dumplings when I cooked these. They're delicious – just sprinkle with flaky salt or dip in soy sauce, popping the beans out into your mouth – don't attempt to eat the pods!

Makes 16

200 g raw prawn tails
1 small thumb of ginger, peeled and roughly chopped
150 g silken tofu (it's best to use Japanese firm silken tofu)
15 ml (1 Tbsp) white truffle oil
75 ml light Japanese soy sauce (if using dark Chinese soy sauce, use half this amount)
2 Tbsp snipped chives
a handful of edamame (fresh soy beans)
16 wonton wrappers
30 ml (2 Tbsp) rice vinegar (or any white vinegar)
5 ml (1 tsp) roasted sesame oil

Place the prawn tails and ginger in a food processor and blitz for 5 seconds. Scrape the side of the bowl down then add the tofu, truffle oil, 2 Tablespoons of soy sauce (less if using dark Chinese soy sauce), three-quarters of the chives and ¼ teaspoon flaky salt. Squeeze the edamame pods to free the individual beans, and reserve 16 of the beans. Add the remainder to the food processor then blitz everything for another 10–15 seconds at which point the mixture should be fairly smooth, but don't turn it into a paste.

Filling the wrappers is quite simple, but it takes a little practice. Assuming you're right-handed, hold the thumb and forefinger of your left hand together to form an O. Lay a wonton wrapper over the O. Take a heaped teaspoon of the mixture and place it in the centre of the wrapper. Using your thumb and forefinger of your left hand, fold the wrapper up towards the top of the filling, but don't actually seal it in. Using the thumb of your right hand to keep the base flat, form it into a 'cube' of filling sealed with the wrapper but with an open top. Alternatively, you can lay a wonton wrapper on a board, dollop on the filling then, using both hands, fold the wrapper over the filling. This will work just as well, but ultimately is a lot slower. Place a reserved edamame bean in the centre of each dumpling.

Line a steamer basket or two with oiled paper, bamboo leaves (as I did) or a banana leaf. Place the dumplings on the oiled surface as you make them keeping them at least 1 cm apart as they'll stick to each other. Once they're all done, put a tight-fitting lid on and place over a steamer running at full heat and cook for 5½ minutes. While they're cooking, make the dipping sauce. Mix the remaining soy sauce with the vinegar, sesame oil and reserved chives.

To serve: Simply take the steamer basket to the table along with the dipping sauce served in a wide dish and let people help themselves.

Marrow bones with pine nut, garlic & Parmesan bone-marrow sauce

I have to say that this incredibly rich and intense 'sauce' is one of my all time favourites. On page 120 you'll see how I serve it with poached venison in a slightly different format, but in this instance it makes a great tapa, spread over toasted sourdough – especially if served with a glass of chilled fino sherry – a match made in heaven really. Any leftovers can be warmed up and spooned over grilled or roast beef. For the marrow bones, I simply asked my butcher to cut marrow bones into 4–5-cm lengths. Once I pushed the marrow out, I gently boiled them with the lid on in very salty water with a cup of white vinegar added for 1½ hours, topping up the water from time to time. They sometimes have sharp edges, so file them a bit with a knife-sharpening steel to round them off. Scrape off any excess fleshy bits, give them a scrub, and they're ready to go – plus you can reuse them endlessly – and even wash them in the dishwasher.

For 24 or so tapas

600-800 g marrow bones, cut into 4-5-cm lengths (the amount of marrow contained will depend on the bones)

30 g butter

150 g coarse sourdough breadcrumbs, made from 2-3 day old crustless bread

50 g pine nuts

300-350 ml simmering jus, or dark chicken stock

50 g Parmesan, grated

a large handful of chopped parsley

3 cloves garlic, peeled and chopped

1 tsp grated lemon zest

Soak the marrow bones in plenty of cold water in a covered container in the fridge for 24 hours, changing the water three times. Using either your finger or a wooden spoon handle, poke the marrow out of the bone. Be careful of very sharp, fine shards of bone which occasionally make themselves known. Rinse the marrow in gently running cold water for a few minutes, then carefully go over them to make sure no bone is attached. Measure out 120 g of marrow and slice into 5-mm pieces.

Put the butter in a wide pan and cook it on a medium–high heat to a *beurre noisette* stage (until it turns nutty brown in colour). Add the sliced marrow and cook for 1½ minutes, stirring as it melts down, although there will still be lumps.

Add the breadcrumbs and pine nuts and cook for another 2 minutes, stirring the whole time.

Add 300 ml of the jus, which will bubble rapidly at first, then cook it for another 1½ minutes, stirring constantly. If it seems too thick, add the remaining jus.

Take off the heat and stir in the Parmesan, parsley, garlic and lemon zest. Taste for seasoning, adding plenty of freshly ground black pepper.

To serve: Spoon into the warmed marrow bones and serve with hot toast, or simply serve in a ramekin alongside hot toast.

My first-ever experience of eating octopus almost ensured I'd never eat it again. Our family was staying at Cape Palliser, which is at the bottom of the North Island of New Zealand. We'd go there several times a year, usually staying in an old woolshed that friends of my Dad owned. The woolshed would be filled with bales of wool, or with bales of agar seaweed – harvested in non wool-shearing months as a way to supplement the farmer's income. Out on the beach were Antarctic fur seals and penguins and the waters were teeming with paua (black abalone), crayfish and kina (sea urchins). It was because of the crayfish we came, though, as Dad was a keen crayfisherman. One fateful day, however, Dad caught an octopus in one of the pots and he decided to cook it for dinner as a treat. He simply threw it on the barbecue and grilled it for a short time. It was absolutely disgusting and the taste remained in my mouth for ages. Since then I've learnt to love eating this strange sea creature. In Turkey and Greece, it is often served simply drizzled with olive oil and lemon after being slowly braised. In this dish I give it a bit of an Asian make-over, and it is truly delicious! In Japan and Hong Kong, you can often buy just one tentacle from the fish markets. If you can only find them frozen don't worry – it won't affect the final result. If you can only find baby octopus, then you'll only need to cook them for around 40 minutes.

For 8

Red wine & star anise-braised octopus with coriander dressing

For the octopus

1 x 1.2–1.5 kg octopus

300 ml red wine (use one with low tannins)

100 ml soy sauce

6 star anise

50 ml extra virgin olive oil

2 tsp flaky salt

300 ml water

Coriander dressing

4 cloves garlic, peeled

1 shallot, peeled and sliced

a small handful of parsley

a handful of coriander, leaves, stems and roots, if possible

1 Tbsp dried oregano

60 ml vegetable salad oil

½ tsp flaky salt

50 ml extra virgin olive oil

juice of 1 lemon

Preheat oven to 170 °C. Prepare your octopus. Cut the head off beneath the eyes and then cut it in half lengthways, removing the eyes and the inside of the head. Using a sharp knife, or scissors, separate the tentacles from each other, and discard the shell-like beak (the mouth) and the mouth area. Place the octopus along with all the other ingredients into a large ovenproof pot and bring to the boil. Alternatively, bring the liquids to the boil and pour over the octopus in a ceramic or stainless steel deep-sided roasting dish. The octopus should be covered with liquid; if it isn't, top it up with extra water. Place a sheet of baking parchment on top of the liquid, then seal the dish really tightly with aluminium foil or a lid and bake in the centre of the oven for 1¾ hours. Take it out and leave to cool. At this point it's ready to be eaten, but it will also be delicious served cold.

For the coriander dressing, using a stick blender or bar blender, blitz everything except the extra virgin olive oil and the lemon juice together until smooth. Stir in the olive oil and then the lemon juice and taste for seasoning.

To serve: One tentacle or less per person with some of the dressing is all that's needed. You can also slice it and scatter over watercress, quartered cherry tomatoes and pitted olives for a lovely salad.

Rice

As a child growing up in Wanganui, New Zealand, rice was rarely eaten. Potatoes, kumara and bread were the carbohydrates of choice for my mother Timmy and step-mum Rose. The times I can remember eating rice in a savoury dish were when mum would cook an occasional Chinese-inspired fried rice, or Rose would make a minced beef or sausage curry and we'd eat it with boiled rice. Rose's father Vic would also make the most delicious hot rice pudding by slowly baking pudding rice with lots of milk, butter, sugar and a little nutmeg – he said slow cooking was the secret to the smoothest pudding and he seemed to always get it right. When I moved to Melbourne, aged 18, I began to eat at Thai and Cantonese restaurants and suddenly realised that rice wasn't just an adjunct to a meal, it was often the main part of a meal. I also discovered Italian risottos and Spanish paellas, Turks and Greeks were stuffing vegetables with rice, vegetarians were making nut and rice loaves. Chinese congee and Indonesian lontong (compressed rice) were both made by overcooking rice in various ways. To this day I am a huge fan of rice in its many forms, colours, textures and varieties – and there are many varieties.

What we know as rice is actually the grain, or edible seed, from an arable plant, also known as rice, that is a cereal. The word *cereal* derives from the pre-Roman goddess Ceres, who it is believed looked after the harvest. Whilst rice appears in many cuisines around the world, for many people it is their main source of carbohydrate and as such is a staple food for tens of millions, providing more than 20 per cent of the kilojoules consumed worldwide. The rice we have made part of our diets globally comes from two different species: one from West Africa (lesser known outside of Africa) and the other originating in sub-tropical Asia, most likely China and its environs. When I first went to Bali in 1985, I was mesmerised by the rice paddy field terraces that littered parts of the island. The artistic town of Ubud, my favourite spot in Bali, is surrounded by rice fields that really do contribute to the character and soothing soul of the area.

It was also in Bali that I ate black rice pudding for the first time. This was made by cooking black glutinous (sticky) rice in water, then finishing it with fresh coconut cream, banana and *gula melaka* – palm sugar. I was hooked on this unusual dessert and have cooked it often myself. As I headed up through South-East Asia I came across many variations of rice, from the Sumatran *lemang* (mixed with coconut milk and cooked inside bamboo stalks over a fire), to sweet green 'cakes' in Malaysia made from rice flour and pandan, to the wonderful sticky rice from Northern Thailand, mostly steamed but occasionally cooked in the same manner as the lemang. Also I came across what I call Thai rice puffs – resembling Rice Bubbles®. Funnily enough, I also ate this style of puffed rice on the streets of Mumbai (or Bombay as it was in 1986) mixed with diced mango, chillies, mint, tamarind and served with *bel poori*. Japanese sake, a much undervalued drink in my opinion, owes its very existence to rice, as does mirin, and where would Japanese cuisine be without either of these? In India, basmati rice might rightly be thought king of the crops for its aromatic and distinctive flavour, but the jasmine rice of Thailand is a personal close second.

Of course, rice didn't stop in Asia or Africa. It was introduced into Europe, the Middle East and the Americas, as so many foods have been, by traders and settlers, invading hoards and missionaries. The Moors brought it to Spain in the 10th century and from there it slowly introduced itself to Italy and France. Rice is versatile and a quick way to extend a meal, and there are numerous varieties, so look out for some different ones next time you go shopping, from Southern France's red Carmargue, or India's unhulled brown basmati through to lovely sticky black glutinous rice from Thailand.

It was Australia, and Melbourne in particular, that initiated and defined my particular approach to food.

My childhood diet in Wanganui was centred around basic, good-quality ingredients: predominantly home-grown vegetables, occasional home-butchered meat plus family-caught fish, whitebait, crayfish and *paua*. However, it was Melbourne, Australia's second largest city, with its mixed population of Australians and vast numbers of migrants from Greece, Italy, Morocco, Turkey and Vietnam – and many other places – that improved my palate and developed my food-shopping abilities – a much underrated skill! Prior to my move across the Tasman Sea to create a new life and start a career, I'd never seen an avocado, drunk a cappuccino, tasted *chinotto* (a bitter cola-based drink for which I developed a strong liking) or doused a salad with olive oil without, literally, having to count the cost. I'd never seen sushi, spaghetti carbonara, goat curry, *masala dosa*, cous cous, rice-paper wrappers or even something as commonplace (these days) as an uncooked fresh prawn still in its shell.

I arrived in August 1981, a youngish 18-year-old, nervous about what lay ahead, but keen to get stuck into a job to earn enough money to put myself through a winemaking course. My sisters Tracey and Donna were living in the tiny settlement of Narracan, near a small town called Moe. It was a bitterly cold and wet spring; they had no heating in their home; the loo was outside and they had snakes on the property. And although everyone spoke English I felt I'd moved to another planet. After joining my sisters and their friends on a protest march on a cold, wet day somewhere in the Latrobe Valley (I think it was something to do with the unemployed), my sisters realised I needed to do something positive. They arranged for me to stay with a friend of theirs in Melbourne and look for work. I also had a cousin called Rae living in town and so I hooked up with her. It was she who actually helped me get my first job.

I became a waiter at Mietta's restaurant on Brunswick Street, at that time one of the most respected restaurants in town. It was an incredible experience for me every minute of the short week I worked there. The floors were tiled – an architectural feature I'd definitely never observed back home in Wanganui. The waiters wore black pants, jackets and ties and white shirts. Up until then, I'd only ever seen that kind of outfit at funerals. Coffee wasn't instant either. It was served as short espressos that the junior staff (i.e. me) would make using an Italian espresso machine (the likes of which I'd also never seen before), then pour into a large silver coffee pot using this to top up people's tiny white cups. The cups were far too small to be satisfying, I thought. I remember one night, in particular, topping up a man's coffee from the aforementioned pot and in the dim lighting, suddenly becoming aware that the pristine tablecloth was slowly turning dark brown as I poured upwards of half a litre of coffee into his thimble-like cup. I was horrified, but the man was clearly amused, and I began to wonder why I was attempting to become a waiter when it had never really been my plan in the first place. After a few days I came to realise that I really didn't want to be a winemaker at all. I became acutely aware of the chefs in the kitchen, in their white jackets and hats, preparing exotic things like duck, rabbit and tortellini, and I suddenly realised that cooking and becoming a chef was my real passion, one I'd carried with me for years. This was what I really wanted to do with my life. After a week working for Mietta I asked her if, instead of employing me as a waiter, she would consider taking me on as a chef. She eyeballed me – then told me she was furious that I had wasted her time and that I'd better collect my things, leave the premises and never come back. Perhaps it was fair comment, but nonetheless, I was really gutted.

Rae and her friends spent the weekend commiserating with me at their house in St Kilda. A few days later one of the flatmates came home and said that Sardi's on Little Collins Street, the restaurant where she was working, was looking to employ an apprentice chef. It was somehow linked to the famous New York restaurant of the same name and was, apparently, very chic and full of celebrities which she said made for some interesting times! I applied for the job and was immediately employed, and thus I began my apprenticeship. I was the happiest I'd ever been in my life, and I took to the work with a vengeance. Early in 1982 I started Catering College at William Angliss thus beginning a lifetime's love-hate relationship with culinary training. At work, I was promoted quite quickly from the lowest in the cheffing ranks to the third from the top – partly because of a lack of staff, but also because I'd actually been cooking for 13 years by this time so I did know a thing or two – at least how to handle a knife and cut a vegetable julienne. Around this time a woman called Suzanne Raidal came to work in the kitchen and we got on incredibly well. She was filling in time until she and her friends opened their own restaurant, which would later become Kew's. After a month cooking together, she asked

me if I'd like to come and work for her when the restaurant opened. And this I did.

My time at Kew's was the most fulfilling and happiest I had in Melbourne, from the painting of the restaurant before it opened through to going to the fish and vegetable markets twice a week to buy the food, working seven days a week, and having midnight feasts in Chinatown with Sue and the team. At this time Mareesa Mayne, or Brie as I still call her, came and worked in the kitchen as an apprentice chef alongside me. Brie and I became close friends, and remain so to this day. Kew's nurtured us in many ways. We cooked food there but also experienced life, enjoyed music and had a lot of fun. My hero Annie Lennox from the Eurythmics had orange hair then, so I dyed mine the same shade. Not to be outdone, Brie turned up at work with multi-coloured, layered hair held up with pegs, no doubt inspired by a crazy new group called Culture Club. We truly had an hilarious time.

During this period, I was flatting with Liz and James. Liz happened to be a food-obsessed nurse and she taught me how to make *ribolata* soup, topping up the thick liquid on the stove each day with extra vegetables, pasta and stock before re-boiling it and taking some out for the night's dinner. James, on the other hand, must have wondered what on earth had hit him when I moved into the flat. I remember very clearly helping him unpack his groceries one day and putting his wine in the fridge. A few hours later he was frantic, wondering where his incredibly expensive claret was – at this point in his career he was a butler at an international hotel. I didn't actually know what claret was but when he found it in the fridge, I was given a very stern lesson in the protocol of red wine.

After a year of happily working seven days a week, Sue decided it would be really healthy if I managed a day or two off. Thus began my exploration of Melbourne's extraordinary culture of ethnic foods. Back in Wanganui we had rarely eaten at restaurants, apart from a place called Big Tex which served such delights as chicken and chips, steak and chips and fisherman's basket. In comparison, Melbourne was the restaurant capital of the universe – or so it seemed. I'd head to the

Thai, Vietnamese, Greek or Italian areas of town and visit their food shops and restaurants. I'd order some unpronounceable thing off a menu and then try to figure out what on earth it might be. Then I'd head to the food stores nearby and buy whatever looked good or interesting – often purchasing something just because I liked the packaging. After months of shopping like this I soon began to build up quite a substantial larder, with ingredients from all corners of the world battling for space in the fridge or pantry. When it came time to cook dinner for flatmates or friends I began to literally mix it all together. No doubt some of my first attempts were dreadful, but with perseverance it soon became clear to me how certain foods could be successfully combined with others, and I began to forget which ingredient had come from which source and which ingredient should or 'had to' be served with another. I definitely wasn't interested in what was supposedly regionally 'authentic' in my kitchen. If I wanted that, I'd simply go out for a meal to a Northern Thai, Sicilian or Southern French restaurant. I wanted to be creative, play with my amazing array of ingredients and have as much fun as was possible in the kitchen. And I guess this is where my Fusion approach to food began. It wasn't a great enterprise, idea or theory I was pursuing or a eureka-like, 'light-bulb has been turned on for me' moment. It was simply a logical place I arrived at, based on what I was doing in my culinary and personal life.

I left Kew's after being told by another of the owners that I had to cut off my mohawk and 'get serious in my life'. Why my haircut should have had any impact on my cooking was beyond my comprehension, but I also realised that I actually did need to leave and get some experience in a different environment. I decided to find a job in a more 'serious' place. So I went to meet a man with a wonderful reputation, Tony Rogalsky, and soon began working at his restaurant, Rogalskys, in South Melbourne. Tony and his wife Adriana were terrific bosses, although we had our moments and I well remember the week I started working with them, as I was almost sacked for the second time in my career. Mogens Bay Esbensen, a Danish-born chef who was instrumental in introducing Thai cooking to Australia, was cooking as a guest chef at Rogalskys one night. I'd never been to a restaurant that featured a guest chef, and as Thai food was still relatively new to me, I was incredibly excited. One of the few jobs I was entrusted with on this very important night was making a raspberry coulis, which necessitated puréeing raspberries with sugar in a food processor then passing the purée through a sieve to remove the seeds. Simple enough, you might think. However, in the excitement of it all, and probably because I wasn't concentrating as much as I should have because I thought all the other jobs were more exciting than mine, I forgot to add the sugar. It wasn't noticed until a customer commented on it. Adriana was keen to sack me on the spot, but Tony managed to convince her to let me keep my job as he himself hadn't checked the faulty coulis. From that point on, I became fanatical about tasting everything I made which now seems to me to be common sense. Yet failing to taste dishes as they are made is still a major fault amongst many young chefs today, even in restaurants I have been involved with.

I was so obsessed with food during this time that Brie and I would eat out whenever our apprentice wages allowed. One memorable meal was at the legendary Berowra Waters just outside Sydney. I worked my Saturday night at Rogalskys as usual and around midnight Brie and I, and two other friends Deb, herself a wonderful chef, and her partner Dave drove to Sydney. Well, actually I drove the whole way as the others slept solidly. We arrived and checked into our hotel before heading off to the restaurant. To get to it, you had to park near a boat jetty then take a water taxi across the river. By this stage I was so exhausted I just wanted to sleep, but that wasn't an option. Gay Bilson welcomed us to her restaurant, possibly the most beautiful I've been to, even to this day, and we ate a fantastic lunch, many courses cooked by my old William Angliss College friend, Huw Roberts, a junior in the kitchen, but one who was rapidly moving up the ranks. The most memorable moment, however, was having Gay tap me and wake me up as I lay asleep, with my head on the table between the serving of the main course and dessert. As I had bright blue hair in those days, I think the tablecloth was probably never the same again. The outstanding dish on that sleepy day long ago was a whole chicken, cooked in a salt bread crust, with green sauce: simple but spectacular.

I attended college every Friday for three years. As I'd been cooking for quite some time previously, you could say that I was somewhat beyond appreciating the joys of learning 50 different potato recipes or 20 versions of hollandaise sauce. Our teachers were, admittedly, well versed in the ways of the European kitchen but unfortunately for me, in very little else. By my second year I wanted to know how to cook with coconut milk and spices; what could be done with tofu; how to make pita bread and focaccia – and, especially, how to wok-fry without burning everything. I brought this up with my tutors many times but they all had the same response: cooking non-European food wasn't really something to aspire to. I mean, take the Japanese for example. They didn't really cook at all. They just ate raw fish. How little my teachers seemed to know, or, how little they were allowed to explore with us within the confines of the educational system at the time. In our third year, we famously had ice-carving classes, which I seem to recall took place over a three-week period. We were painstakingly shown how to carve a large chunk of ice into a basket. As I watched the lesson, I knew this whole circus was going to drive me mad. I knew that, personally, I would never, ever have need of this skill. It annoyed me intensely that we were having such old-fashioned and pointless subjects drummed into us weekly, i.e. how to make *chaud-froid* (béchamel sauce set with gelatine to cover poached poultry) plus ice sculpture, when we could have been exploring, for example, modern or ethnic cookery techniques. I hatched a plot – my way to fight the system. At the last of our ice classes, we had to present a work to the rest of the students. My ultimate creation was a cube of ice about 2-cm square. The teacher was furious, but as I explained, to me, it seemed the only useful thing I would ever need ice for – an ice cube to put in a gin and tonic! Nowadays, of course, I really do appreciate the skills involved in this and other crafts such as margarine carving, even though I doubt I'll ever pursue them myself, and I think it's admirable, but for me, a 21-year-old hungry to learn about the world's vast array of foods, it was a complete waste of my time. Nevertheless, I managed somehow to graduate as top theory student in my final year, which is when I realised that perhaps the tutors were also battling the system to bring about change. Things have definitely moved on from those days in colleges around the world, but it pays to keep in mind that not that long ago the culinary world was quite a different place.

I left Australia on 19 November 1985, aged 22, and headed to Bali, thinking I was going to spend a few weeks there before travelling to Greece to see if I could find a job on a cruise ship. My eventual plan was to get to London and begin working in a fancy hotel like the Savoy or the Ritz. My plans went out of the window, however, on 21 November when I realised that in Bali something extraordinary had been kick-started inside me, something I hadn't even been aware of until my culinary horizons were violently expanded in this new country. Blown sky-high, actually. I remember not enjoying it at all for the first 48 hours. I hired a motorbike and got totally lost. I couldn't speak a word of Indonesian and I thought everyone was cheating me. Then one day I awoke, smelt the scents in the air, saw the plants and colours, heard a melodious language, observed so many smiling and happy people – and I thought I was in paradise. I ended up spending four weeks in Bali before heading overland through Java and Sumatra, and every single day I experienced a thousand new sensations: realising I adored the flavour of chillies (not just the heat); snorkelling on Nusa Lembongan and Nusa Penida off the coast of Bali; eating my first mangosteen and thinking it was the most incredible thing ever; having a smoked duck all by myself at a restaurant in Ubud overlooking the river and rice paddies. I climbed Mount Bromo in Java to see the sunrise and I explored Borobodur, an incredible Mahayana Buddhist monument that had once been abandoned. I ate bananas of all shapes, colours and sizes and wondered why previously I'd never liked them. I took a 12-hour boat trip to the Sumatran island of Nias, accompanied by flying fish, dolphins and whales in the distance, and bought a coconut wood and brass necklace that I still have to this day. I ate crayfish caught in the lagoon, watched surfers from the shore whilst drinking beer and walked through villages where they would lay their dead out on stone slabs rather than bury them. The island smelt incredible due to the millions of clove trees grown all over it (mainly for the production of Indonesian *kretek* – clove-flavoured cigarettes) and I stayed in a bamboo hut on the beach. The boat trip back to the mainland was the scariest I've ever experienced, as we hit a mini typhoon. Waves were washing all over the deck and the boat almost capsized when the captain failed to turn it around in order to head back to Nias. It was almost 24 hours later when we pulled into the town of Sibolga and we all kissed the ground as we got off (except, of course, those who were so seasick that they couldn't walk). Never one to miss out on a food experience, even after recently cheating death, I decided that I ought to at least try eating a durian - apparently a near-death experience in itself for the uninitiated - as I was clearly not going to drop dead just yet. The fruit has a reputation of smelling and tasting like excrement and I have to say that I pretty much support that viewpoint. Ten months later I arrived in London, after having travelled through Malaysia and Singapore (see pages 109-113), Thailand and Burma (as it was then called). I had stopped off in Bangladesh, trekked through the Anapurna Himalayas of Nepal for a month and spent three months in India.

The next time I visited Australia would have been in 1987 while I was head chef at The Sugar Club. I flew to Sydney to see my eldest sister Vicki and to catch up with my chef friend Huw again. Whilst in town, Huw took me to two restaurants that really changed the way I perceived restaurant food. One was called Bluewater Grill in Bondi, where a young chef called Neil Perry was wooing diners with his modern Australian food with a French influence. The other restaurant was Oasis Seros, where Philip Searle was creating his amazing food. A few months later I saw an article in a magazine and the accompanying photo showed Philip's kitchen team. One person, in particular, stood out wearing chefs' pants made from a blue and white striped apron - with braces - and for having the whitest of dyed blonde hair. Also around this time I ate one of my most memorable meals at a restaurant in Roselle called Tetsuya's. To this day I can still recall the first mouthful of his legendary slow-cooked Tasmanian trout with seaweed. Years later my sister Vicki took me to eat at one of her favourite Sydney restaurants, Paramount. It turned out that this was owned and run by Christine Manfield (the blonde chef from the photo) and her partner Margie Harris. The food was sensational - so original and exciting, with flavours that spoke and sang of distant lands and cuisines. Chris and Margie have since become good friends and we have had some hilarious times together, most memorably one recent summer, on a *Gulet* (the traditional wooden Turkish sailing boat) with Tarik and Savas from Istanbul's Changa restaurant and nine other friends. I also adore Chris's wonderful book, *Fire*, which she released in 2008. Like her food, it is both intricate in content and clear in direction.

Australia's indigenous foods (often called bushfoods) are truly fantastic, ranging from *quandongs* (rambuttan-like with their hairless skins) and Davidson's plums, through to flavourings like that of wattleseed (with its aroma of coffee), aniseed myrtle and lemon myrtle, and produce such as bunya nuts (like massive pine nuts), macadamias (native to Australia) and finger limes (tangy fat fingers of caviar-like pearls). In fact, my youngest sister Tracey and her partner Roesheen set up a bakery in Byron Bay many years ago selling biscuits and slices containing these foods, such as macadamia and ginger biscotti and lemon myrtle slices.

Tracey came to London and helped me prepare and cook some of the dishes in this book, and if you look closely you'll see she did a spot of hand modelling too - check out the pandan croissants on page 180. Meanwhile, my middle sister Donna makes her life as a chef, and she is living not far from Narracan, where my Australian journey started decades ago, with her partner Carmen. My eldest sister Vicki makes her living as a music producer in Sydney, with her partner Alana, but when she's not eating at the newest or best restaurant in town you'll find her forever cooking up a storm in their kitchen. All up, food appreciation and preparation is an intrinsic part of many Australians' lives, and it is part of Australia's history. Thanks to many decades of migrants from different parts of the world bringing ingredients and their cooking skills and styles to the country, a global culinary mecca has been created on one continent. If heaven is both a restaurant and a food market, then Australia would be a strong contender for the title.

Potatoes

This wonderful vegetable can be found in the diet of almost every country. For the British, the thought of living without ever eating a spud, or tattie, is unthinkable, and for a fan of Indian cuisine, like myself, the thought of not eating *saag aloo* ever again is too much to bear. The Swiss grate them and make them into *rösti*, Americans turn them into French fries to be served alongside hamburgers and the French bake slices of them smothered in cream to make a *gratin*. Hash browns, potato bread, Jansson's temptation, *pomme purée*, potato salad and my own father's mock whitebait fritters – they all need potatoes.

The potato is a wonder food in many ways, from the enormous amount of protein, vitamin C and nutrition it can produce per hectare compared with other crops, through to the vast array of differing climatic conditions in which it can thrive. In fact, it's such an important food crop that the United Nations declared 2008 the 'International Year of the Potato'.

However, these delicious tuberous roots, a relative of the tomato and aubergine, started their life way back, high up in the Andes of South America, in the lands we now think of as Peru and Bolivia. In fact, the shores of Lake Titicaca have recently been credited as being the most likely site of the original potato as we know it today. Potatoes were introduced into Europe throughout the 1500s, but when they first appeared on European shores there was some dissent as to whether they were safe to eat as they belong to the Deadly Nightshade plant family and some people felt they might be poisonous. Eventually though, the potato won over the sceptics and it soon began its absorption into the world's myriad evolving cuisines. European traders and migrants took the plant with them on their travels, planting them wherever they would grow and thus potatoes arrived in India, North America, Africa and pretty much everywhere else. The first British settlers brought plants with them to Australia and New Zealand, and these days a typical Kiwi Sunday roast just wouldn't be complete without roast potatoes – alongside our other imports lamb and mint sauce!

I like nothing better than a boiled new potato, lightly salted and drizzled with olive oil or melted butter. Add some shredded mint leaves and they're the perfect accompaniment to everything from grilled lamb chops through to a whole baked fish. On the other hand, in the middle of winter I love to mash large floury potatoes with an excessive amount of cream, mustard and butter and serve it with a meaty stew or sautéed field mushrooms and buttered cabbage. There are over 5000 varieties of potato, but it's unlikely you'll ever see more than a handful – unless you head to Lima, Peru, and do some research through the International Potato Centre. On the other hand, they're incredibly easy to grow, and as with most vegetables these days, there's a resurgence in so-called heirloom or heritage varieties, which will broaden your experience.

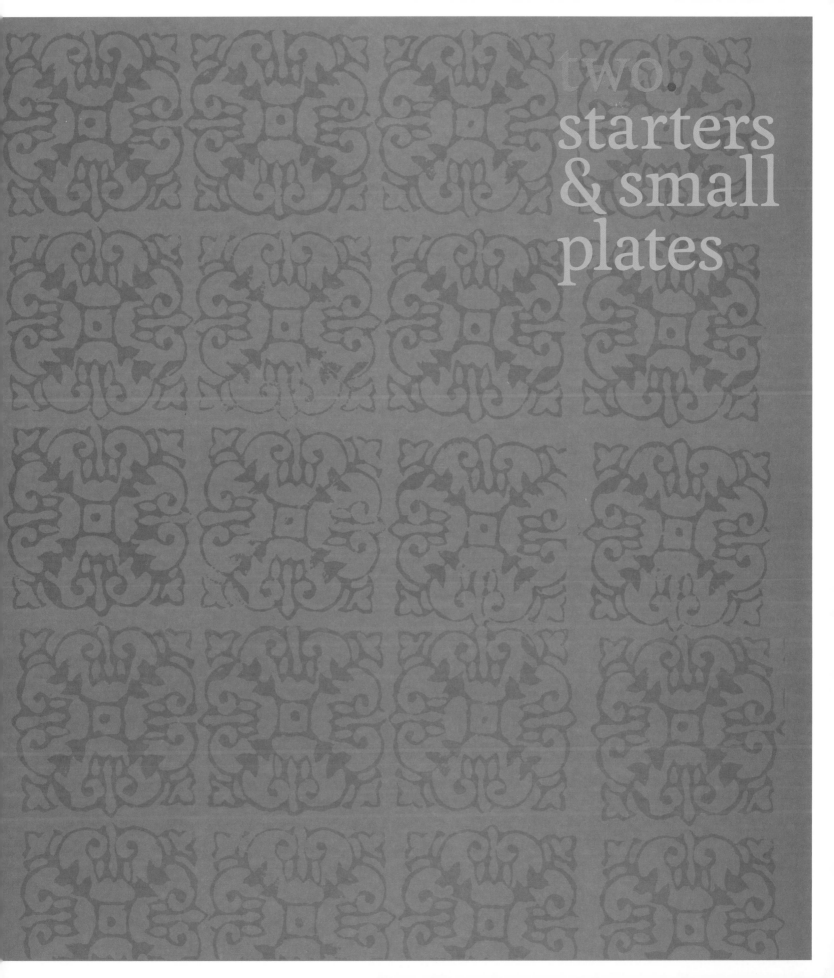

two.
starters
& small
plates

Sea urchin panna cotta with dashi jelly & seaweed

In June 2008, we celebrated Matariki at The Providores restaurant for the first time. Matariki is what's best described as Maori New Year and it takes its name from a cluster of stars normally seen in June, signifying the start of a new year to many cultures around the world, including the Japanese, Greek, Australian Aborigines, Chinese and Hindu. However, rather than being an excuse for a party to see in the new year, it symbolises the start of the planting of new crops, and a time to remember relatives, friends and ancestors who have passed on. As part of our own celebrations we sourced many New Zealand indigenous ingredients and used them to stunning effect on our menu. This dish was probably the biggest hit, and it was certainly a fusion of many cultures in itself. *Kina* is Maori for sea urchin, an acquired taste, but there truly is nothing quite so delicious as the coral from a freshly 'shucked' kina, or what the Japanese call *uni*. If you can't source it fresh, you may be able to source it frozen from Asian food stores, or replace it with the fresh coral from scallops, or use whole oysters for a more earthy taste. For the seaweed, head to your local health food shop, or Asian food store, and see what they have to hand. If you can find the lovely crunchy vegetable samphire, use it as a garnish. Simply pick off any dry or discoloured branches and blanch and refresh twice in unsalted water. It has a lovely briny taste.

For 6–8

1 x 10-cm piece kombu seaweed, rinsed briefly under warm water and wiped dry

50 ml soy sauce (avoid dark soy sauces, a Japanese one is best for this)

50 ml mirin

550 ml filtered water

6 g dried shaved bonito flakes (a very small handful)

7 sheets leaf gelatine

350 ml cream

10 ml (2 tsp) fish sauce

60 g fresh kina/sea urchin coral or 2 Tbsp dried kina powder

dried seaweed to garnish, soaked in cold water

a small handful samphire, blanched

First make the dashi. Place the kombu, soy sauce, mirin and filtered water into a pan and very slowly bring almost to the boil – make sure it doesn't boil though. Turn the heat off then add the bonito and give it a brief stir. Let it settle for 10 minutes. Strain it through a fine sieve and it's ready to be used. The amazing thing about this stock is that it's so simple to make, and yet so incredibly delicious.

You'll need 6–8 jelly moulds, preferably metal (they demould easier) of around 150–200 ml volume each. Soak three of the leaves of gelatine in icy cold water for a few minutes. Bring 100 ml of the dashi almost to the boil, then drain the gelatine and mix this into the hot dashi to dissolve it. Mix in another 200 ml of dashi then divide this amongst your moulds. Leave to cool, then place on a tray in the fridge and leave to set.

Place the remaining dashi, the cream, fish sauce and 1 teaspoon flaky salt in a pot and slowly bring almost to the boil. Using a stick blender, purée the kina with 100 ml of the hot liquid, or whisk the kina powder with 100 ml of the hot liquid, then add back to the pot. Soak the remaining 4 sheets of gelatine in icy cold water for a few minutes, then drain and mix into the cream mixture. Strain into a metal bowl, placed in an iced water-bath and leave to cool, stirring every few minutes until it begins to set, and has cooled to below body temperature. Carefully ladle it in on top of the jelly, then cover with plastic wrap and place back in the fridge to set. Leave for at least 6 hours.

To serve: Unmould the panna cottas by dipping them very briefly in hot water, or briefly run hot water over them inverted under a tap, and place on a plate upside down. Hold the base of the mould and gently wobble until you feel it pop out. Garnish with the seaweed and serve with hot toast if you like.

Baked rhubarb with sashimi & a beer-battered oyster

It may seem a little odd to serve rhubarb, usually associated with desserts, with fish, but the combination works surprisingly well. I've read old British cookbooks which mention the combination of mackerel and gooseberries, so this really is just a contemporary reworking of a classic dish. The sourness of the rhubarb works well with oily fish like salmon, mackerel or tuna but it also goes well with elegant but firm fish like the halibut I used in the photo. The crispy oyster works a treat too – that wonderful combination of crunch and gooey centre. What is important is that the rhubarb is served at room temperature, the fish needs to be icy cold, and the oyster piping hot! If you can't get hold of any verjus then use a mixture of equal quantities of lemon juice and water.

For 4

200 g rhubarb, washed then cut into 6-cm lengths

½ thumb of ginger, peeled and thinly sliced (or use candied or sushi ginger)

150 g caster sugar, plus 1 tsp for the batter

120 ml verjus (sometimes spelled 'verjuice')

40 g flour

20 g cornflour, plus a little extra for dusting the oysters

8 g (1 Tbsp) baking powder

100 ml beer

250 g fish fillet, all bones and skin removed – it must be perfectly fresh and chilled

vegetable oil for deep-frying

4 oysters, removed from the shell

a small handful of cress or sprouts

light soy sauce, to be served separately

Preheat oven to 160 °C. First bake the rhubarb – this can be made up to 5 days in advance if kept covered in the fridge. Choose a non-reactive roasting dish that will be just large enough to hold the rhubarb in one layer. Place the ginger on the bottom, cover with the rhubarb, then sprinkle with the sugar. Drizzle over the verjus then bake in the oven for 15–20 minutes until you can just squeeze the rhubarb between your fingers – if you overcook it it will go mushy. Leave it to cool in its juices in the roasting tray then place in the fridge.

Make the batter by sieving the flours, baking powder, 1 teaspoon sugar and ½ teaspoon fine salt together. Slowly pour in the beer, whisking continually to avoid lumps, to form a smooth batter then set aside for 5 minutes.

Slice the fish into 8–12 pieces, then place on a chilled plate and keep in the fridge until you need them.

When you're almost ready, take the rhubarb from the fridge and divide it amongst four plates along with some of its cooking juice. Heat 4 cm of oil in small pot to 180 °C. Dust the oysters with the reserved cornflour as this helps the batter to stick. Give the batter a quick stir, then add the oysters to it. Using a fork or a pair of tongs, carefully lower the oysters into the hot oil, making sure you keep them apart, and cook until crispy, flipping over after 12 seconds. They'll need no more than 20–25 seconds all up. Remove with a slotted spoon and drain on kitchen paper.

To serve: Lay the fish across the rhubarb, tuck in some cress and sit an oyster on top. Serve with a small jug of soy sauce on the side.

Grilled wagyu beef on horseradish creamed potato with soy buttered shimeji & pickled enoki mushrooms

Wagyu simply means 'Japanese cattle' with *wa* meaning Japan. It must be one of the most expensive, sustainable luxuries in the foodie larder. It's expensive for many reasons, the most obvious being that there is a lack of high-quality wagyu cattle on the market. You can buy wagyu from many countries, but the best will be from Japan (Kobe beef being the best of the best) with the wagyu from Hawke's Bay in New Zealand coming along closely behind. The beasts are fattier at the front, with their omega-3 and -6 rich fat tapering off to the rear, so the joints nearer the head are more marbled, although not necessarily the most tender. As you can see in the photo, wagyu beef is marbled with fat, but this fat has a higher proportion of unsaturated fats than regular beef fat – so don't worry too much about it. The other animal whose fat isn't as bad as you might think is the Iberico pig from Spain which eats lots of acorns on the *dehesa* (the oak fields) in the last 18–24 months of its life. And, just like wagyu, it's incredibly expensive. Having said all that, this dish works absolutely fine with regular beef, and if using regular beef it makes a great main course if you increase the portions of everything. The combination of soy and butter in the mushrooms has become a firm favourite of mine, two ingredients from completely different cuisines working harmoniously together. Perfect.

For 4

100 g shimeji mushrooms
100 g enoki mushrooms
100 g butter
50 ml soy sauce
80 ml rice vinegar (or any white vinegar)
2 Tbsp caster sugar
500 g floury potatoes
150 ml cream
1 Tbsp freshly grated horseradish, or use horseradish from a jar (more or less to taste)
15 ml (1 Tbsp) olive oil or rapeseed oil
4 x 60-g steaks of wagyu sirloin, fillet or rib-eye, trimmed of sinew, at room temperature
cress or something pretty to garnish

Cut the base from both types of mushroom then separate each mushroom from the clump – keeping them separate. Heat up a frying-pan and add half the butter and cook until it begins to turn golden. Add the shimeji and cook over a moderate heat, stirring, until they begin to wilt. Add 40 ml of the soy sauce, put a lid on, and turn the heat quite low. Leave them to cook/steam for 5 minutes, shaking the pan from time to time, and keep warm.

Put the vinegar and sugar into a pan with 150 ml water and 1 teaspoon flaky salt. Bring to the boil, add the enoki and take off the heat. Leave to cool in the liquid then decant into a bowl.

Peel the potatoes and halve them, then boil in lightly salted water until cooked. Drain the potato into a colander and put the pan back on the heat with the remaining butter and the cream. Bring to the boil, return the potato to the pan and mash it all together with the horseradish. Season with salt and keep covered and warm.

Heat up a heavy-based pan or skillet over a moderate–high heat. Rub the oil over the wagyu steaks and season generously with black pepper and salt. When the pan is hot, place the steaks in and cook until well coloured, then turn them over and cook the same on the other side. Sear all sides of the wagyu so it's brown and caramelised. Take from the heat, but keep warm and covered. Rest for 5 minutes. Don't overcook them or all their lovely flavour will be lost.

To serve: Divide the mash amongst four warmed plates. Slice the steaks in half and rest on the mash, tuck the shimeji in and then place some of the drained enoki on top. Add the wagyu cooking juices, remaining soy sauce and a little of the enoki pickling liquid to the shimeji pan juices, and use this to sauce the dish. Garnish with cress.

Smoked ham hock & seared scallop salad with green mango, pecans, palm heart, peas & avocado

This little mixed salad works so well because the various flavours are distinctive and the textures work wonderfully together. We have been lucky enough to get delicious crunchy fresh coconut palm hearts from Thailand in London – you can see slices of it in the photo. If you have to use canned palm hearts they'll be okay, but you may prefer to use either thinly sliced raw kohlrabi or *jicama* (yam bean) instead for the crunch factor. Please make sure you serve the coral from the scallop in this salad – too many people discard it, yet it has a lovely, almost bitter, flavour whilst also being quite rich. I use green mango that's ripened a little on the windowsill – it remains a little sharp, but also becomes a little sweet. Use fresh uncooked peas for this, although frozen ones (defrosted) will be fine, and make sure the avocado you choose is ripe and tasty. As for the ham hock, one hock will give you enough meat to make 20 salads – but it's worth cooking a whole one and using the leftovers in a pasta or risotto dish, mixed into scrambled eggs for breakfast, or used as a pie filling.

For 8

1 brined ham hock or gammon knuckle (1–1.2 kg)

1 whole head of garlic, unpeeled and cut crossways

2 chillies, split lengthways

10 black or white peppercorns

4 bay leaves

15 ml (1 Tbsp) olive oil

20 ml (1 Tbsp and 1 tsp) avocado oil

20 ml (1 Tbsp and 1 tsp) lime juice

100 g palm heart (see note on left)

1 green mango

1 avocado

150 g scallops, cleaned

2 large handfuls mixed micro-greens, cress or sprouts

16 toasted pecan nuts, snapped in half

a handful of raw peas

2 juicy limes, cut into quarters

Place the ham hock into a large deep pot along with the garlic, chillies, peppercorns and bay leaves. Pour on enough cold water to cover by 5 cm and bring to the boil. As it has been brined it won't need any salt. Put a lid on the pot and rapidly simmer for 1½–2 hours, topping up with hot water from time to time if the cooking liquor falls below the level of the meat. It's cooked when you can pull the meat off the bone. Leave it to cool in the poaching liquor then take it out, pull the fat off and discard it, and take the meat from the bone. Pull the meat apart, as in the photo, and put to one side.

Make the dressing by mixing the olive oil with 15 ml of the avocado oil, the lime juice and some salt and pepper.

Slice the palm heart thinly and put to one side. Peel the skin from the green mango, then peel the flesh off in strips and put to one side. Run a knife around the avocado and twist it open. Flick out the stone then, using a spoon, scoop the flesh out in one piece. Cut into chunks.

Cut the coral from the scallops then slice them into 5-mm thick discs. Toss gently with the remaining avocado oil and season with salt and pepper. Heat up a pan and when it's really hot place as many scallop slices and coral as will fit comfortably in the pan at once. Cook the scallops for 5 seconds on each side. Take from the pan and place on a warmed plate.

To serve: Toss everything together and then divide the salad amongst eight plates. Shake the dressing again and pour it over the salad. Serve with the lime wedge tucked in.

Scallop sashimi with watermelon & feta dressing

This is a really wonderful summer's dish. It is so simple that the ingredients need to be as near to perfect as you can get them. The watermelon needs to be sweet and chilled, the scallops as fresh as possible and the feta needs to be made as it should from ewe's milk, not the awful cow's milk varieties that occasionally pop up. The coral of the scallops really does make a difference here – the slight rich bitterness they have contrasts perfectly with the sweetness of the watermelon.

For 4

4 large scallops, with coral attached
 (or 6-8 smaller scallops)
¼ small watermelon
30 ml (2 Tbsp) soy sauce
30 ml (2 Tbsp) lemon juice
50 g feta, cut into small dice
15 ml (1 Tbsp) extra virgin olive oil
cress to garnish
1 lemon, cut into wedges

Clean the scallops, removing the tough muscle, which sits opposite the coral and looks like white gristle, if it's still attached. Remove the coral and cut roughly into dice – you'll need 1 Tablespoon worth in total. Slice each scallop into three discs of even thickness, place on kitchen paper on a chilled plate, cover with plastic wrap and place in the fridge.

Cut the rind and any white pith from the watermelon. Cut into 12 slices or wedges, removing as many pips as you can. Don't butcher the melon in the process though – a few pips won't hurt anyone. Place in the fridge to chill down for 20 minutes.

Mix the soy and lemon juice together in a small bowl and add the scallop slices. Leave to marinate for just 20 seconds then remove them and drain.

To serve: Lay a slice of watermelon on each plate, lay a scallop disc on top and repeat this until you have three slices of watermelon and the scallops are used up. Scatter the feta and coral on top. Sprinkle with a little flaky sea salt, drizzle with the olive oil, sprinkle with the cress and place a lemon wedge on each plate. Eat immediately.

Seared tuna on nori sauce with green papaya, mango, jicama & fresh coconut salad & wasabi tobikko

Tuna is one of the loveliest tasting fish, rich, slightly oily, firm and robust. Its flesh is more meaty than most others, and it must be the most popular of all sushi fish. However, it's also very susceptible to bad fishing practices. Make sure you only ever buy (from a shop or a restaurant) sustainable tuna. This will mean it has been caught from areas where tuna depletion isn't a risk, and that it has been caught in ways that are not a threat to other marine life (from dolphins through to bird-life) and where it hasn't been trawled out of the ocean in massive nets, killing other species indiscriminately. Once you've got your tuna sorted you can make this fabulous dish! The *nori* sauce is a creation of Satoshi Kikuchi, a chef who cooked at my restaurant in New Zealand for several years, and who also taught us how to make the best tempura batter and sushi rice ever. The dish itself came about when I was asked to create a tapas-style menu for a Providores customer's son's bar mitzvah in London. If you can't source *jicama*, green mango, green papaya or fresh coconut, then simply use only one of these, or replace them with a combination of celeriac, kohlrabi, nashi pear or carrot.

For 8 – although you'll have a lot of salad garnish left over

500 g tuna loin

30 ml (2 Tbsp) sesame oil

6 sheets nori

80 ml mirin

80 ml sake

60 ml (4 Tbsp) soy sauce

30 ml (2 Tbsp) balsamic vinegar

1 green papaya

1 jicama (yam bean)

1 green mango

1 coconut

6 sprigs of coriander

1 Tbsp wasabi tobikko (optional – or use any other fish roe mixed with a little wasabi paste)

30 ml (2 Tbsp) extra virgin olive oil

2 limes, quartered

Depending on the shape of the tuna, cut it into 5-cm x 3-cm batons (approximately). Rub with the sesame oil then sear in a hot pan on all sides, one minute in total. Immediately wrap it tightly in plastic wrap and plunge into a bowl of iced water. Place covered in the fridge for up to two days.

Toast four of the nori sheets over a medium open flame or a very hot electrical element until it goes dark green. Crumble the toasted nori into a bowl along with the untoasted sheets. Bring the mirin, sake, soy and balsamic vinegar to a simmer in a medium-sized pan, then stir in the nori and cook for 20 seconds, stirring constantly. Blitz into a paste with a stick blender and leave to cool.

Peel the papaya, jicama and mango, then julienne enough of each of them to give you a good handful.

Crack open the coconut and coarsely grate enough to give you a very small handful and add to the julienne.

Pick the leaves from the coriander, then cut the stalks into 1-cm long pieces and add both to the salad ingredients.

Cut the tuna in half lengthways then cut into slices 5 mm thick.

To serve: Dollop the nori sauce onto your plates along with a mound of green papaya salad next to it. Lay the sliced tuna on the sauce, sprinkle with flaky sea salt, spoon on the wasabi tobikko and drizzle with the olive oil. Serve with a lime wedge.

Grilled wild & regular asparagus with sweet miso dressing, watercress, Cape gooseberries & macadamia nuts

This incredibly simple salad makes for a lovely refreshing course, although it's also great when served as part of a multi-course meal. When we started shooting this book in June it coincided with the end of the season for what is called (in restaurant speak) wild asparagus. In the photo they're the thin green stems with what looks like a wheat head on them. The reality is that there is actually asparagus which only grows wild but it is becoming quite rare. In the UK it's only found in a few sites in Cornwall and a handful of other areas. However, for this recipe, any of the various asparagus will work. If you buy asparagus that is fat stemmed and firm, then you'll need to slice the ends off and peel the green stem which will be quite fibrous. If you buy thinner stems then you can simply bend them at their base ends until they snap – no need to peel them. Macadamia nuts originated in Australia, but have spread around the world and in Hawaii they're a huge attraction for the tourist dollar. Cape gooseberries, or *physalis*, are South American in origin and are a wonderful addition to a salad for their colour and their acidic sweet flavour.

For 4

500-600 g asparagus
45 ml (3 Tbsp) virgin rapeseed oil or extra virgin olive oil
a handful of wild asparagus
30 ml (2 Tbsp) sweet white miso (shiro miso)
45 ml (3 Tbsp) lemon or lime juice
12 Cape gooseberries
a handful of macadamia nuts, lightly toasted
2 handfuls watercress, picked over to remove any bad leaves or woody stems

Prepare the asparagus depending on its size as described on the left. Toss it with 1 Tablespoon of the oil, some salt and pepper. Heat up a skillet, heavy pan or barbecue and when it's hot place the asparagus on. If the spears are thin they'll need barely 30 seconds in total to cook, if fatter then around 1½ minutes, turning them as they colour. They should still be a little undercooked on the inside.

At the same time, bring a pot of salted water to the boil and add the wild asparagus. Boil for 40 seconds, then drain and refresh in cold water for a minute.

In a small bowl, whisk the miso with the lemon or lime juice, then mix in the remaining rapeseed oil and season with salt and pepper.

Cut the Cape gooseberries in half, and roughly chop or slice the macadamia nuts.

To serve: Divide two-thirds of the asparagus between four plates and lay the wild asparagus on top. Place the remaining asparagus on top, drizzle with the dressing then scatter with the Cape gooseberries, nuts and watercress. Eat straight away so that the watercress doesn't wilt.

Tempura enari pocket stuffed with spinach & shiitake rice with chilli pickled bean sprouts & braised lotus root

I bought the plate for this dish in Kyoto, knowing I'd be serving this recipe on it. I have to say that the flavours and textures of the finished dish equal what I think is a most beautiful photo. *Enari* are like a tofu pita bread in that they come flat but can be easily pulled apart. You'll find them at Asian food shops and some health-food stores, and they're most often used for serving vinegared rice topped with vegetables – like a vegetable sushi sandwich! We have served versions of this at various restaurants I've either owned or cooked at, and when you fill the enari up to almost bursting, they make a great vegetarian main course served with lots of vegetables. Lotus root can be found fresh and frozen at most Asian food markets and it has the most wonderful texture when cooked this way. I had thought about using sushi rice for this dish, but the Arborio risotto rice on my shelf was wanting to enter the Fusion debate so I cooked that instead and it worked a treat.

For 8

1 medium beetroot – ideally a raw one, but a cooked one will work okay
200 ml rice vinegar
60 g caster sugar
1 bird's eye chilli (or other chilli), split lengthways
150 g mung bean sprouts
200 g lotus root, peeled
100 ml soy sauce
1 thumb of ginger, peeled and julienned
4 star anise
150 g risotto rice
6 shiitake mushrooms, stalks discarded, caps thinly sliced
100 g spinach, washed and drained, then coarsely shredded
30 g Parmesan, grated
8 enari pockets
50 g flour, plus 4 Tbsp extra
50 g cornflour
20 g baking powder
vegetable oil for deep-frying the enari
cress to garnish

If your beetroot is raw, put some gloves on, peel it, then coarsely grate it. If it's already cooked, then wear the gloves and grate it. Place it in a pot with 150 ml of the vinegar, all but 1 Tablespoon of the sugar, the chilli and 250 ml of water. Bring to the boil then simmer for 5 minutes. Rinse the bean sprouts in cold water briefly, then place in a heat-proof jar or bowl. Strain the pickling liquid over them through a fine sieve and cover tightly while still hot. Leave to cool down then place in the fridge for at least 4 hours or up to a week.

Slice the lotus root ½ cm thick and rinse under cold running water for a few minutes, rubbing it a little to help release some of the slimy texture. Place in a saucepan and cover with cold water. Add the remaining vinegar and sugar, along with the soy sauce, ginger and star anise. Bring to the boil then simmer until cooked – at which point you'll be able to just pass a sharp skewer through the flesh. Leave to cool in the liquor then store, covered, in the fridge for up to a week.

Rinse the rice with cold running water in a fine sieve for 30 seconds then place in a pot with 300 ml water, the sliced shiitake, 1 teaspoon flaky salt (less of fine salt) and cover with a tight-fitting lid. Place over high heat and bring to the boil, then turn the heat down, keeping the lid on, and cook for 15 minutes. At this point the rice should be cooked, the liquid should have evaporated, and the rice should be sticking to the bottom of the pan, turning golden and tasting toasted. If not, keep it cooking a little longer. Take the pan from the heat and, keeping the lid on, tilt it under a tap of running water to cool the base down. Alternatively, dunk the base of the pot into a bowl of cold water. Scrape the bottom bits up and mix into the rice then stir in the spinach and Parmesan and taste it for seasoning. Divide the mixture into eight 50 g portions and roll into a fat cylinder shape.

Take one enari pocket at a time and pull it gently apart. Tuck in one of the rice portions, gently flatten it into the enari to even it out, then dip the open mouth into 2 Tablespoons of the flour and press it firmly shut. This will help seal it. Do the same to the rest of the enari. Dust them gently with the other 2 Tablespoons of flour.

Make the tempura batter by sieving the remaining flour with the cornflour, baking powder and ½ teaspoon fine salt. Whisk in 120 ml cold water and leave for a few minutes – it will froth up a little but don't worry.

Heat 6 cm of vegetable oil in a wok or pot to 180 °C.

Give the tempura batter a stir, then dip the enari in, one at a time, to coat them then lower into the hot oil. You can cook four at a time, more if you have a huge deep-fryer. Take from the oil after 3–4 minutes at which point they'll be golden brown and piping hot. Drain onto kitchen paper and cook the remainder.

To serve: Lay some of the drained bean sprouts on a plate along with a slice or two of the lotus root. Cut the enari in half and sit this on top then scatter with some cress – I used red shiso leaves.

Laksa is a Peranakan dish (a fusion of Malay and Chinese cultures) originating in Malaysia, although Singapore and (less common but equally delicious) Thailand make wonderful versions as well. I first came across laksa when I was hitch-hiking around South-East Asia in 1986 and what I loved about it, and its 'cousin' *bakso* from Indonesia, was that there was always a wee tweak here and there depending on the cook making it. In Penang it was an aromatic dark sweet and sour broth served with round fat white rice noodles, in Ipoh it was somewhat more sour with a tamarind-based stock redolent of shrimp paste, and in Singapore it was yellow with turmeric and coconut milk, served with vermicelli noodles and fried tofu. Since those days I've always had a laksa on my menu in whatever restaurant I've cooked in, and although I've been criticised for ruining a classic dish, I figure I've just adapted one of the world's great soup-meals as I witnessed myself. Sweetcorn originates in North America and by cooking it over a high heat as in this recipe, it develops a lovely smoky, sweet taste and crunchy texture. Soba noodles are Japanese in origin, and their lovely buckwheat flavour and firm texture rounds off this coconut-sweet and aromatic soup. For the curry paste you can simply buy one from a Malaysian or Thai food store, although I also give a simple recipe on the following page.

For 4–6

Duck & coconut laksa with grilled sweetcorn, soba noodles, squid & coriander

4 shallots, peeled and sliced

1 thumb of ginger, peeled and finely chopped or grated

4 cloves garlic, peeled and sliced

10 ml (2 tsp) vegetable oil

1–2 Tbsp curry paste (to taste)

2 Tbsp palm sugar

30 ml (2 Tbsp) fish sauce

4 lime leaves (or use the peel and juice of 1 lime)

½ tsp Sichuan peppercorns (optional – but they add a real zing to this)

1 heaped Tbsp tamarind paste (you can also use the paste that's full of fibre and seeds that usually comes in a block, you'll just have to pick out the chunky bits as you eat it)

400 ml unsweetened coconut milk or coconut cream

1 duck breast, skin scored with a sharp knife to give many ridges

2 tsp garam masala or other spice mix (see my garam masala recipe on page 29)

1 corn cob, cut in half

100 g soba noodles

a small handful each of Thai basil and coriander

100 g squid, cleaned, the heads cut into rings, the legs separated

crispy shallots to garnish

Heat up a medium-sized pot and sauté the shallots, ginger and garlic in the vegetable oil until just beginning to caramelise. Add the curry paste and fry for 1 minute, stirring often, until it releases its aromas. Add the palm sugar and fish sauce and fry until they form a boiling syrup. Add the lime leaves, Sichuan peppercorns and tamarind paste and cook until the leaves soften. Add the coconut milk or cream and 300 ml hot water and bring to the boil, then turn to a simmer and cook for 20 minutes.

Heat up a deep-sided pan large enough to hold the duck breast and place the duck in, skin-side down. Cook over a moderate heat for 5 minutes to render some of the fat from it and to colour it golden brown. Remove the duck and dust it on both sides with the garam masala.

Place the corn halves in the pan and cook over a moderate–high heat in the duck fat until it's coloured all over. Remove from the pan and return the duck, continuing to cook for 2 more minutes on the skin side, then turn over and cook on the other side for 2 minutes. Turn the heat off and leave it to rest in the pan and it will be nicely pink when you eat it.

While the duck's cooking, bring 2 litres of water to the boil in a large pan. Add the noodles, gently stirring them to prevent them from sticking, and bring back to the boil. Add a cup of cold water to the pan then drop the temperature to a rolling simmer and cook until they're supple, but still with a little bite to them – around 10 minutes. Drain and rinse under cold water then cover with a little water to prevent them sticking.

Cut the corn kernels from the cob and put to one side. Pick some Thai basil and coriander leaves from the stalks and thinly slice the duck.

Taste the laksa broth for chilli heat, sweetness and seasoning, adding either some fresh chopped chilli, palm sugar, fish sauce or salt to taste. Bring it to a gentle boil and stir in the squid. Count to 20 and it's ready to serve.

To serve: Drain the noodles and divide amongst preheated bowls. Ladle on the broth making sure everyone gets some squid, then place the sliced duck, corn, Thai basil and coriander on top. Scatter on the crispy shallots and it's ready.

Simple curry paste

6 red chillies, roughly chopped, don't discard the seeds
2 stalks lemongrass, cut the base off, discard the outer 3 layers and cut as much from the base up as you can until it begins to turn fibrous
2 thumbs of ginger, peeled and sliced against the grain
6 cloves garlic, peeled
4 lime leaves, shredded
15 ml (1 Tbsp) sesame oil
1 Tbsp ground coriander seeds

Place everything in a small food processor with 2 Tablespoons cold water and blitz to a fine paste. This will keep for 10 days in the fridge, or spread it out on a parchment-lined baking tray and freeze it before breaking it into pieces and storing in a suitable container.

Seared scallops on plantain coconut fritters with papaya & lime salsa

The first time I saw a box of plantain was in 1989 on Portobello Road in London's Notting Hill. I thought they were actually big bananas rotting in the sun. It was a Ghanaian chef who first cooked them for me, and in *The Sugar Club Cookbook*, I wrote this, which still holds true, about them: 'For those not familiar with plantains, they are those huge "bananas" that you may have seen in Caribbean or African food stores and markets. They are sold in shades from green (hard, starchy and unripe) to yellow (firm and semi-sweet) to mottled brown (soft and sweet). When ripe they are very banana-like in taste, but their main use is as a source of starch in tropical cooking – and for this the less ripe fruit is normally chosen.'

For this recipe you want to use plantain that are yellow and just a little soft. I used large Scottish-diver-caught scallops for this dish but you may have to settle for smaller ones. I truly believe you should always serve the coral on your scallops – it still amazes me that the majority of restaurant chefs discard this part of the scallop. If you don't eat shellfish, then this combination of fritter and salsa, without the scallop, is really tasty as it is, with the addition of some salad leaves instead.

For 4 as a starter or 8 tapa-sized dishes

1 yellow-skin plantain, as described on the left
¼ tsp baking soda
¼ tsp baking powder
3 Tbsp desiccated coconut, or freshly grated coconut
½ red chilli, sliced (more or less to taste)
1 egg
5 ml (1 tsp) soy sauce
a handful of shredded coriander, plus some coriander leaves to garnish
½ papaya, peeled and deseeded
1 spring onion, thinly sliced
finely grated zest and juice of 1 lime
6 basil leaves, shredded
30 ml (2 Tbsp) extra virgin olive oil
8 large (or 16 smaller) scallops, cleaned, coral attached
vegetable cooking oil

Peel the plantain and weigh the flesh – you want roughly 180–200 grams. Cut into a fat julienne around 5 mm thick, or simply grate it coarsely or slice into thin rounds. Sieve the baking soda and baking powder and mix with the coconut, chilli and ¼ teaspoon salt, then mix this into the plantain. Using a fork, beat the egg with the soy and mix this into the plantain along with the coriander. Leave to one side.

Cut the papaya into small dice. Mix with the spring onion, lime zest and juice, basil and olive oil. Taste for seasoning, adding a little salt.

Toss the scallops with 1 Tablespoon cooking oil and leave to come to room temperature while you cook the fritters.

Heat a frying-pan over a moderate heat and add enough oil to give a 5-mm depth. Give the plantain fritter mixture a stir, then drop spoonfuls of it into the hot pan (you want 8 fritters) and cook for 2 minutes or so, before flipping over carefully and cooking on the other side until golden. Keep warm on a plate in an oven set to around 100 °C. Once all of the fritters are cooked it's time to cook the scallops. Tip the excess oil out, wipe the pan with kitchen paper and put back on the heat, turning it to medium–high. Place the scallops in and cook for 1 minute, then flip over and cook for another minute – at which point the scallops will be done. Smaller scallops need less cooking – and be careful not to overcook as they become quite rubbery in texture.

To serve: Place two fritters on warmed plates, sit a scallop atop each, then spoon the salsa over and sprinkle the coriander leaves on top.

Crab, ginger & tofu fritters with Sichuan pickled vegetables

What I like about these fritters is that they use silken tofu instead of the more traditional egg and cream in the mousse mixture to bind it all together. When I was doing my apprenticeship in Melbourne in the 1980s, we were taught that the best savoury mousses were always made with the addition of cream and eggs. What I've found is that by using silken tofu the mixture is much lighter and more pure-tasting. I often use Japanese tofu from a tetra-pak, it's easy to source and store in the pantry – although if you can get fresh silken tofu, all the better. There are varieties of tofu that are light brown in colour, quite firm and almost rubbery. These are lovely to use in braised dishes, but they'll make this mousse too dense. On page 160 you'll see that I've used this same mixture to provide the crust for a fish main course, but another thing you can do with it is to roll them into marble-sized balls before deep-frying then serving them as canapés, topped with wasabi *tobikko*. The pickled vegetables will keep in the fridge for up to a week, so they can be made in advance.

For 4–6, although the vegetables will make a little more than you need

1 carrot, peeled
½ cucumber
2 tsp Sichuan peppercorns
vegetable cooking oil
200 ml rice vinegar (or any other white vinegar)
100 ml mirin
120 g white fish fillet, skin and bones removed, roughly diced
120 g firm silken tofu
½ tsp shichimi spice mix (a Japanese spice mix – or simply use paprika)
2 spring onions, thinly sliced
2 Tbsp firmly packed and drained gari (sushi ginger) shredded (or use 2 tsp grated fresh ginger)
100 g white crab meat, all shell removed
50 g honey panko breadcrumbs (or regular breadcrumbs)
vegetable oil for frying
fresh coriander leaves

Julienne the carrot and put to one side. Slice the cucumber into ½-cm thick slices and put to one side. Place the Sichuan peppercorns in a saucepan with 1 Tablespoon of the vegetable oil and turn the heat to medium. Keep stirring the pepper as the oil heats up, and at the point when they become aromatic, slowly add the vinegar and mirin mixed with 300 ml warm water, and 1 teaspoon fine salt. Bring to the boil and cook for 2 minutes. Add the carrots to the pan and bring back to the boil then take off the heat and add the cucumber. Give it a gentle stir, put a lid on and leave to go cold, then decant into a clean jar, seal well and store in the fridge. Best left for at least a day before using.

Make the mousse by placing the diced fish and tofu in a food processor and blitz for 15 seconds, scraping the sides halfway through. Scrape the sides again then add the shichimi spice, spring onions and some salt and blitz for another 5 seconds. Tip the mousse into a bowl and mix in the gari and crab meat. Place in the fridge and leave for at least an hour to firm up. Divide the mixture into 12 and roll each one in the breadcrumbs, gently pressing the crumbs onto the mousse's surface. Place on a plate and put back in the fridge.

Set up a deep-fryer with 5 cm of oil in it heated to 180 °C. Lower several fritters at a time into the hot oil from a slotted spoon and cook as many as will comfortably fit in the pan until golden. Remove and place on kitchen paper to drain.

To serve: Place two or three piping hot fritters alongside some of the pickled vegetables and coriander leaves.

Sautéed snails & hazelnuts on chorizo mash

The first time I ate a snail, I have to say, was almost my last. My 3rd and 4th Form French teacher, Miss Dunsmuir, had returned from New Caledonia, I think it was, and had brought back some French goodies for our class to try. One of the goodies was a tin of snails. She lined us up and made us all eat one – cold, from the tin, with no other flavouring. I have to say that I'd always imagined my first snail would be served with sizzling garlic and parsley butter and be somewhat romantic! This was like a blind date with an elephant seal. Twenty years later, I bought a can of snails and cooked them in sizzling butter with garlic and parsley and whilst they were a marked improvement, I still felt they were just a bit too much like … well … muddy-tasting, chewy pellets. A few years later I was in Cáceres in Spain, and I was served a tapa of what appeared to be cold mashed potato mixed with minced chorizo. It wasn't even vaguely tasty, although I knew if it were served hot it would have been much better, but I suddenly remembered those snails and realised that they would be the perfect match. So here it is, the dish which for me justifies snails, and a dish that's been incredibly popular on our menu at the restaurant.

For 6

500 g boiling potatoes, peeled and cut into large chunks
200 g cooking chorizo sausage
15 ml (1 Tbsp) olive oil
a good pinch of cumin seeds
30 g butter
4 cloves garlic, peeled and sliced
48 snails, briefly rinsed under cold water then drained
60 g hazelnuts, roasted, peeled and roughly chopped
15 ml (1 Tbsp) black vinegar or sherry vinegar
100 ml reduced roast-chicken, veal or pork stock
a few sprigs of flat parsley, roughly chopped

Boil the potatoes in lightly salted water until cooked, then drain and mash. While they're cooking, peel the chorizo and chop it into chunks. Heat up a pan and add the oil, chorizo and cumin and cook over a lowish heat, stirring often, so as to render fat from the chorizo and cook it through – it will start to stick a little, so just keep giving it a good stir. Once it's cooked and the potatoes are mashed, mix them together, taste for seasoning, then keep warm.

Heat up a wide frying-pan or pot over a moderate–high heat and add the butter. Cook it until it turns a nut-brown colour then add the garlic and cook that until it turns golden, stirring all the time. Add the drained snails and the hazelnuts and keep cooking for 20 seconds, stirring constantly. Add the vinegar and boil to evaporate most of it, then add the stock and cook over high heat until it thickens.

To serve: Taste the snails for seasoning then stir in the parsley and serve immediately atop the chorizo mash.

Miso risotto with chicken livers & plum compote

50 g butter

260 g (1½ cups) risotto rice

2 smallish red onions, peeled, halved and thinly sliced

⅓ leek, thinly sliced, washed if gritty

4 cloves garlic, peeled and sliced

2 star anise

1 Tbsp fresh thyme leaves

1 tsp fresh rosemary leaves, chopped

60 g miso - any miso will work - I used hatcho miso

60 ml mirin (or 2 Tbsp sugar)

30 ml (2 Tbsp) soy sauce

1.2 litres unsalted chicken stock, keep it simmering

80 g mascarpone

20 g Parmesan, grated

10 ml (2 tsp) vegetable oil

250 g chicken livers, cleaned of sinew and fat

4 red plums, halved and stone removed, then thinly sliced

1 Tbsp Chinese black vinegar, balsamic or sherry vinegar

a handful of flat parsley leaves

Italian purists may hate this 'so not classic' risotto recipe – but they should remember that rice is Asian in origin, as are miso, mirin and soy. So actually, one could argue, and I often have, just to be annoying, that this dish sticks to its roots more properly than your usual risottos that come out of Italy. But then, I think anything that tastes good is worth doing, so what do I really care? The combination of earthy miso, tasty soy and rich butter gives a lovely unexpected sweet–savoury taste to the dish. The livers and plums really do complete the dish, but if you're liver-phobic then I'd suggest you replace them with either bacon lardons, pecan nuts or just leave them out.

For 8

Heat up a 2–3 litre pan then add the butter and cook until it stops sizzling, stirring as it melts. Add the rice and cook for a few minutes over medium heat, stirring constantly until it begins to turn a light golden colour. Add half the sliced onions, the leek, garlic and star anise and cook for another 4–5 minutes, stirring often, until the onions and leek wilt. Add the thyme, rosemary, miso, mirin and soy sauce and bring to a boil. Stir in enough simmering stock to cover the rice by 1 cm. Bring to the boil, then turn to a simmer. As the rice cooks, absorbing the stock, keep topping it up, stirring really well each time you add more stock. Make sure the rice is always covered by at least 1 cm of stock. The rice will take 20–30 minutes to cook. If the stock has run out before the rice has cooked, simply add boiling water. When the rice has the faintest bite to it, stir in the mascarpone and Parmesan and taste for seasoning. Put a lid on the pan, turn the heat off and leave to rest for 5 minutes.

While the risotto is cooking, place a wide pan over moderate heat, add the oil and remaining sliced onion. Sauté to caramelise the onions, then add the livers and cook evenly all over to colour them. Mix in the sliced plums and cook for a minute to soften them, then add the vinegar, a little salt and lastly the parsley.

To serve: Stir the risotto once more, taste it, then divide amongst eight warmed bowls and spoon the liver and plum compote on top.

Green tea noodles & arame seaweed with teriyaki smoked eel & avocado

Green tea noodles (called *cha soba* in Japan) are a firm favourite of mine. They are the most gorgeous colour and they have a lovely firm texture and subtle earthy flavour. If you can't find any, use plain soba noodles instead. *Soba* (the Japanese word for buckwheat) noodles are made with varying percentages of buckwheat flour and wheat flour – the latter giving them elasticity. However, the most expensive soba in Japan are made from 100 per cent buckwheat and they're more brittle, hence I prefer ones that are around 70–80 per cent buckwheat. If ever you find yourself in Japan, head to a soba restaurant, they specialise in soba noodles as well as soba dumplings and various other delicious treats. The first time I combined smoked eel and avocado was back in 1987 at The Sugar Club restaurant in Wellington, New Zealand. I put them together in an omelette and they seemed perfectly suited. Over the years I've developed a fondness for Japanese teriyaki-style cooking, where a mixture of soy sauce, mirin and sometimes sake is used as a glaze and marinade for grilling fish, meats and tofu. When cooked over a char-grill, or on the barbecue, the resulting smokiness that is created when the sugars in the teriyaki sauce drip down and caramelise over the hot embers adds a lovely dimension to the food you're cooking. Failing that, it's a good idea to use a non-stick pan when cooking this as the sugars can end up sticking to your pan and burning a little.

For 4

250 g smoked eel fillet, all skin and bones removed
50 ml soy sauce (choose one that isn't too salty)
30 ml (2 Tbsp) mirin
100 g green tea noodles (or use soba noodles)
10 g dried arame or hijiki seaweed
5 ml (1 tsp) toasted sesame oil
2 tsp toasted sesame seeds (white or black seeds)
½ avocado, peeled, cut into dice
sprouts or cress to garnish

Cut the eel into eight even-sized pieces. Mix the soy and mirin together and place in a flat dish. Sit the eel in, give it a mix then leave for 10 minutes. Turn over and leave for another 10 minutes.

While the eel's marinating, cook the noodles. Bring a large pot of very lightly salted water to the boil and add the seaweed and noodles, making sure they don't all clump together when you add them. Give the pot a stir from time to time to ensure they cook evenly. When the water comes back to the boil it can sometimes boil over on the stove. Just before it does this add 200 ml cold water to the pan and again bring back to the boil. Add another 200 ml cold water to the pan then turn to a simmer and cook until they're done – they are best with the slightest bite to them – a lovely texture. Drain into a colander and refresh under cold running water. Leave to drain for a minute then tip into a bowl and toss with the sesame oil and half the toasted sesame seeds then divide amongst your bowls which have been previously chilled in the fridge.

Take the eel from the marinade, reserving it. Place a non-stick frying-pan over a moderate heat and when it's hot add the eel pieces, as many as will comfortably fit in the pan at one time. Cook for 1 minute then flip over and cook on the other side until coloured. Once all the eel is cooked add the marinade back to the pan with the eel and cook over a high heat until it mostly evaporates and develops a lovely sheen. Take off the heat and sit the eel on top of the noodles, drizzling on the pan juices.

To serve: Scatter the avocado, remaining sesame seeds and sprouts or cress on top.

Orecchiette with chorizo, scallops, broad beans, coconut & black vinegar

Orecchiette are lovely ear-shaped pasta originating from Puglia in the heel of Southern Italy. I must admit I used to think they were more like belly buttons than ears, but then it's tortellini that have that anatomical honour – must be that I have a funny-shaped belly button. Whatever, I have to say that they're one of my favourite wheat-based pastas as I love the way that they hold sauce in their cavity and they are usually quite firm to the bite and chewy. They're mostly produced in smaller artisan 'factories' rather than being one of the many mass-produced long pastas such as spaghetti or fettuccine. Here I mix them up with lovely spicy Spanish chorizo, aromatic Chinese black vinegar, rich scallops and coconut milk and crunchy broad beans. It's a delicious combination and one that seems quite simple to get to, once you've done the shopping.

For 6 as a generous starter

250 g spicy cooking chorizo, sliced into 5-mm rounds
30 ml (2 Tbsp) olive oil
1 red onion, peeled and thinly sliced
4 cloves garlic, peeled and roughly chopped
30 ml (2 Tbsp) black vinegar (or sherry vinegar or chardonnay vinegar)
250 g podded broad beans
360 g dried orecchiette
8-12 scallops (depending on their size)
200 ml coconut milk
a handful of coriander

Bring a pot of water to the boil and add 1 Tablespoon of salt.

Meanwhile, heat up a pan and add the chorizo and half the olive oil and fry for a few minutes, stirring frequently, until the fat begins to render from the chorizo.

Add the onion and garlic and continue to cook over a moderate heat, stirring frequently, until the onion caramelises. Add the vinegar to the pot and cook until evaporated then take from the heat.

Add the broad beans to the boiling water and cook for a minute, then remove them with a sieve and refresh under cold water. Hull or peel them if they're larger than your small fingernail, as the skins from larger ones can make them a little bitter.

Add the orecchiette to the boiling water and cook until a little softer than al dente – about 8–14 minutes depending on your brand of pasta.

While that's cooking, heat up a frying-pan over a high heat. Slice the scallops into 2–3 discs each, depending on the size of them, making sure to keep the coral intact. Gently toss with the remaining oil and a little salt and pepper. Place in the hot pan and colour briefly on both sides, making sure you don't overcook them. Tip from the pan onto a warm plate. Add the chorizo mixture to the pan along with the coconut milk and bring to the boil, then cook to reduce by half. Return the scallops and broad beans to the mixture and turn the heat off.

Drain the pasta and tip into a large warmed serving bowl, then tip the chorizo mixture on top and gently toss it all together before serving in warmed bowls. Tear the coriander up and scatter it over the top and serve piping hot.

Now this is really quite a mixture of cultures on one plate – a really happy mixture it has to be said. At The Providores we've been using a black pudding (sometimes called blood sausage) from Stornoway, a town on the distant Outer Hebrides island of Lewis, north-west of Scotland. This particular black pudding is the most delicious I've eaten because it's a little crispy when fried with a meltingly rich and tasty centre. They are really large, resembling a fat rolling pin more than a sausage and they have none of the stodginess that I find many other black puddings and French *Boudin Noir* have. My second favourite would have to be the rice-based *morcilla de Burgos* from Spain as again, once cooked it's a little crunchy and rich. Here I team this pig's blood-based breakfast staple with freshly made rice flour-based *hor fun* (or *shahe fen* or *kway teow*) noodles, which you can buy fresh in most Chinese food stores, and which surprisingly reheat best of all in a microwave – although a steamer is slightly more authentic. If stored in the fridge these become really firm and are less successful when reheating. Look for dried rice noodles if you can't find them freshly made. Fresh, they have a lovely chewy, almost sticky texture and they pair well with the richness of the black pudding. The Chinese have a love of the pig and so along with ginger, peanuts, shiitake and other things used often in the Cantonese kitchen, this is an intriguing and tasty dish.

For 4

Fresh rice noodles with black pudding, peas, peanuts, spinach & shiitake ragout

200 g black pudding, any skin or binding removed, cut into 1-cm dice
5 ml (1 tsp) sesame oil
5 ml (1 tsp) peanut oil
1 small onion, peeled and thinly sliced
8 shiitake mushrooms, thinly sliced (discard stems if too woody)
1 large thumb of ginger, peeled and julienned
50 ml mirin
50 ml soy sauce
60 g roasted peanuts
100 g spinach, blanched and refreshed
100 g peas, blanched and refreshed
400–500 g fresh hor fun noodles

Heat up a wide pan. Add the diced black pudding and cook over a moderate heat until the fat renders out. Remove from the pan. If your particular sausage isn't fatty at all, you'll need to add some oil to the pan. If, however, you find a lot of fat renders out then once it's cooked and slightly crispy, scoop it out with a slotted spoon onto a warmed plate and discard the fat in the pan.

Return the pan to the heat and add the two oils along with the onion, mushrooms and ginger and fry, stirring often, until they caramelise. Add the mirin and soy and boil until they've practically evaporated.

Add the peanuts, spinach and peas to the pan along with the black pudding and 60 ml warm water and gently heat it, mixing it as it warms up.

While that's reheating, place the noodles in a suitable bowl and cover with plastic wrap, poke a few holes in the top and microwave until hot. Alternatively, place them on a plate and steam over boiling water for a few minutes until hot.

To serve: Divide the noodles amongst four warmed plates and then spoon the ragout on top.

In summer, there's not much better than a bowl of chilled soup on a hot day. The most popular chilled soup would undoubtedly be Spain's *gazpacho*, but the reality is that many hot soups, if served cold, are also quite delicious, and many chilled soups, if heated, are likewise. However, this soup isn't one of them. Don't think that in the midst of a snowy winter you might serve this hot and it will still be delicious – when I tried it I found it to be a little strange, even for my taste. All the ingredients work in harmony in this soup, possibly because they're all quite rich in texture and flavour, and the chilling of the soup helps to keep them mellow. In some ways, this soup owes its genealogy to the legendary chilled leek and potato soup called *vichyssoise*, but if you were to characterise that soup as a humble French country peasant, then this must be the exotic, distant cousin who decided to become a global back-packer. It's really important that the avocados you use for this are ripe, with no discoloured pieces. If they're not ripe the soup will be bland.

For 4

Chilled avocado, kumara, coconut & ginger soup with radish

300 g peeled kumara (or use white-fleshed sweet potatoes)
2 thumbs of ginger, peeled and sliced against the grain
400 ml coconut milk
10-cm pandan leaf, tied into a knot, or 2 lime leaves
 or 1 bay leaf
2 ripe avocados
30 ml (2 Tbsp) extra virgin avocado oil or extra virgin
 olive oil, plus a little extra to garnish
20-30 ml (1-2 Tbsp) lime or lemon juice (to taste)
a handful of radishes, sliced

Slice the kumara thinly and place in a saucepan with the ginger, coconut milk and pandan leaf. Add 1 litre water and place over a moderate heat. Bring to the boil, stirring occasionally, then put a lid on and simmer until the kumara is cooked. Take off the heat and leave to cool, or to speed things up, transfer it into a clean wide bowl and leave it to cool. Run a knife around the avocados and twist them open, then remove the stones. Using a large spoon scoop out the flesh and add this to the mixture, reserving a quarter of an avocado to be used for garnish. Add the avocado oil to the mixture then purée it using either a stick blender or a bar blender. Season with salt and freshly ground white pepper.

Put the puréed soup in the fridge and leave it to chill for at least 3 hours.

Just before serving, stir in lime juice (to taste), the soup needs a little acidity to cut through the rich flavours. Add extra salt if needed as well. Cut the reserved avocado into chunks.

To serve: Pour into chilled bowls, scatter with sliced radishes and the reserved avocado then drizzle on the extra avocado oil.

Heirloom tomato, Manouri cheese, green chilli, fig & summer truffle salad

Late summer, when figs are at their best, summer truffles are around (and nowhere near as expensive as white winter truffles) and there are heirloom tomatoes in the markets, is the time to make this incredibly simple salad. This recipe relies on the best, ripest, sweetest produce. In many ways this is really a recipe to inspire you to get what's best and available and do almost nothing to it. The green chilli dressing gives all the sweetness a little kick, and the fried Manouri ewe's milk cheese gives it a savoury edge. Manouri comes from Greece and it is quite a flaky, soft cheese, which benefits from a quick fry over moderate heat. If you can't find any, then use either haloumi cheese or feta, although the latter won't benefit from frying. If you do use haloumi then the best thing you can do is slice it 1 cm thick and soak for 4–5 hours in plenty of warm water – this trick, passed down from Tarik and Savas in Istanbul, softens the cheese and removes some of the excess salt. If you can't find truffles then don't despair, whilst they do add a certain wow factor to the dish, it will still be lovely as it is without them. Or, you could add a few drops of truffle oil to the dressing.

For 4

5-6 heirloom tomatoes, of varying shapes and colours
2 figs
½ green chilli (more or less, to taste)
10 ml (2 tsp) lemon juice
150 g Manouri cheese
1 summer truffle (more or less, to taste)
30 ml (2 Tbsp) extra virgin olive oil (the best you can afford)

Slice the tomatoes and mix them up between your plates. Remove the stem from the figs then slice them and place on top of the tomatoes.

Mix the chilli with the lemon juice and a little salt.

Slice the Manouri into eight pieces then fry on both sides in a pan over a moderate heat, adding a little oil if it looks like it needs it (you won't need any in a non-stick pan). Sit this on top of the salad, then shave the truffle over that – a potato peeler or a mandolin works well for this unless you happen to have a truffle slicer at hand!

Mix the olive oil into the chilli and lemon juice and drizzle this over the salad and eat while the Manouri is still warm.

Chorizo, curry leaf, ginger & chickpea soup

This is such a simple-to-make soup, but one that is incredibly flavoursome, and the sort of soup that is excellent to serve on a really cold day. If you don't eat pork, then you can get nearly the same effect by adding two teaspoons of smoked paprika (sweet or spicy) to the onion mixture when you are sautéing it. Ginger isn't the flavour companion any of my Spanish friends think of when teaming something with chorizo, yet both possess a warmth and earthiness to them that it seems it was only nature not growing the plant originally in Spain that is to blame. Curry leaves can be easily frozen, so when you're shopping for them, get a decent-sized bag and store them this way, and if you can't find any just make the soup without it, adding another herb such as dried oregano instead. To make this soup quickly I used canned chickpeas but obviously you can cook your own chickpeas from their dried state if you'd prefer. Whenever I cook dried chickpeas, I soak them overnight in cold water, then drain and refresh. Place in a deep pot and pour on plenty of cold water, do NOT add any salt. Bring to the boil and cook for 5 minutes, then turn the heat down, skim off any scum that rises to the top, add a 10-cm piece of rinsed kombu seaweed and continue to cook over a gentle boil until they're done – which will take around an hour depending on how fresh or large they are. The kombu helps them cook a little quicker (much like adding baking soda) and adds nutrients to them – which has to be good.

For 6–8

2 red onions, peeled and sliced
6 cloves garlic, peeled and sliced
a small handful of curry leaves
30 ml (2 Tbsp) olive oil or avocado oil
200 g cooking chorizo, peeled and cut into chunks
2 thumbs of ginger, peeled and chopped finely
1 x 10-cm sprig rosemary, leaves removed from the stem
2 bay leaves
1 large potato, peeled and diced
1 x 400-g can chickpeas (to give 250–300 g cooked weight), drained and rinsed
8 tomatoes, chopped (or use canned tomatoes)

Heat up a pot and sauté the onions, garlic and curry leaves in the oil, cooking over a moderate heat, until they begin to caramelise, stirring occasionally. Add the chorizo, ginger, rosemary and bay leaves and cook another few minutes, stirring often to prevent them sticking to the pot. Stir in the potato, the drained chickpeas, chopped tomatoes, 400 ml water and 2 teaspoons flaky salt.

Bring to the boil then simmer in a covered pot for 30 minutes. Taste for seasoning and serve it piping hot – although it also reheats really well the next day.

Aubergines

In India, it is often referred to as the 'king of vegetables', and it's no wonder as it is such a brilliant ingredient. Just like the tomato, it's actually the berry of a fruit from the nightshade family – it's not technically a vegetable. Unlike the tomato, potato and chilli (all members of the nightshade clan), the aubergine originates not in the Andes, but in India where they're called *brinjal*. In Australia they're known as eggplant, Italy names them *melanzano* and Thailand has *makreua*. These days a lot of the bitterness associated with the more usual violet-and-purple-skinned variety has been bred out, and they can be cooked without disgorging them. However, some still need to be sliced and soaked in cold salted water to help remove this trait. In Thai cuisine, the bitterness can in fact be one of the appealing aspects to them, especially for the pea-eggplant. You'll find these added to rich coconut curries, and when you bite into one of them it creates a wonderful contrast to the curry, but perhaps one that takes getting used to. Thailand also has the *maeuk*, a hairy golden eggplant that is lovely eaten raw in salads – just make sure you scrape the hairs off with the back of a knife before slicing and serving straight away before it discolours.

Aubergines have been lovingly embraced by various cuisines throughout the world, although mainly in countries of temperate climate where they can easily be grown. Unlike the tomato, it's not documented how the aubergine got from one place to another, but it would no doubt have been a slow process of Asian migrants taking their favourite foods with them to new places and traders swapping and selling goods and produce. It seems they have been grown and eaten in China and Japan for many centuries, as well as in Turkey, Egypt, Greece, Thailand and Malaysia. At some point they entered Europe and that spawned the creation of many recognisable dishes such as *ratatouille* from France, Greece's moussaka and Italy's *melanzane alla Parmigiano*. In the Levant, there are numerous versions of *babaganoush* – which is made by grilling the aubergine to give it a smoky flavour, then chopping the pulp and mixing it with lemon, garlic, tahini paste and sometimes strained yoghurt. The Turks also dry out smallish ones and sell them in strings in the marketplace, and all you need do is rehydrate them in cold water, stuff with a minced-lamb-based stew and bake slowly in the oven – delicious.

When I was a teenage apprentice chef living in Melbourne, Australia, I can remember my sisters cooking a dish that seemed so thoroughly exotic to me at the time. They sliced eggplant (as we called it) and salted it, then fried it and layered it with a sauce made from canned tomatoes, tonnes of garlic and raw grated carrots. It seemed crazy at the time, but that dish is what firmly established my love for eggplant – something I'd not eaten previously. I remember eating a wonderful dish of charcoal-grilled, sweet miso-marinated Japanese eggplant at a restaurant called Kuni's – the texture was incredibly silky and soft and the flavour rich, almost buttery. In India, in 1986, I found myself on a camel in the Thar desert for three days, setting out from the desert town of Jaiselmere. Food on that trip, cooked by the camel man for just the two of us and our two camels, was pretty basic. Every night we'd have freshly made chapattis served with a topping of raw onion, unripe tomatoes, and bitter brinjal. I have to say if it wasn't for the scenery (wild peacocks flying for brief stretches, waking up to see a scorpion a few centimetres from my face, and herds of small, wild deer-like creatures) I might have gone off them forever, but I simply put it down to the fact that it was a culinary experience.

Of all the South-East Asian countries in which I found myself backpacking as a 23-year-old, it was Malaysia that had the biggest impact on me foodwise.

It was my culinary favourite. Previously, I had really enjoyed eating my way through the various regional cuisines of Indonesia, from the subtle, spicy food of Hindu Bali to the fiery chilli dishes of predominantly Muslim Java and Sumatra. Indonesia is an enormous archipelago of over 17,500 islands with over 230 million people living on them. Within this Islamic republic there are hundreds of ethnic groups with varying religious beliefs from Animism through to Hinduism, Buddhism, Christianity and Islam, but to a certain degree, they all seem to stay quite distinct from each other when it comes to their diet. Like Indonesia, Malaysia is a Muslim nation. The bulk of its population is Islamic Malaysian, the remainder being made up of people of Chinese origin with Buddhist beliefs, various Christian minorities and Indians who regard themselves as Hindu - although these various peoples, as in the rest of the world, can be of different faiths. Geographically, Malaysia is made up of two territories: Peninsula Malaysia (or West Malaysia) and Eastern Malaysia, which is in the north of a massive island known more commonly as Borneo. This area, which shares borders with Brunei and Indonesian Kalamantan,

contains the states of Sarawak and Sabah. Altogether, Malaysia is a country of over 27 million people, who inhabit some of the most beautiful land in the world and who enjoy an amazing variety of cuisines.

Whilst quite distinct in themselves, occasionally these various cuisines have come together, such as in the Peranakan or Nonya cuisine that is based around Malacca and Penang. Early Chinese settlers who arrived in these areas (and also in what is now known as Singapore) intermarried with local Malays. This new 'race' became known as Peranakan. Nonya is an endearing term that means auntie or Madame, and has become synonymous with the local cuisine which is in itself a blend of both Chinese and Malaysian kitchens. This came about as the new migrants had to adapt their repertoire to the new ingredients they discovered as well as making do when they could no longer source customary ingredients. What came out of this fusion is a cuisine that brings together key Malaysian ingredients in often non-traditional Malaysian ways. Candlenuts are used to thicken and flavour sauces and curries (they must be cooked as they can be toxic); coconut milk is used to temper the astringency of tamarind; pandan leaves and laksa leaves are used for subtle flavouring; galangal gives heat and aroma to foods; kaffir lime leaves add citrus notes; and *jicama* (also known as yam bean) gives crunch. It could be said that this cuisine encompasses those of Thailand, China and Malaysia and indeed that's what I came to appreciate. It was in Penang that I first ate *laksa asam*, which is a spicy noodle soup made sour with the addition of lots of tamarind, and although I'd eaten laksa before in Australia, this one was memorable for its sourness. When I travelled down into Singapore I was served the more familiar *laksa lemak* - a coconut-based broth. Both were nonya dishes, both were quite different.

My travels were confined to the peninsula as I hitchhiked down from Penang (an island just off the north-west coast), through the towns of Ipoh and Kuala Lumpur towards Singapore, then back up through the centre to the Perhentian islands off the north-east coast. In my backpacking days, I had to travel between towns which had American Express offices as it was here I would collect my money for living. This sometimes meant that I would be travelling with little or no money on me, depending on how I'd budgeted and made my cash stretch. The most memorable time I actually ran out of cash was on a bus ride from Jakarta in Java to Bukkittingi in Sumatra, which is where I spent New Year's Eve in 1985. This bus ride took three days, and it involved crossing the equator, but the reason I ran out of cash was that I'd had my wallet emptied by the guy who ran the hostel I'd been staying at in Jakarta. In one year of backpacking, that was the only time I ever had anything stolen, and now looking back at it, it seems simply part of the experience. At times when I'd run out of money I would turn to hitchhiking to get around and it was surprisingly easy to get a ride - I think the sight of a white guy on the side of the road was quite intriguing. Occasionally, I'd find myself stranded for a day or so in a place that wasn't particularly Westerner-friendly (Udorn Thani in north-east Thailand was memorably hostile - but that was back in 1986). Worse than that though, were several days when I had to go hungry, unless scrounging food off other travellers or picking wild fruit, as I literally had no money. It probably seems unbelievable that a 'comparatively rich' Western tourist had so little cash on him he couldn't eat in this part of the world, but it happened to me a few times, and the food in Malaysia being so amazing it was heartbreaking! I kept a diary for most of my year's travels and the following are extracts from the travel journals I wrote in Malaysia and Singapore. Bear in mind that I was 23 at the time and I was experiencing the ingredients, smells and sights, and sheer wonder of Asia for the first time, eyes wide with awe and excitement.

On 14 January 1986 I boarded a boat in Indonesian Sumatra bound for Malaysian Penang. Efficient boat - leaves on time too - Malaysian not Indonesian. Leave Sumatra to tunes of Eurythmics on walkman and lightning on horizon.

15/01 No breakfast on boat as no Malaysian cash. Suffering from diarrhoea. Georgetown seems a really nice place - lots of ice cold drinks - drink heaps - especially soy milk without sugar. Have curried veggies, egg and rice for lunch. Visit tourist office, walk to Blue Bus station (steamed pork buns and veggie dim sum along the way) and go to Batu Ferringhi - tourist mecca of eight international hotels - find place in village with Chinese people (Ang and Ung). Huge bed and mosquito net. Eat sour laksa soup with fat rice noodles - spicy - like Indonesian bakso.

16/01 Up for two *roti canai* (pronounced chanai) - Indian-style thin bread patties (oil, flour, egg, water) with veggie curry sauce (dahl). Go to beach with local guy Zul and others - lazy day watching fat tourists being lazy and parasailing.

17/01 Quiet day and night - go to fishing village during day - long walk back. Last night here.

18/01 Go to Georgetown, post parcel of things I bought on Nias Island (Indonesia) back to Wanganui and it uses up 'all' my money, now not enough to catch bus to Kuala Lumpur (called KL). Stay in New China Hotel dormitory for $5.50. Zul shouts me dinner at 4 a.m. of Horlicks and roti canai.

19/01 Hitchhike Georgetown, Butterworth, Ipoh. Too hot for hitching - some rain. One sweet bread for breakfast, get to Butterworth (on bus) and start hitching, walk 1½ hours before first ride, beaten up Mercedes truck. Indian driver – good guy, so bloody hot and too hungry to be hungry. Next ride in air-conditioned Mercedes saloon with Malaysian guy – wowsy! Get ride to Ipoh, can finally afford a 70 cent noodle soup. Shower at Zul's parents' house. Go to city – hang around with his friends – stay at his friend's place – noodles in chicken booster tasting broth for dinner – sleep like a rock.

20/01 Hitch Ipoh to KL. Hot again. Farewell to Zek, walk one hour before I get a ride in Malaysian's Cortina – he seems nervous to pick up hitchhikers. Get 1/3 way to KL – next ride only 10 minutes later, in Government truck with no load and a super aware Indian Driver – talks about politics a lot – interesting – have had no breakfast – get to KL just after midday. Yong (52) grabs me and escorts me to a Coca Cola – the best ever – cold! Then to bus station to dump rucksack and shouts me *mie goring* (fried noodles) for lunch. Then to Amex office to get traveller's cheques. Now he asks me for M$220 loan to pay for repairs to his Volvo (he owns 5 cars, a plywood business and has 2 servants . . .) – a bit suss and he gets angry – says I don't trust him even though he has said I can go with him and his family to Singapore and have Chinese New Year with them. Anyway, he tells me to wait at the bus station and he'll come get me later. He never comes back – glad – saves hassles. Eat an amazing dessert called *es kacang* (iced peanut) made from shaved ice, boiled peanuts, lumps of jelly and colouring and reduced milk from a can – delicious. Stay at Leng Nam Hotel, $15 a night (expensive – mahal), go to laundromat, heaven. Duck and noodles for dinner. Chinatown market, good clothes but expensive.

21/01 Three Chinese custard tarts for breakfast. Walk to museum – great place, everything's there. Roti canai for lunch, go to the Batu caves – amazing – a place of Indian worship. Indian/Muslim dinner, hair cut $4.50 – look like a marine. Go to movies to see *Cocoon* – some trashy American movie about extra terrestrials who give eternal life to a group of oldies – Baarf!! A pineapple and watermelon juice for supper.

22/01 KL–Singapore, fine and humid. Bus KL–Malacca, then on to Singapore. They ask me at customs if I'm in the army due to my hair cut. Stay at Simms Guest House $4 first night, then $3 after. Food market is excellent, in car park building. Singapore laksa is yellow with turmeric and made with thin vermicelli noodles. Sleep on mattress on floor.

23/01 Fine/warm. Shopping day: yellow and black checked trousers, leather sandals, a camera lens, 6 cassettes (2 x Jean Michel Jarre in China, Prince, Simple Minds, Bowie, Jon and Vangelis). Lots of walking, 2 books *Moby Dick* and *Huckleberry Finn*. Visit temple of 1000 lights (Buddhist), give up trying to find Bugis Street. See Indian temples, GPO is fairly lavish. Passionfruit and peach yoghurt for lunch. Indian breakfast. 10 p.m. bus to KL.

25/01 Arrive youth hostel 6.30 a.m., sleep on steps till open with a Swiss guy, Laurent. Tonight Thaipusam festival starts at Batu Caves so hostel closing between midnight and 5 p.m. Hindu festival whereby people who have made promises to the gods must now pay them back. This includes lots of piercing their tongues, cheeks, lips, etc., they carry large ornaments, etc. hung from hooks onto their bodies. I'm tired.

26/01 Full moon. Up at 5.30 a.m. Laurent and I take bus to Caves – thousands and thousands of people, music, drums especially, flutes, colour, incense. Coconuts thrown and if broken in half they'll bring good luck. Statues drenched in coconut milk. Kavadis are the people who carry the huge spear-holding and hook-holding heads/body enclosures. They walk up the 250+ steps and still in a trance they are relieved of their burden. (They start at the river where they're first pierced.) Women and a few children also carry these metal contraptions. Monkeys all the way up the steps to the caves. Lots of noise and chaos. Many peacock feathers, bells, tinsel paper, statues used to decorate the headsets, hand pieces, etc. People have either hooks in their backs/bellies, some suspending limes, some leaves. Really emotional time, especially this early in the morning. At the time the spears are removed a friend or 'priest' would take a mouthful of cold 'drink' and putting his lips close to the devotees he would spurt it into the others and at the same time remove the spear. A few fires in the cave where people would toss camphor incense cubes and smashed coconuts. Whole coconuts tossed in, which explode like bombs. As the sun rises birds high up in the caves start swirling around – just incredible. Down on the flats, below the caves, there is a real carnival atmosphere – hand-powered Ferris-wheels, merry-go-rounds. Hare Krishna devotees spreading the word, yoga devotees likewise. Many food stalls, especially Indian sweet cakes and nuts. Roti canai, poppadoms, *mie goring*, etc. So many people, what an amazing atmosphere, hustle bustle, push-push.

27/01 KL to Kuala Lipis. Overcast, fine. Miss the bus to Lipis by 30 seconds! Laurent and I take the next one. Lipis is nice and cool, not a lot to do except jungle treks and River tours. We buy tinned curried fish, kaya (coconut and egg 'jam') and shrimp sambal and 2 loaves wholemeal bread and pig out for lunch. They say Kuala Lipis is cowboy country!

Saturday 1 February 1986, I took a boat from Kota Bahru in the north-east over to the uninhabited island of Pulau Perhentian Besar, hoping to stay at the government-run bungalows that I'd read about in a guide book. Unfortunately for me, the bungalows were closed as the manager had had to go to KL for a funeral. Luckily for me, there were five Malaysian students on board and they invited me to camp with them – which was just as well, as although I'd brought enough food for four days, I hadn't included a tent or cooking equipment. So I camped out with Sani, Kamil (Rambo), Syed (Arab), Nik and Sam as they awaited exam results. They cooked the first night's meal which included coconut fresh off the palm tree, baby cuttlefish cooked two ways, fried baby fish, a casserole of *ikan bilis* (tiny fish), chilli and soy, rice and coconut milk. Over the wonderful days that followed we saw a huge turtle just off the jetty and stingrays (we caught and ate one of the latter – delicious), witnessed flying squirrels in the island's interior and a man from the neighbouring island encouraging his big monkey to collect older coconuts from the palms to make copra. We caught and ate tons of fish, swam lots and took in the stars, the blue skies and the crystal clear water. It really was a paradise.

On 5 February we were picked up by a boat and we headed back to the mainland and then to an army camp where Syed's father was based resettling Vietnamese refugees. Here we ate noodles, *pulu* spring rolls and drank tea before heading to the guys' home village, called Kampung Pau. Over the next four days I found myself living with them and their families, playing soccer, kite flying, partaking of midnight feasts of barbecued chicken – even having a duck killed in my honour which was then dutifully

rubbed with fresh turmeric, ginger, garlic, sugar and salt before being barbecued and basted with soy and vinegar. It was the most amazing meal I'd ever had, the environs contributing to its taste as much as the ingredients, I guess. Nik's cousin Noh came around during this time and took us out for drives in her car to the beach and forests and I really felt I'd come to experience a side of Malaysia that simple backpacking wouldn't have allowed me. So it was with real sadness that I drove Noh's car to the border with Thailand at Ratu Panjang on 9 February, said my farewells to Nik, Noh and their friends and walked across the bridge to Sungei Golok in Thailand.

Malaysia – its people, its lands and its unique culture will always occupy a special place in my mind which is at one and the same time the consciousness of a well-travelled, middle-aged man and the impressionable awareness of that 23-year-old backpacker. Its food is still an inspiration to me.

Chillies

Chilli, chile, chili - they're all the same thing and one of my favourite ingredients. Chillies (I'll use the British spelling) are a versatile and inspiring addition to anyone's pantry. As a seasoning added to savoury dishes, the use of them is truly global - from flavouring and colouring Spanish chorizo, creating sometimes agonisingly spicy Sichuanese dishes and Goan vindaloos, through to Mexican guacamole, Japan's *schichimi* spice mix, a red duck coconut curry from Thailand, Indonesian beef rendang, Hungarian goulash or *kirmizi-biber*-flavoured Turkish kofte. When I was a child the only chilli I ever experienced was either sparingly dropped onto freshly shucked oysters from a bottle of Tabasco sauce, or a pinch of cayenne pepper added to cheese scones, or ground Hungarian paprika added to minced beef. Always added very subtly, just a hint of the potential heat was what was decided was best for the family. When I moved to Australia I discovered fresh chillies, as well as exotic cuisines. I found myself eating Indian chickpea-flour-battered whole green chillies, chilli- and cumin-spiced Moroccan tagines and Tex Mex dishes such as turkey tortillas drowned in cheese and 'chile sauce'. Young men seemed to think it a sign of their manhood as to how hot a chilli they could eat and then drown with beer (although plain yoghurt is a better mouth cooler). If you like the flavour of chillies (yes, they offer more than just heat) then you should split the chilli in half lengthways and use a small teaspoon to scrape out the seeds and the membrane that holds them in - these contain the most capsaicin, the ingredient that gives chillies their heat. Not surprisingly perhaps, it's capsaicin that is the primary ingredient in pepper spray - used for personal defence, riot and crowd control (often controversially).

Research shows that chillies have been eaten in the Americas since at least 7000 BC, and were being cultivated in Ecuador around 6000 BC. Related to potatoes and tomatoes (the nightshade family), they spread overland south into Peru then north into Mexico and North America. The West encountered this spice in the Caribbean, allegedly when Christopher Columbus tried it, and it was this first taste that, like so many everyday foods, started the spread of the plant into Europe (starting in Spain around 1494) and Greater Asia. Sailors took it with them to the Philippines and India, from where it spread into Korea, Japan and China, as well as overland through the Middle East into Turkey and Hungary, readily becoming absorbed into local cuisines and in many ways creating new dishes as it was popularised. It's impossible to think of the cuisines of Thailand or Malaysia without using chilli. Mind you, peanuts and coriander aren't indigenous to those parts either - thank God for the introduction and fusion of foreign ingredients, I say.

Whilst a scorchingly hot beef and pumpkin curry made from a mixture of fresh Caribbean Scotch Bonnets, dried smokey Mexican chipotle and reasonably mellow kirmizi biber from Turkey to give the heat many layers of flavour can be a thing of beauty, chillies can also be used in far more subtle ways. Try poaching stone fruit with a little fresh red chilli added to the syrup, or adding a teaspoon of the fantastic Spanish *pimenton dulce* (sweet smoked paprika) to your next lamb stew (along with some soy sauce) for a flavour enhancement that people won't be able to pinpoint, but one which will be welcomed. Purée a few fresh or crumbled dried chillies with plain yoghurt, buttermilk or coconut milk, some ginger, garlic and spices and use to marinate pork chops or duck breasts for six hours before barbecuing or grilling them. If my parents were happy to add seemingly exotic cayenne pepper to their cheese scones in New Zealand back in 1968, then there's really no excuse for you not to experiment. And if you have a garden free from frosts, then there's no excuse for you not to grow your own. There are a huge variety of chillies out there, just waiting for you to welcome them to your repertoire.

three.
main
meals

Lamb & quinoa kofte with anchovy & olive dressing & cucumber sumac yoghurt

Kofte are a great snack in Turkey and mostly made from meat, although there are vegetarian versions as well. One of my favourite kofte is made from wheat, shaped like small rugby balls and stuffed with meat. Lots of cloves and cinnamon in them gives a lovely sweet but savoury taste. Quinoa, originating in the Andes of South America like so many of our everyday foods, was one of the great Inca foods, held sacred by them. It's a grain that is one of the world's super-foods – full of protein, essential amino acids, fibre and a host of other goodies. *Kirmizi biber* are delicious oily chilli flakes from Turkey – also referred to as *Aleppo* pepper flakes – you can substitute these with regular chilli flakes but use a little less. Sumac is a berry from a flowering bush that seems to have been used all over the world for various culinary uses. The most common is in the Middle East, where the berries are ground to produce an astringent powder used for sprinkling over salads, grilled breads and fish, tossing it with tomatoes and olive oil and many more uses. For a snack, one kofte is a lovely portion, although you could sit it in a flat bread filled with lots of salad, tomatoes, plenty of sumac and cucumber and serve it as a light meal.

For 8 kofte

100 g quinoa grains

500 g lamb mince (lean to medium-lean is best)

30 ml (2 Tbsp) soy sauce

a handful of parsley, shredded

a handful of coriander, shredded

a handful of dill, roughly chopped

1 tsp ground cinnamon

1 tsp toasted cumin seeds

½ tsp ground cloves

2 tsp kirmizi biber

6 anchovy fillets in oil (or use 2 salted anchovies, rinsed with bones removed)

4 cloves garlic, peeled

2 handfuls mint leaves

45 ml (3 Tbsp) olive oil, plus some extra for cooking

50 g (just over 2 heaped Tbsp) green olive paste

60 ml white or cider vinegar

½ cucumber

150 g thick yoghurt

15 g (1 heaped Tbsp) sumac

Bring a pot of water to the boil. Rinse the quinoa under hot running water for 20 seconds (this removes the bitter coating) then add to the water. Add 1 teaspoon salt and cook for 8–12 minutes, the grains will have opened somewhat and be cooked – they will always have a nutty crunch to them. Drain and leave to cool. Place in a bowl with the next nine ingredients and mix really well, almost kneading it, for 1 minute. Cover and leave to rest in the fridge for at least an hour. Divide the mixture into eight balls then roll into a sausage shape. Leave as they are, or thread them onto a skewer.

While the mixture is resting make the dressing and cucumber yoghurt. Ideally pound the anchovies, garlic and mint into a paste with a pestle and mortar, although a small food processor will work. Mix in the olive oil, the olive paste and vinegar. Taste for seasoning and leave to one side.

Cut cucumber lengthways into quarters, remove seeds then cut into dice. Mix with the yoghurt and sumac. Leave to come to room temperature.

Rub a little oil over the kofte and grill over a moderate–high heat, turning them as they colour. They'll only take 3 minutes in total to cook.

To serve: Simply pile the kofte on a platter and serve the dressing and the cucumber yoghurt on the side.

Ginger-poached venison with bone-marrow Parmesan sauce & broccoli cous cous

This was the dish I demonstrated in more cooking demos than any other in 2008–2009. It's a dish that seems incredibly difficult on paper, but which in reality is very simple – so long as you have your bone marrow sorted (see page 50). The sauce is truly fabulous and in this version it works so well with the refreshing broccoli cous cous which in itself is a very simple but great recipe to have up your sleeve – try replacing the broccoli with spinach, peas, carrots or cauliflower. It was the Maghreb region of North Africa (Morocco, Algeria, Tunisia and Libya) that introduced cous cous to the culinary world, and these days you're likely to buy instant cous cous that simply needs water or stock added. The handy hint for this is to never pour on boiling, or even simmering, stock or water – which unbelievably almost every packet says to do. Only ever add tepid or cold water or stock, which will ensure the grains remain fluffy and loose, and will prevent them sticking into one lumpen mass. Once the cous cous has absorbed the liquid you can then warm it up in a covered bowl set over a pot of simmering water, or in the microwave. Mind you, I prefer to eat my cous cous at room temperature as the sauces and garnishes are invariably served piping hot. Try using beef fillet, or lamb neck fillet in place of the venison. I like to make this using farmed New Zealand venison, as wild venison may be too rich for some people, but both will be fine.

For 4

600 g venison loin, trimmed, portioned into 4

6 cloves garlic, chopped (no need to peel them)

1 thumb of ginger, sliced (don't peel it unless it's dirty)

a small handful of hard herbs (rosemary, thyme, sage or oregano)

15 ml (3 Tbsp) olive oil

1 glass robust red wine

2 litres dark veal or chicken jus, approximately

50 g butter

50 g bone marrow sliced 5 mm thick, extracted fresh from bones

40 g coarse sourdough breadcrumbs, made from 2-3-day-old crustless bread

30 g Parmesan, grated

broccoli cous cous

cress to garnish

Season the venison generously with freshly ground black pepper and leave to come to room temperature.

Heat up a saucepan (large enough to hold the meat in one layer) and fry the garlic, ginger and herbs in the olive oil to colour, stirring as they cook. Add the venison to the pan and colour the meat all over. Add the wine to the pan and bring to the boil – it will splutter a little so be careful. Add enough jus to cover the meat and bring to the boil. Lower the heat to a rapid simmer and cook for 3 minutes then turn the heat off and flip the meat over. At this point the venison will be rare to medium–rare which is great for lean meats like venison. If you're making this with lamb neck fillets, they'll benefit from another 5 minutes gentle cooking. Leave the meat in the pan to rest for at least 5 minutes.

Before you make the marrow sauce read the recipe on page 50 to get a feel for it. Cook the butter to a nut-brown colour then add the sliced marrow and cook until it begins to render down, stirring frequently. Add the breadcrumbs and cook to colour for a minute, then add 150 ml of sieved cooking jus from the venison. Bring it to the boil then simmer for a minute. Add the Parmesan and season with pepper and a little salt if needed.

To serve: Spoon the cous cous into the centre of a plate. Slice the rested venison against the grain and lay on top, then spoon the marrow sauce over and sprinkle with the cress.

Broccoli cous cous

For 4 as part of a larger dish

90 g instant cous cous
120 ml tepid water
250 g broccoli, cut into pieces, peel the stem if woody
a very large handful of fresh mint leaves off the stem
15 ml (1 Tbsp) extra-virgin olive oil

In a medium-sized bowl, mix the cous cous with the tepid water and a little salt and leave it to absorb the water, around 10 minutes, stirring from time to time to loosen the grains.

Boil or steam the broccoli for no more than 90 seconds then drain in a colander and immediately plunge into a bowl of iced water and leave for 5 minutes. Drain well and place in a food processor with the mint leaves and olive oil then blitz in several short bursts, scraping down the sides of the bowl each time to produce coarse 'crumbs'. Mix these crumbs into the cous cous with a generous amount of freshly ground black pepper, adding salt to taste.

This is lovely eaten at room temperature, but you can warm it up in a covered bowl set over a pot of simmering water or in the microwave.

It will keep covered in the fridge for a day, just mix it with a fork to loosen it up before serving.

Five-spice roast crispy pork belly with apple & sweet potato mash, roast shallots & coriander salsa verde

Pork belly, roasted like this, is always a favourite at any restaurant I've cooked at. I guess people find it hard and fiddly to prepare at home, so tend to eat it when they dine out. Sweet potatoes and apples aren't naturally occurring bed fellows, but I think they're a match made in heaven – the sourness from the apples works as a lovely foil to the rich buttery potatoes, and the combination goes so well with the pork. The coriander *salsa verde* gives the whole dish a South-East Asian feel and the freshness that coriander offers again works well with the fatty belly. At work, leftover trimmings from this get blitzed up in a food processor and cooked out with coconut milk, chilli paste, *gapi* (shrimp paste) and fish sauce to be served on betel leaves as a tasty canapé. Or we cut the trim into cubes and braise it briefly with star anise, soy and boiled potatoes – for the best staff meal ever.

For 8

2 kg pork belly, rib bones removed
3 Tbsp five-spice
5 large carrots, peeled and halved lengthways
8-16 banana shallots (depending on their size)
4 star anise, roughly crushed
15 ml (1 Tbsp) sesame oil
45 ml (3 Tbsp) olive oil
700 g potatoes, peeled and cut into large chunks
700 g sweet potatoes, peeled and halved lengthways
150 g butter
3 Granny Smith apples
1 Tbsp rosemary (or sage) leaves, roughly chopped
4 Tbsp grain mustard
3 Tbsp capers, drained or rinsed and roughly chopped
zest and juice of 2 limes
a small handful of coriander, leaves and stem, shredded

Score the rind and fat of the belly in lines 1 cm or less apart, avoiding cutting down into the flesh. A Stanley knife, or a sharp boning knife is the best thing to use for this – or ask your butcher to do it. Mix the five-spice with 50 g of fine salt and rub this into the skin side of the belly. Place in a deep plastic container or casserole, skin side facing down and leave for 20 minutes in a cool place. Pour on enough cold water to cover by 2 cm (although the belly may float) and place in the fridge for 24–48 hours.

When you're ready, take the belly from the brine and discard the brine. Turn the oven to 190 °C. Line a roasting dish with baking parchment and lay the carrots in it side by side to form a trivet large enough to hold the belly. Sit the belly on top, skin side facing up, pour on 200 ml of water and roast for 2 hours or so, until the skin has bubbled up and become golden and crispy. You can in fact serve the pork at this stage straight from the oven, but what we do in the restaurant is slightly more time-consuming. Place the cooked belly on a clean tray lined with baking parchment, sit a sheet of paper on top of the belly and sit another tray on top. Balance a 2–3 kg weight on top (a few saucepans are good, or some bottled water or canned chickpeas!) to flatten the belly a little, without actually crushing it. Leave it to cool then place in the fridge, minus the weights, and it'll be ready the next day. At this point the belly will keep for 4–5 days in the fridge. The next day take it from the fridge and cut it into 8–16 even-sized portions – using a serrated knife makes it a lot easier.

Turn the oven to 180 °C. Place the shallots in a roasting dish with the star anise, sesame oil and 1 tablespoon of the olive oil, then pour in 120 ml of hot water. Roast in the lower part of the oven until you can easily insert a skewer through the shallots – around 45 minutes to an hour. After 20 minutes, you'll need to cook the pork belly. Heat up a heavy-based pan and drizzle in a few teaspoons of vegetable oil. Place the belly pieces in, skin side down, and cook over medium–high heat until the crackling begins to blister and pop – be careful as it can splatter a little. If the skin side of the belly is uneven and won't cook as in the photo then simply press it down into the pan using the back of a pair of tongs or something similar. Flip it over and cook for a minute on the flesh side. If you can't fit all of the pieces into the pan at once then cook them in batches. Tip out any excess fat from the pan, otherwise it will be really smoky in the oven. Place the pan, if it's ovenproof, into the upper part of the oven (or transfer it to a roasting dish lined with baking parchment) and roast for 30 minutes or so, at which point the skin will be lovely and crisp and the flesh tender.

While the belly is roasting boil the potatoes and sweet potatoes in a pot of lightly salted water until cooked – you can also make this using only kumara. Once cooked, drain and return to the pot. While that's cooking heat the butter in a pan and cook to a nut-brown colour. Peel the apples if you want to (it's not necessary) and cut into quarters. Remove the seeds and chop each quarter into 4–5 chunks. Add to the nut-brown butter along with the rosemary, put a lid on, and cook over medium heat until the apples have stewed down and most of the juice has evaporated, stirring from time to time. Mash this into the potatoes and season with salt and pepper.

To make the coriander salsa verde, mix the mustard into the remaining olive oil along with the capers, lime zest and juice and a little salt, then stir in the coriander.

To serve: Divide the mash and the roast shallots amongst your plates and place one or two chunks of roast pork belly alongside, then simply drizzle with the salsa verde and any roasting juices from the roast shallots.

.125

Coffee, star anise & liquorice-braised pork belly & quince with mushrooms

The first time I'd ever heard of cooking pork with coffee was when speaking to an Indian chef who was cooking in a hotel in Guangdong province in China. We were talking about Fusion as a culinary concept and he said that in a country like China, which has such a history to its food, it was often hard for people to adapt to change. But this had all begun to change in recent years as foreign ingredients were arriving in China and young chefs were keen to experiment with them in dishes which had previously been classics, or commonplace. Obviously this can be a good and a bad thing, depending on the palate of the chef, but he said young Chinese were having fun, and that's got to be good. He also mentioned that he'd cooked a dish of pork with coffee. When I was thinking about a braised pork dish for this book, his dish came to mind, so here's my take on his dish. I've added quince to mine, which I think is a great thing – they have a slightly sour taste and add another dimension of texture to the dish. The coffee beans you use will have a big impact on the flavour of the finished dish – so you'll need to adjust the coffee quantity to suit your taste – and you can actually stir in an espresso or two at the end which also works really well. This dish goes remarkably well with plain mashed potatoes, as well as with steamed rice and steamed greens.

For 6–8

1.5 kg pork belly, ask your butcher to remove the rib bones in one piece but keep them

60 g white sugar

6 star anise

6 cloves

a few quills of cassia (or 2 cinnamon sticks)

15 g dried liquorice root (or 2 pieces unflavoured liquorice)

2 thumbs of ginger, peeled and sliced

8 cloves garlic, peeled and halved

1 onion, peeled and thickly sliced

2 quince

15 ml (1 Tbsp) toasted sesame oil

80 ml soy sauce

80 ml black vinegar (or 100 ml Shaoxing wine or dry sherry)

24 roasted coffee beans, roughly crushed

250 g mushrooms (I used shiitake and porcini, cut into large chunks)

2 spring onions, sliced, to garnish

Cut the ribs between the bones and separate them. Cut the belly into large chunks with the skin intact.

Place the sugar in a large pot and cook over a moderate–high heat until it caramelises, stirring from time to time to help it cook evenly. Once it begins to melt, stop stirring and leave it to cook to a dark caramel colour. Add the belly and bones, star anise, cloves, cassia and liquorice and stir it together. Eventually the caramel will melt into the meat. Keep cooking to brown the pork. Add the ginger, garlic and onion, pour on 500 ml water and stir it well and bring to the boil. Wash the quince, rubbing off any furry coating. Cut into quarters and cut out the pips. There's no need to peel them, but cut them in half again, so that you get eight chunks per quince. Add these to the pot and stir them in, then add sesame oil, soy sauce and vinegar and bring back to the boil. Sit a paper cartouche (see page 147) on top of the mixture and turn to a rapid simmer, put a lid on and cook for one hour. Alternatively, if it's ovenproof, place the pot in the oven set to 130 °C.

Stir the coffee beans and mushrooms into the stew. There should be lots of simmering juices – add some extra hot water if it needs it.

Cook for another 20–30 minutes, at which point the meat should be tender and the aroma magnificent. Taste for seasoning and serve scattered with the spring onions.

Green chilli, cardamom & green peppercorn-braised shoulder of lamb with minted baby potatoes & ginger peas

I love the differing flavours of all sheep meat, whether it be lamb, hogget or mutton. A lamb is technically from a newborn to around 12 months old. Hogget is the next stage in a sheep's life, so long as they have fewer than two incisor teeth, and mutton are older still, from 18 months and upward so long as they're a wether or a ewe. Sheep appear in cuisines from all around the globe, from New Zealand (where we have around 10 sheep for every person) to Greece and Turkey, India and the Middle East. The wonderful thing about sheep meat is that it has a good amount of fat, which carries the flavour, and a lovely variety of textures. Pyrenean milk-fed lamb is pale pink and extremely succulent (although a little lacking in flavour for me), Welsh salt-marsh lamb has a distinctive briny character and the weird North Ronaldsay hogget, from the Orkney Islands, is something from another world – which makes sense seeing as how these Neolithic sheep live on the beaches of the northern Isles and survive almost entirely on seaweed. This dish pays homage to India, where I've had some amazingly delicious lamb curries and samosas, and although I use the shoulder you can use the leg as well. The best way to serve this is to take the shoulder from the pan, strain the cooking juices into a clean pan, skim the fat off, and reduce the juices until they're thick and tasty – and keep tasting it. Pull the meat from the bone (it should come away easily) and cut it into chunks.

For 6–8 when served with lots of vegetables

1 lamb (or hogget) shoulder – around 2.2–2.8 kg in weight with bone included

2 onions, peeled and thickly sliced

2 large green chillies, split in half lengthways

6 bay leaves

4 stalks green peppercorns, peppercorns removed from the stalks (or 2 Tbsp brined peppercorns)

2 large sprigs rosemary, pull the leaves off

12 green cardamom, crushed flat with a pestle

1 Tbsp coarse sea salt

600 g baby potatoes

a handful of mint on the stalk

30 ml (2 Tbsp) extra virgin olive oil

400 g baby peas (frozen work fine)

1 large thumb of ginger, peeled and finely chopped

60 g butter

Preheat oven to 180 °C. Using a thin sharp knife, prick the lamb all over in 20 places, piercing until you hit the bones. Lay the sliced onions, chillies and bay leaves in the bottom of a deep-sided roasting dish, lay the lamb shoulder on top and pour over 150 ml hot water. Mix the peppercorns, rosemary, cardamom and sea salt together and sprinkle this over the lamb. Lay a sheet of baking parchment on top of the lamb and then seal the dish tightly with foil. Place in the middle of the oven and bake for 2½ hours. Take the foil off the dish along with the baking parchment and ladle the pan juices over the lamb and bake for another 25 minutes. At this point the lamb should be tender and you should be able to pull the meat away from the bone. Cover lightly with foil and rest in a warm place for 10 minutes.

Fifteen minutes before the lamb is ready, place the potatoes in a pot with half the mint and some salt, and cover with warm water. Bring to the boil and cook until ready. Drain, discard the cooked mint, add the leaves from the remaining mint and the oil and toss together, then keep covered in a warm place.

As soon as the lamb begins its 10 minutes' resting period, bring a pot of lightly salted water to the boil and add the peas, then cook for 2 minutes. Place the ginger and butter in a pan and slowly cook until the ginger begins to sizzle. Drain the peas and add these to the butter, season with plenty of freshly ground black pepper and toss it all together adding salt as needed.

To serve: Lay chunks of the lamb on plates, spoon over some of the cooking juices and scatter the peas and potatoes on top.

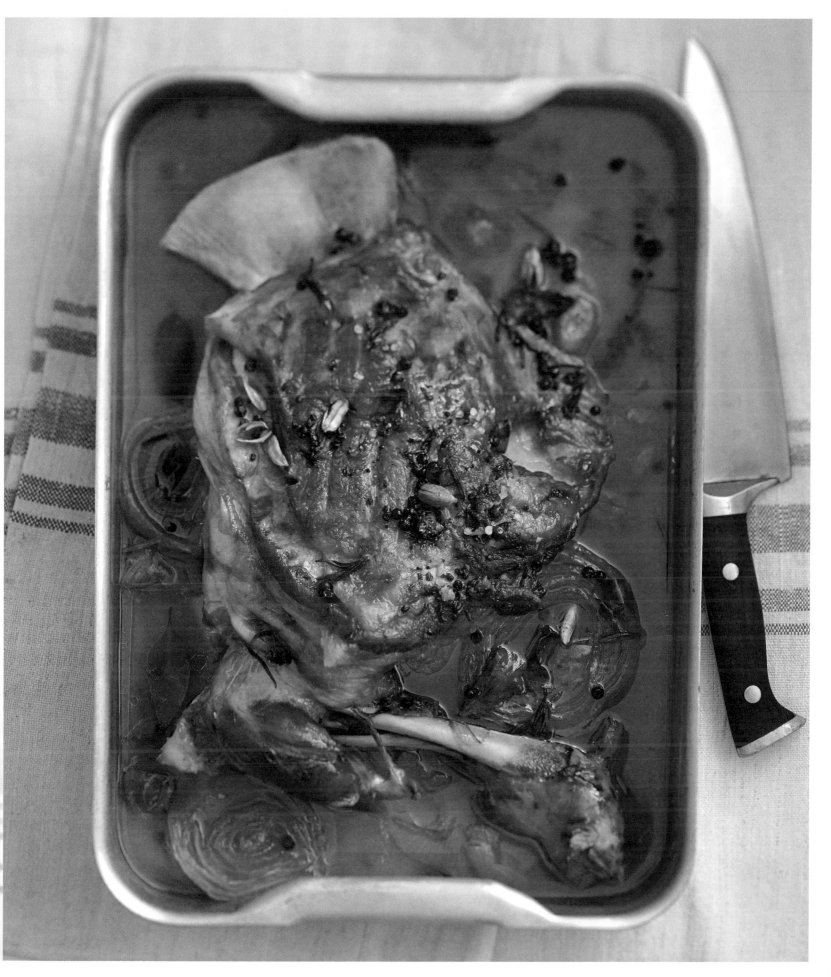

Roast rack of lamb on Israeli cous cous with tomato, tamarind & coriander relish

Coming from New Zealand, where I think most of the world's tastiest lamb and mutton comes from, I had eaten my fair share of lamb by the time I left, aged 18, to train in Australia. I have to say that I had never eaten a dish like this in my youth, but I like to think I would have loved it. I discovered Israeli cous cous in London in the mid-'90s and was intrigued by it as I'd only ever seen the small granular cous cous so familiar to the North African kitchen. To me it seemed more like a pasta than anything else. A few years later I came across *fregola* which looked almost identical to Israeli cous cous but which is in fact a toasted pasta from Sardinia. At this point I have to admit to cous cous confusion. Around 2005 we had an Israeli pastry chef, Aner Zalel, come and work with us at The Providores and he showed me how to cook Israeli cous cous, firstly by toasting it and then cooking it almost like a risotto. Since then I've played around with it a bit and have found my favourite additions are soy and hijiki or arame seaweed – which give it a lovely texture, taste and colour. The addition of tamarind and ginger in the tomato relish works a treat with the lamb and gives the dish an almost Indian feel to it. Luckily India isn't known for any cous cous dishes so that saves me from being even more confused! In this recipe you can simply replace the Israeli cous cous with fregola and it will be just the same.

For 4

Israeli cous cous

30 ml (2 Tbsp) olive oil
200 g Israeli cous cous (or fregola)
1 red onion, peeled and diced
3 cloves garlic, peeled and thinly sliced
10 g dried hijiki or arame seaweed
30 ml (2 Tbsp) soy sauce

Heat half the oil in a wide deep pot and add the cous cous. Fry, stirring constantly to prevent it getting too dark and when evenly coloured tip it into a bowl.

Add the remaining oil to the pot and fry the onion and garlic until coloured and beginning to caramelise. Return the cous cous to the pot along with the seaweed and soy sauce.

Add 500 ml hot water and bring to the boil, stirring several times as it heats up. Cook on a rapid boil for 8–10 minutes, stirring occasionally until it's just cooked. If it dries out at all add a little extra hot water. Take off the heat, put a tight-fitting lid on and leave for 15 minutes to finish cooking.

This will keep for 2 days in the fridge. Bring to room temperature before serving.

Tomato, tamarind & coriander relish

4 shallots, peeled and thinly sliced into rings
1 thumb of ginger, peeled and julienned
30 ml (2 Tbsp) olive oil (or any vegetable oil)
4 large tomatoes, cut into large chunks (peel them if you
 want to but it's not necessary)
30 ml (2 Tbsp) tamarind paste
a small handful of coriander on the stalk, coarsely shredded

Caramelise the shallots and ginger in the oil in a wide pan over
moderate heat. Add the tomatoes and bring to the boil, then cook for
5 minutes, stirring frequently. Add the tamarind and cook another few
minutes then taste for seasoning and take off the heat. Leave it to cool
for 5 minutes, then mix in the coriander and leave to cool. It's best
eaten quite fresh but you can store it in the fridge for up to one day.

Roast rack of lamb

4 x racks of lamb (allow around 180-220 g each,
 including bones)

Preheat oven to 150 °C. It's the fat that makes lamb so tasty, but too
much of it can also make it unpalatable. Score the fat on the racks
into quite a tight cross-hatch pattern, cutting into the fat but avoiding
cutting into the meat itself.

Heat up a wide frying-pan and place the racks in fat-side down then
cook over a moderate heat to render the fat from them and also to
colour the fat a lovely dark golden brown. You won't need to add any
fat to the pan. Once coloured, tip excess fat from the pan and discard.

Season the racks all over quite generously with salt and freshly
ground black pepper. Turn them over in the pan and cook to colour
the underside of the racks.

If your frying-pan is ovenproof then place it in the oven, or transfer
the racks to a roasting dish. Roast for 10–15 minutes. Turn the oven
off, open the door and leave the racks to rest for at least 5 minutes
before cutting them into individual cutlets if you so wish.

To serve: Place the lamb rack on top of the still warm cous cous and
tuck in some steamed greens such as spinach. Spoon some tomato
relish on top and it's ready.

Sautéed star anise & ginger poached lambs' brains on chickpea panizza & Asian greens

Lambs' brains are an acquired taste, but they are really rich and delicious and they have a texture much like a firm creamy mousse. They take a little preparation, but nothing so hard that they aren't worth it. The first time I ate them they were cooked in 'burnt butter' and had capers and lemon juice added to them, both of which cut through their richness. They were intriguing, but not amazing. Since then I've eaten brains in many ways, and my favourites are always when cooked with rich aromatic flavours, with chillies and ginger, or when they're crumbed and deep-fried, or cooked in a crunchy tempura batter, which contrasts so well with their own texture. Here I poach them in something akin to a Chinese Master Stock and then team them with Asian greens – I used wing beans, shiitake and gai lan. The last part of the dish is *panizza* – a sort of set polenta that's made from chickpea flour. This was taught to me by my chef friend Gianni Vatteroni, a native of Carrara in Tuscany, who has cooked with me at various restaurants. It has a lovely texture and one which goes so well with the brains.

For 4 main courses or 6 entrées

6 sets of brains (12 lobes in total)
100 ml cider vinegar (or white wine or red wine vinegar)
250 ml soy sauce
100 ml black vinegar
10 star anise
1 cinnamon stick
1 small onion, peeled and thinly sliced
2 thumbs of ginger, thinly sliced
12 baby carrots, washed and cut on an angle
110 g chickpea flour
1 tsp five-spice
50 g butter
15 ml (1 Tbsp) mirin
5 ml (1 tsp) roasted sesame oil
peanut oil or sunflower oil for sautéing
8-12 shiitake mushrooms, discard stalks if too woody
a handful of wing beans, cut on an angle (or use snow peas or mange-tout)
a bunch of gai lan or similar Asian green, cut into 6-cm lengths

Place the brains in a large bowl of cold water and run water gently through them for 5 minutes then drain most of the water from them. Dissolve 50 g fine salt in a cup of warm water and add this to the brains along with the vinegar and barely cover with cold water. Leave them to sit in the 'brine' for 30 minutes.

While they're doing their thing, place all but 20 ml of the soy, the black vinegar, star anise, cinnamon, sliced onion and ginger in a large pot with 1 litre of cold water. Bring to the boil and simmer for 5 minutes then turn the heat off and leave to cool to body temperature.

Once ready, drain the brains and place these in the pot, making sure they're not too tightly packed in. Add the carrots as well and place a paper cartouche on top of the liquid (see page 147) and slowly bring to the boil. Simmer for 4 minutes then turn the heat off and leave them to cool completely. Once they've cooled, carefully remove the brains from the poaching liquid, pull the lobes apart and lay these on a tray lined with a kitchen cloth. Strain 200 ml of the liquid into a jug and pick the carrots out. You can discard the rest, although you could freeze the strained stock to be used for a meat stew at a later date.

Make the panizza by sifting the chickpea flour, five-spice, and ¼ teaspoon freshly ground black pepper. Mix in 100 ml cold water and make a paste. Bring 400 ml water to the boil with 1 teaspoon salt. Turn the heat down then gently whisk the chickpea paste in. The mixture will thicken just like polenta or porridge and when it does, turn the heat down and cook over a low–moderate heat, stirring constantly but gently. Take from the heat and stir in 20 g of the butter then tip onto a lightly oiled main course plate, or a tray, and leave to cool down and set before cutting into 6–8 wedges, depending on whether you're serving it as a starter for six or a main for four. When you're almost ready to serve this dish, heat up a pan and add a few Tablespoons of peanut or sunflower oil and fry the panizza for a few minutes on each side until lightly coloured. Keep warm in a low oven.

Return the pan to the heat, wipe it of excess oil then add the remaining 30 g of butter. Cook over a moderate–high heat until the butter sizzles and turns golden brown. Add the brains and cook until coloured all over. Add the carrots and the reserved poaching liquor and bring to the boil, then simmer for 4 minutes, turning the brains over halfway through until they're warmed.

Mix the reserved soy sauce with the mirin and sesame oil. Heat up a wok or a wide heavy-based pan. Once it's really hot add a few teaspoons of the peanut or sunflower oil and then the shiitake and wing beans. Cook over a high heat, tossing frequently, until the vegetables colour. Add the gai lan and then the mirin mixture at which point it will steam up and sizzle. Toss the vegetables until it's all but evaporated.

To serve: Place a wedge of warmed panizza on warm plates, add the vegetables and the brains, then spoon over the poaching liquor.

Lemon-poached chicken on Manchego polenta with Sichuan pepper, spinach, pine nuts, peas & beans

I'm a real fan of chicken. A simple roast chicken and potatoes with peas and broccoli is a perfect meal as far as I'm concerned. However, my second favourite way of eating the humble chook would be to have it poached. It becomes incredibly moist and plump and you then have the added benefit of having masses of delicious stock to play around with as well. I like to serve the chicken at room temperature, which obviously suits summertime, but if you want to eat this piping hot, then once it has sat in its stock for the required time you'd need to turn the heat up and bring to a simmer. In China, the chicken is placed into the pot whole, but I prefer to separate the legs and thigh from the crown as legs do need that extra cooking time. However, in this recipe I brown the meat a little which gives a deeper flavour to the stock. Soft polenta is one of the culinary world's great things – you can whip it up really quickly, flavour it with whatever you feel like, from shredded blanched spinach through to blue cheese, toasted cumin or roast garlic. It wasn't until I went to China in 2005 that I realised how often pine nuts are used in Cantonese cuisine – I'd always thought of them as peculiarly Italian. So in this dish I've linked the cuisines of Italy and China together though the pine nut. Or at least tried to. Keep the poaching stock from this, strain it, then boil it to reduce to just 500 ml and freeze it for later use.

For 4–6

1 chicken (around 2 kg)

45 ml (3 Tbsp) olive oil

1 head garlic, unpeeled, cut in half horizontally

2 banana shallots, peeled and thickly sliced, or 1 white onion or 6 round shallots

2 carrots, peeled and cut into 4

1 lemongrass stem, bash it with the back of a knife or with a pestle to bruise it

a small handful of thyme and rosemary

2 tsp flaky or coarse smoked salt (use regular salt if you can't find it smoked)

125 g instant polenta (sieved through a coarse sieve to remove lumps)

30 g Manchego, grated (or use Parmesan or pecorino)

a handful of green beans, topped and halved lengthways

a handful of peas

2 tsp sesame seeds

½ tsp coarsely ground Sichuan peppercorns

3 Tbsp pine nuts

200 g spinach, washed and drained – if using large leaves, shred them coarsely

Cut the legs and thighs off the chicken carcass, then cut them in half at the knee joint. Heat up a large saucepan (it will need to be around 5–6 litres – big enough to hold the chicken comfortably), add half the olive oil and then the chicken thighs and legs and cook over medium heat until the chicken has browned all over. Remove the chicken but keep the pot on the heat. Add the garlic, shallots, carrots and lemongrass and fry until the shallots are coloured, stirring frequently. Return the legs and thighs to the pan along with the herbs, a few teaspoons of salt and the crown of the carcass (the body with the two breasts attached). Pour on enough cold water to cover the chicken by a few centimetres then bring to the boil. Turn to a simmer and cook with the lid on for 8 minutes. Remove the carcass using a pair of tongs, or two forks, and place it in a bowl. Turn the heat up to a gentle boil and continue to cook the legs and thighs for another 6 minutes. Return the carcass to the pan, put the lid on and turn the heat off. The chicken will continue to cook in the latent heat in the pot, and it will be cooked all the way through in 20–30 minutes.

To make the polenta, remove 650 ml of the stock and pass it through a sieve into a 2-litre pan along with the smoked salt, and bring to a rapid simmer. Put the sieved polenta into a jug (it makes it easier) then slowly pour it into the simmering stock, whisking gently but continuously until it has all been added. Turn the heat up to moderate and swap your whisk for a spoon or spatula, then cook for 1–2 minutes, stirring constantly to prevent lumps forming, then mix in the Manchego. Taste for seasoning, adding extra salt or Manchego if needed.

Bring a pan of lightly salted water to the boil, add the beans and peas and cook for 2 minutes or so, until just cooked, then drain. In a wide frying-pan or pot, place the sesame seeds, Sichuan pepper and pine nuts along with the remaining olive oil and cook over a moderate heat until the pine nuts are golden – stirring constantly. Once they've coloured, add the spinach and cook it until it wilts. Add the beans and peas to the pan and season with salt and freshly ground black pepper, give it a good toss and stir, then cook for a minute to warm it all through.

To serve: Remove the chicken carcass, legs and thighs from the stock – tongs are best for this. Cut the breasts from the carcass using a thin sharp knife and slice into 4–5 pieces. You can either leave the bones in the legs and thighs, or remove them. Spoon the polenta onto your plates and sit the spinach mixture on top, along with the chicken meat. Drizzle with the poaching stock as you would a gravy.

Pan-roasted duck breast on lime leaf & peanut mash with mango dressing & roast tamarillo

The flavours in this dish may appear quite sweet and sour, but in many ways they're no more so than the classic *duck à l'orange* where the duck is roasted, then a sauce is made from orange juice, often an orange or mandarin liqueur, and sugar. Sweet and sour – but done in a French fashion. Tamarillos are what I grew up knowing as tree tomatoes but I think their name changed sometime in the late '60s, as had happened to Chinese gooseberries (now known as kiwifruit). Several years ago, The Providores set up a restaurant in the wonderful London department store Selfridges during a promotion they ran called Body Craze. One of the people we worked with was from Bolivia and we got to talking about tamarillos which she said she'd never heard of. I said that was strange as I knew they originated in the South American Andes of Bolivia, Ecuador, Peru and Chile. She then realised that what I was talking about were in fact *tomate de árbol*, or tree tomatoes! If you can't find any, then this works really well with roast nectarines, apricots or peaches. My mango dressing came out this amazing colour due to the fact that I used a delicious bright yellow Alphonso mango, but any ripe mango will give a lovely, rich sweetness to the dish.

For 4

4 duck breasts – around 150–200 g each
2 tamarillos
1 tsp caster sugar
50 ml extra virgin olive oil
4 potatoes, peeled (700 g) and halved
6 lime leaves (or use bashed lemongrass or sliced ginger)
4 cloves peeled garlic, sliced
50 g butter
½ mango, peeled and the flesh removed from the pit
½ thumb of ginger, thinly sliced against the grain
¼ tsp finely grated lime zest
15 ml (1 Tbsp) lime juice
¼ red chilli (more or less to taste)
1½ tsp nam pla fish sauce
30 ml (2 Tbsp) vegetable oil (use peanut or sunflower oil)
60 g coarsely chopped roasted skinless peanuts (also delicious made with roasted hazelnuts)

Score the fat side of the duck breasts cross-hatch style. Don't actually cut into the flesh of the breast, just the fatty skin layer on top. The closer the cross-hatch lines, the crisper your duck skin will become. Season the fat side lightly with salt, and the flesh side with freshly ground pepper. Place on a plate and cover with plastic wrap.

Preheat the oven to 160 °C. Cut the tamarillos in half lengthways and lay on a tray lined with baking parchment. Score the flesh with a small sharp knife cutting in towards the skin, but avoiding cutting through the skin. Sprinkle the sugar over them and drizzle with a little of the olive oil, salt and pepper. Bake until they begin to resemble oven-roasted tomatoes, around an hour, then take from the oven and turn it off.

Place the potatoes into a pot of lightly salted water with the lime leaves and garlic and bring to the boil, then cook on a rapid simmer until done. Drain then mash with the remaining olive oil and the butter and taste for seasoning, keep warm and to one side.

Place the mango, ginger, lime zest and juice, chilli, nam pla and vegetable oil into a blender – or use a stick blender – and purée thoroughly to give you a smooth dressing. Taste for seasoning, adding extra nam pla or salt to taste.

To cook the duck, heat up a frying-pan that you can fit the breasts in easily, but not so large they get lost. Your pan will also need a lid. When the pan is smoking place the breasts in fat-side down – you won't need any oil. Once they begin to sizzle, turn the heat down and cook for 5–8 minutes over a moderate heat until the skin becomes golden (see the photo) and the fat begins to render off them. I always place a slightly askew lid on the pan, don't seal it, this stops the fat splattering over your stove. Once they're properly coloured, take them from the pan and discard most of the fat – be careful as it'll be hot. Return the breasts to the pan, this time with the skin-side facing up and put the lid tightly on. Cook over a moderate heat until the breasts have cooked to rare – around 3–4 minutes. If you like your duck cooked more then do so. Turn the heat off, make the lid askew again to stop the skin going soggy from the steam in the pan and rest for 5 minutes. At this point they will have become medium-rare.

Place the duck onto a warm plate and turn the heat in the pan back on. Add the peanuts to the pan juices and heat them up, stirring constantly, until any liquid has evaporated, then mix the mash in.

To serve: Slice the duck against the grain. Spoon the mash onto your plates and lay the duck on top, place a tamarillo on top and drizzle the duck with the dressing. If you've some cress at hand then put that on as well.

Roast yoghurt-marinated pigeon on seeded potato quinoa rösti & roast cauliflower with umeshu plum relish

Pigeons can be either domesticated or wild. The latter will be more gamey in flavour and also possibly more lean – which means they can dry out when cooking as they have little excess fat. Restaurants tend to use farmed squab pigeons, which are consistent in quality and size and incredibly tasty. This yoghurt marinade takes its inspiration from the tandoor marinades of India: the enzymes contained in the yoghurt tenderise the meat. The Swiss introduced the world to rösti and I've eaten more versions than I can remember. Memorable ones included the addition of grated hard cheese, bacon lardons or apple to the usually starchy potato. Here I mix the potato with seeds and ground quinoa which adds a really lovely crunch and flavour to them, and also I bake them first before shallow-frying them. I created these rösti at The Providores many years ago, and they then crossed the Atlantic to appear on the brunch menu at PUBLIC restaurant in New York, a restaurant The Providores was instrumental in setting up with the owners. *Umeshu* is a delicious sweet Japanese liqueur made by macerating unripe *ume* fruit (much like a plum) with sugar and alcohol. The flavour pairs really well with the plums in the relish and goes incredibly well with the pigeon – if you can't find it, then any good-quality plum or apricot liqueur will suffice. I also give a recipe for a pigeon stock which is lovely drizzled over the dish, although it can be frozen in ice cube trays to be used at a later date too.

For 4

4 x squab pigeon, plucked, livers will ideally still be intact in the body cavity

100 g plain thick yoghurt

4 cloves garlic, peeled and finely chopped

½ tsp roasted cumin seeds, ground

½ tsp roasted coriander seeds, ground

1 red onion, peeled and thinly sliced

1 thumb of ginger, peeled and chopped

1 tsp ground star anise

½ tsp chilli flakes (or use fresh chilli or chilli sauce)

2 Tbsp toasted white sesame seeds

4 large firm but ripe plums, washed, halved, stones discarded, cut into chunks

200 ml umeshu liqueur

80 g unrefined caster sugar

30 ml (2 Tbsp) cider vinegar

3 large floury potatoes (around 750 g peeled weight)

3 Tbsp uncooked quinoa, ground into a coarse powder in a spice grinder

1 Tbsp poppy seeds

1 Tbsp fresh rosemary leaves, roughly chopped

1–2 tsp curry powder (use a commercial blend or make one yourself)

1 medium-sized cauliflower, separate the florets and cut each lengthways into 2–3 pieces

50 g butter (although you can use oil to cook the pigeon in)

a handful of rocket, pea shoots or watercress to garnish

Cut the legs from the carcasses and then remove the breasts – you may want to ask your butcher to do this for you. Mix the yoghurt with half the garlic, the ground cumin and coriander and ¼ teaspoon salt. Use this to generously coat the breasts and then place them, covered, in the fridge for 12–36 hours.

Make the relish. Heat up a medium-sized pot, add 1 Tablespoon cooking oil, then sauté the onion, ginger and the remaining garlic until they begin to caramelise over a moderate heat, stirring frequently. Stir in the star anise, chilli flakes and half the sesame seeds and sauté another minute. Add the plums, umeshu liqueur and sugar and bring to a boil, then put the lid on the pot and cook for 5 minutes. Take the lid off, give it a stir and increase the heat and cook until the liquid has reduced by three-quarters. Add the vinegar, bring back to the boil then take off the heat, taste for seasoning and spoon into a clean container and seal while hot. Once cooled this will keep in the fridge for a week.

Make the rösti. Preheat the oven to 180 °C. Grate the potatoes coarsely then squeeze out any excess moisture between your hands. Mix with the ground quinoa, poppy seeds, the remaining sesame seeds, the rosemary, 2 teaspoons flaky salt and some freshly ground black pepper. Line a baking tray with parchment and lightly oil it. Using a 10-cm round cookie cutter, or something similar, press a quarter of the mixture in firmly to give you a fat disc. Use the remaining mixture in the same way to give you four röstis. Drizzle a little oil over each one then bake for 20–30 minutes, until they're beginning to turn golden. Leave to cool on the tray then remove, and turn the oven to 200 °C.

Mix the curry powder in a medium bowl with 1 Tablespoon cooking oil and a little salt then add the cauliflower and toss it all together. Lay the cauliflower on the same tray you baked the rösti on and cook until the florets turn golden – around 6–10 minutes. Remove from the oven.

To cook the pigeon, wipe off excess yoghurt marinade and discard it. Place an ovenproof pan large enough to hold all eight breasts over a moderate–high heat and then add the butter and 1 Tablespoon vegetable oil. Once the butter has been sizzling for 30 seconds place the breasts in skin-side down and cook for 2 minutes, before turning over and cooking for 1 minute. Place in the oven and cook for a further 2 minutes then take out and leave to rest in the pan, in a warm place, for 2 minutes. At this point they will be between medium –rare and medium – you may prefer to cook a little less or more.

To cook the rösti, heat up 1 cm of vegetable oil in a deep-sided pan (or you can deep-fry them) and when it gets to 180 °C place the rösti

in, as many as you can fit comfortably and cook on both sides until golden and crunchy. Take from the oil, drain of excess oil and keep warm while you cook the remainder.

To serve: Place a hot rösti on each plate and lay some rocket on top. Place the roast cauliflower on top, then two pigeon breasts and finally some of the plum relish. Drizzle with the pigeon stock (if making it) and eat straight away.

Pigeon stock

the 4 pigeon legs and carcasses
1 onion, unpeeled, sliced
1 carrot, peeled and sliced
1 thumb of ginger, sliced
1 head garlic, unpeeled, cut crossways into 4
6 star anise
200 ml red wine
2 bay leaves
2 egg whites
50 ml Chinese black vinegar or balsamic vinegar (or any
  dark aromatic vinegar)

Heat up a 3–4 litre pan and add 2 Tablespoons vegetable oil then the pigeon legs and carcasses and fry them, stirring constantly, until browned. Take the carcasses and legs from the pot then add the onion, carrot, ginger and garlic and fry to colour it. Return the pigeon to the pan along with the star anise, red wine and bay leaves and 1 litre cold water. Bring to the boil and simmer for 1 hour. Whisk the egg whites with the vinegar and 50 ml cold water then mix this briskly into the simmering stock. Simmer over a low heat for a further 20 minutes then strain it through a sieve, shaking the juice through rather than pushing it through. Place back on the heat in a clean pot, bring to the boil and reduce by half. Pass through a fine sieve and it's ready to use.

Roast guinea fowl on celeriac, pear & satsuma salad with watercress

It's amazing that we don't eat more Guinea fowl. You cook them exactly as you would a chicken, which they generally have more flavour than, and they're not hugely expensive. You can feed 3–4 people from your average bird, so perhaps it's more a budgetary thing when you consider you can buy a large battery-reared chicken for much less – much less flavour, too, mind you. Guinea fowl are native to Africa but it was the Portuguese who brought them to Europe from their colony in Guinea around the 16th century, and they've been reared in Europe since – the French being particularly fond of the young ones which they call *pintadeaux*. The Romans were also known to be partial to them and there are images of them in ancient Egyptian art. The brown meat from the legs benefits from being slowly poached, so I like to cook them separate to the breasts, which I roast on the crown. The braised celeriac salad is a modern-classic dish from muzedechanga restaurant in Istanbul which the gorgeous Tarik and Savas run, alongside their changa restaurant. At muzedechanga they have reinvented their mothers' and aunties' recipes, creating delicious dishes from often simple vegetables and basic ingredients. Visit them in summer, sit on their terrace overlooking the Bosphorus and think how lucky you are. The celeriac salad is best made at least the day before as its flavour slowly develops.

For 3–4

1 guinea fowl (around 1.6–2 kg)
1 onion, peeled and thickly sliced
½ lemon, cut into 4, skin and all
1 tsp coriander seeds
50 ml soy sauce
a small handful of thyme
2 Tbsp (30 ml) vegetable oil
3 large banana shallots, peeled and sliced into rings (or 1 white onion)
1 medium-sized celeriac, peeled and cut into 2-cm chunks
2 pears
2 satsumas, cut in half crossways, then each half cut into 8 (or use seedless clementines or oranges that aren't too bitter)
50 ml lemon juice
50 ml satsuma juice
60 ml extra virgin olive oil, plus extra for roasting the bird
a bunch of watercress, washed, excess stalks discarded

Cut the legs and thighs from the carcass, then cut them in half at the knee joint and place in a 1-litre pan. Add the sliced onion, the cut lemon, coriander seeds, soy sauce and thyme. Cover with cold water by 1 cm. Place on high heat, bring to the boil, then simmer with a lid on the pot for 1 hour. Leave to cool in the pot.

While the legs are cooking prepare your braised celeriac. Heat a medium-sized pot and add the oil then the sliced banana shallots and 1 teaspoon flaky salt, and sauté, without colouring, until wilted. Add the celeriac and stir well, then put a lid on the pot and cook over low–moderate heat, stirring every few minutes, for 12 minutes. Cut the pears into quarters, remove the seeds and stalk and cut each quarter into four, add these to the celeriac along with the satsumas, lemon juice, satsuma juice and extra virgin olive oil. Stir well, place a paper cartouche (see following page) on top of the mixture, put the lid back on and cook for 15–20 minutes, until you can insert a knife through the celeriac with a little resistance. Leave to cool in the pot then taste for seasoning and, if making in advance, store covered in the fridge.

Turn the oven to 170 °C. Rinse the inside of the carcass with cold water, pat dry with kitchen paper and lightly season it. Drizzle some extra virgin olive oil over the carcass, sprinkle with salt and rub it in. Line a roasting dish with aluminium foil and sit the carcass in – sitting on its wings with the breasts facing up. Pour 100 ml hot water into the dish and place in the centre of the oven to roast for 25 minutes. Take from the oven and fold the aluminium foil over the bird to keep it warm while it rests.

To serve: Pull the meat from the poached legs, discarding bones, then cut or shred into pieces and mix with the watercress and place on your plates. The celeriac salad is best eaten at room temperature, but if serving this in winter you may want to warm it up gently before plating up. Carve the breasts off the carcass and serve alongside the salads, drizzling any roasting-pan juices over as you do so.

How to make a cartouche

A cartouche is a round of baking parchment that is placed on top of a simmering stew or on poaching fruit. It sits on top of the liquid, therefore not allowing it to evaporate too much, keeping in the aromas and moisture. The simplest way to make a cartouche is to sit the lid of the pot you're cooking the stew in on top of a sheet of baking parchment then, using a non-toxic pencil or pen, draw an outline and cut out the circle with scissors. Using a sharp knife, poke it twice near the centre. Once the liquid has come to the boil, turn to a simmer and gently press the cartouche on top.

Roast ostrich on smoked mashed potatoes with moromi miso aubergines & apple-braised cavolo nero

Africa brought us the ostrich, the largest living bird, just as it gave us the somewhat smaller guinea fowl. Ostriches were once also found throughout parts of Syria, Iraq and the Arabian peninsula but, just like New Zealand's native moa (a flightless bird even larger than the ostrich), they were hunted to extinction by man. These days you're just as likely to see an ostrich farm in your own country (even winter-cold Sweden breeds them) and their meat, leather and feathers are found all over the world in expensive kebabs, handbags and dusters. The smoked mashed potatoes may well be something that you restrict to summertime barbecues, but this recipe is incredible. At my Auckland, New Zealand, restaurant, dine by Peter Gordon, we also make soft polenta using the same principle – smoking the cream from which it's made. The smoking matter I use is a mixture of equal quantities of untreated wood chips (neither too fine nor too chunky), black tea and rice, but you may have a mixture of your own. It's worth investing in a smoker – the best place to find one would be your nearest outdoor or camping store. The first time I ate *cavolo nero*, which means black cabbage in Italian, was in Florence in 1990 when I visited friends there. It had been slowly cooked with butter beans and garlic and was served on bruschetta – delicious. If you can't find *moromi* miso then any miso paste will work.

For 6

1 kg (peeled weight) starchy potatoes

100 g smoking matter (a mixture of untreated wood chips, tea and rice)

300 ml double cream

200 g butter

500 g cavolo nero

1 large onion, peeled and thinly sliced

6 cloves garlic, peeled and sliced

30 ml (2 Tbsp) olive oil, plus more for cooking the ostrich

1 apple, core removed, cut into small dice (choose an apple that isn't overly sweet)

100 ml apple juice (choose one that isn't too sweet)

50 g moromi miso

50 ml sake

30 ml (2 Tbsp) mirin

1 thumb of ginger, peeled and julienned

½ red chilli, julienned

1 large aubergine, stalk removed, cut into 10 lengthways wedges, then each in half again

10 ml (2 tsp) sesame oil

1 kg ostrich breast meat, cut against the grain into 6 even-sized pieces

30 ml (2 Tbsp) extra virgin olive oil

1 lemon, cut into 6 wedges

Boil the potatoes in lightly salted water until cooked. While they're cooking set up your smoker and when smoke begins to issue from it place the cream, in a shallow heat-proof dish, on the smoking rack inside, put the lid on the smoker, and smoke over moderate–high heat for 6–8 minutes. Every few minutes give the cream a stir as the smoke settles on the fatty surface and you want to infuse this throughout the rest of the cream. Once it's ready, turn the heat off and carefully remove the container of smoked cream. Pour it into a pan, add the butter and slowly warm through until the butter has melted. Drain the cooked potatoes then mash with the warmed cream and season with salt.

Tear the leaves from the fibrous central stalks of the cavolo nero and rinse in a sink of cold water then drain. Sauté the onion and garlic in the olive oil until just beginning to caramelise, stirring often, then add the apple and drained cavolo nero and give it a good stir. Add the apple juice, bring to a boil then put a lid on the pot and cook on a rapid simmer for 20 minutes, stirring occasionally. Season with salt and pepper.

While that's cooking, preheat the oven to 180 °C. Mix the miso, sake, mirin, ginger and chilli together in a bowl along with 50 ml warm water. Add the wedges of aubergine to the bowl and toss it all together. Line a baking tray with parchment and place the aubergine on top, skin-side down. Drizzle the juices from the bowl on top, then the sesame oil, and bake for 15 minutes or so, until the flesh has softened and coloured.

Pat the ostrich steaks dry with kitchen paper, then lightly season and rub with olive oil. Leave to come to room temperature. Heat up a wide frying-pan over a moderate–high heat then place the ostrich steaks in, as many as will fit comfortably in one layer, and cook to medium–rare (although you can cook ostrich meat more it will be quite dry as the meat is lean). You can also grill ostrich on a barbecue which is great.

To serve: Spread some of the mash on warmed plates and place the cavolo nero and aubergines on top. Slice the steaks into 3–4 pieces and lay these on top, then drizzle with the extra virgin olive oil. Serve with a wedge of lemon on the side.

Whole salt-baked fish stuffed with lemongrass, thyme & jasmine tea

This cooking technique may seem like a huge waste of salt – but I promise you your fish will be really tasty and incredibly moist. A few years ago The Providores restaurant owners were in Istanbul for our AGM and we ate dinner at a restaurant on the Asian side of the Bosphorus. Part of the meal consisted of two huge sea bass cooked in this style, although without any herbs added, and it was one of the top three fish I have ever eaten. I've also eaten a massive 5 kg turbot cooked the same way in a huge roasting dish and it was equally delicious. Cooking fish in this style is quite a novel thing to do, and when served as part of a dinner party it makes for a great talking point as it's a real 'get stuck in' affair. There's no need to remove the scales from the fish, but you will need to remove the guts, and it pays to remove the sharp dorsal spines with a pair of scissors so that none of your guests prick themselves. Cut the tail off if your fish is larger than your baking dish, then gently wash the stomach cavity with cold water and pat the whole fish dry with kitchen paper. The flavour from the jasmine tea will be most noticeable in the flesh closest to the stomach cavity, so make sure you divide that up evenly. A fish this large will serve 4–6 people, depending on what else is being served for the meal, but it goes well with baby potatoes, steamed greens or a tomato, rocket and feta salad.

For 4–6

2 lemongrass stems, bashed, then roughly chopped
a handful of thyme
2 Tbsp jasmine tea leaves
1 whole lemon, roughly chopped with the skin still on
1.5 kg coarse sea salt
1 x 1.5–2 kg whole fish, prepared as on left (I used a lovely 1.5 kg bream)
1 egg (optional, but it makes the whole thing work better)

Preheat the oven to 250 °C and place a rack in the centre of the oven. Ideally choose a ceramic baking dish large enough to hold the fish, but not so big that the fish gets lost. If you have to use a metal dish, line it with baking parchment – the salt can damage aluminium dishes. Mix the lemongrass, thyme and jasmine tea together with 1 Tablespoon of the salt and half the lemon and pack a third of this into the stomach cavity of the fish. Scatter the remaining lemon on the base of the roasting dish.

Mix the remaining lemongrass mixture with the remaining salt and the egg and lay ½ cm of it on the bottom of the dish. Place the fish on top, then pile the remaining salt on top of the fish, making sure it's completely covered. Put in the oven and bake for 20 minutes. Take from the oven and rest for 10 minutes, at which point the fish will be perfectly cooked.

To serve: You need to break apart the salt-crust. The best way is to use something like an oyster knife or a wide flat-head screwdriver. The salt will fly all over the place if you're too rough, so take it easy. Once you've exposed the fish, pull the skin off (the scales help to keep the skin in one sheet) and using a fork or spoon carefully scrape the flesh from the upper side of the fish. There will be the odd bone, but that's what you get with a whole fish. Pull the skeleton up from the fish to expose the lower part of the fish. Carefully pull the flesh up using a fork or spoon, leaving the skin in the dish, and again, look out for bones.

Monkfish steamed with ginger & yellow beans on tomato basmati rice

In 2005, I was lucky enough to travel around Guangdong, China, for 19 days filming a TV show about the delights of Cantonese cuisine. In the show I cooked a dish very similar to this in beautiful Daya Bay using whole tiger groper. This style of steaming fish is very much a traditional recipe from many parts of South-East Asia and China, but what I have found is that it actually goes really well with this tomato rice originating in Turkey. In 2007, our friends Tarik and Savas, who own changa and muzedechanga restaurants in Istanbul, had hired a gorgeous 'Captain Pugwash'-type boat for us all to have a summer break on. They're both excellent cooks and the tomato rice that Tarik made on that voyage has since proven to be a great all-rounder with most fish dishes – the light acidity of it especially complements the yellow beans in this recipe, although I use basmati rice in place of the short-grain Turkish rice that Tarik used. Although I used monkfish tail (skinned and cut through the bone), hake, sea bass, turbot or skate wings will work equally as well, just adjust the cooking times as needed. A salad made from rocket, watercress, spinach and fresh herbs goes really well with this, as does steamed buttered spinach, asparagus and mange-tout.

For 4

2 thumbs of ginger, peeled and julienned, or thinly sliced – keep the ginger peelings
60 g salted yellow beans (bottled in a brine)
15 ml (1 Tbsp) soy sauce
4 lime leaves
5 ml (1 tsp) peanut oil
5 ml (1 tsp) sesame oil
4 x 200-g chunks of fish on the bone
200 g (1 cup) basmati rice
2 ripe tomatoes, cut into chunks
15 ml (1 Tbsp) extra virgin olive oil

Place the ginger, yellow beans, soy, lime leaves, peanut oil and sesame oil into a bowl and slosh it around. Add the fish and mix it with the marinade. Cover the bowl with plastic wrap and leave to marinate for 10 minutes in a cool place, but not in the fridge.

While it's marinating, make the rice. Rinse the rice for 20 seconds in a sieve under cold running water then drain it. Place in a saucepan with the tomatoes, olive oil, 350 ml cold water and ½ teaspoon fine salt. Put a lid on, place over a high heat and bring to the boil. Give a quick stir, then turn to a simmer and cook for 10 minutes with the lid on. Turn off the heat and rest with the lid on for 10 minutes.

Place the ginger peelings in the bottom of a steamer along with 2 litres of hot water, turn the heat on and let it boil for a minute with the steamer lid on.

Place the lime leaves onto a heat-proof plate or a dish that will comfortably fit into the steamer basket (it needs to have sides on it so that the marinade juices don't completely run off), then sit the fish on and pour the ginger and yellow beans on top with the marinade juices. Place the plate in the steamer then put the lid back on and steam for 8–10 minutes, at which point the fish should be cooked. To check, take the lid off after 8 minutes being careful not to burn yourself from the steam, and poke a thin sharp knife into the flesh around the bone – the flesh should be translucent.

To serve: Give the rice a gentle stir and divide amongst four warmed plates, sit a portion of fish on top and drizzle with the steaming juices.

Fish & shellfish saffron & coconut stew with spice-roasted pumpkin

This dish takes a bit of prep, but it's absolutely delicious and full of amazing textures, flavours and colours. You'll need to get your hands stuck into it when you eat it, all those shells and things, but it's worth it. Although I give a recipe for braised octopus on page 52, which you could use here, I also wanted to give you an alternative way of cooking it. I also used baby octopus, although you could use squid, and it's important that you cook the clams like this as they're notoriously gritty and it's a real shame to go to the effort to cook this and have it full of grit. The saffron I used for this was actually grown in Otago, New Zealand, and its flavour is incredibly intense with the aroma and colour very earthy. I love to pair pumpkin (or butternut squash) or sweet potatoes with saffron, so it seemed a good idea to add large chunks of roasted pumpkin to the dish – as it sits in the broth it slowly absorbs some of the flavour – which gives it a lovely taste.

For 6

1 white onion, peeled and sliced

6 cloves garlic, peeled and sliced

vegetable oil for sautéing

300 g large octopus legs, cut into 5-10-cm lengths

½ lemon, sliced (keep the skin intact)

10 peppercorns

600-800 g pumpkin or butternut squash, seeds removed

1 tsp cumin seeds

4 whole allspice

1 Tbsp sesame seeds

1 tsp chilli flakes

30 ml (2 Tbsp) extra virgin olive oil

250 g cleaned clams (soak in cold, gently running water for 20 minutes to help remove grit)

3 shallots, peeled and sliced

1 thumb of ginger, peeled and julienned

2 green chillies, split lengthways and cut into 4

12 baby octopus, gutted

2 pinches saffron - crumbled into 100 ml warm water and left to soak for 10 minutes

300 ml coconut milk (although you could also use cream)

6 large scallops, cut in half crossways (or 12 smaller scallops)

200 g monkfish fillet, sliced into 6 (or try using cod, hake, john dory or swordfish)

First prepare the octopus legs. In a large pan with a tight-fitting lid, sauté the onion and garlic to colour in a little vegetable oil. Add the octopus and give it a stir, then add the lemon, 1 litre of water, 2 teaspoons flaky salt and the peppercorns. Sit a cartouche (see page 147) on top of the liquid and bring to the boil. Turn to a simmer, put the lid on, and cook for 80 minutes. Turn the heat off and leave it to cool in the liquid. Once it's cool, remove the octopus from the liquid, strain the liquid, pour it back over the octopus and place in the fridge.

Preheat the oven to 180 °C. Line a roasting dish with baking parchment. Cut the pumpkin into 12 even-sized chunks – there's no need to peel it unless you want to. Pound the cumin, allspice, sesame seeds and chilli flakes with 1 teaspoon flaky salt and sprinkle this over the pumpkin, drizzle on the olive oil and 50 ml water. Roast until you can insert a thin sharp knife through the flesh of the pumpkin.

Heat up a wide, deep pot and when it begins to smoke tip in the clams, all at once, and put a lid on. Cook for 4 minutes, shaking the pan from time to time. Turn the heat off and discard any clams that haven't opened. Tip the clams into a colander and leave to drain, then strain the pan juices through a fine sieve and reserve for later use – it makes a great addition to a fish and shellfish soup and is lovely mixed into a tomato-based sauce for pasta, or mixed into a seafood risotto.

Rinse the pot out then sauté the shallots, ginger and chillies in 1 Tablespoon of the vegetable oil until beginning to caramelise. Add the baby octopus and give it a good stir, then add the saffron and its soaking liquid and coconut milk and bring to the boil. Put a lid on and cook over a high heat for two minutes. Add 200 ml of the octopus cooking liquid and bring back to the boil, then add the clams, octopus, scallops and monkfish and give it a very gentle stir. Simmer for no more than 2 minutes with the lid on then turn the heat off, taste for seasoning, and leave for a few minutes.

To serve: Place two chunks of hot pumpkin into preheated bowls then ladle over the fish and shellfish and plenty of the broth.

Crab, ginger & tofu-crusted halibut on wok-fried greens with red lentil coconut broth

I created this dish when we opened my Auckland restaurant dine by Peter Gordon. I'd been making the mousse to use as a crust on fish for many years, often adding some coconut cream, shredded kaffir lime leaves or prawn mince to give it a twist. However, I wanted to create a signature dish for the restaurant, and I had a hunch this would be it. We serve it on top of roasted kumara and plenty of wok-fried Asian greens and the fish we mostly use is the lovely hapuku – a meaty but tender fish native to New Zealand's waters. The addition of red lentils gives the sauce a great texture and a wonderful earthy taste, and the pandan adds an almost vanilla aroma to the dish, although don't fret if you can't find pandan leaves, the flavour is terrific, but not essential.

For 6

6 x 120–140-g portions of halibut fillet, skin and bones removed

1 x recipe of the tofu crab mousse from page 88

80 g red lentils (orange split peas)

¼ leek, thinly sliced and washed to remove grit if needed

100 g ripe plantain, peeled and sliced (see page 86) or use a semi-ripe banana if you can't locate a plantain

1 pandan leaf, tied into several knots (optional, but tasty)

½ thumb of ginger, peeled and thinly sliced

2 black cardamom

300 ml coconut milk

50 ml tamarind paste

15 ml (1 Tbsp) fish sauce

50 g panko crumbs

vegetable oil for frying

a handful of Asian vegetables – choose a mixture of any of the following: bok choy, gai lan, pak choy, enoki or shiitake mushrooms, wing beans or long beans, etc.

5 ml (1 tsp) toasted sesame oil

10 ml (2 tsp) soy sauce

10 ml (2 tsp) mirin

Lightly season the fish on one side, then spread the tofu crab mousse evenly over the other side to form a coating. Place on a tray or plate, cover with plastic wrap and put in the fridge while you prepare everything else.

Put the lentils, leek, plantain, pandan leaf and ginger in a pan and add 500 ml water. Bring to the boil, stirring occasionally, and cook on a rapid simmer until the water has all but evaporated and the lentils are cooked and bursting. Add the black cardamom, coconut milk and another 200 ml water and simmer with a lid on for 20 minutes, stirring occasionally. Remove the pandan leaf and cardamom then mix in the tamarind and fish sauce. Purée using a stick blender or bar blender and taste for seasoning. This can be made up to 3 days in advance if stored in the fridge once cooled.

Preheat the oven to 190 °C. Place the panko crumbs onto a plate then press the mousse side of the fish into them gently to give an even coating. Place a frying-pan over a moderate heat and when it's hot add vegetable oil to give a ½ cm depth. Place the fish in (as many portions as will fit comfortably), mousse-side down, and cook until the crumbs are a deep golden colour. Carefully flip the fish over and cook for 1 minute, then transfer to a baking tray (if your pan doesn't hold all the fish at once). Place in the oven and cook for 3–5 minutes, depending on the thickness of your fish – to test if it's cooked poke a small sharp knife into the thickest part – it should be translucent. Turn off the oven and open the door to keep it warm while you cook the vegetables.

While the fish is cooking, heat up a wok or a large wide pan or pot, and add a splash of vegetable oil. Add the Asian vegetables and toss or stir them for 30 seconds, keeping the wok on the heat. Mix the sesame oil, soy and mirin and add to the wok. The vegetables will only need a minute of cooking – you want them to stay crunchy.

To serve: Ladle some broth into six bowl-plates. Pile the vegetables in, then sit a portion of fish on top with the crumbed side facing up.

In many ways the salad under the mackerel is a free-for-all. In London we're lucky to have a great selection of Thai fruit and vegetables made available to us through various shops, but also through the lovely Australian authority on Thai food – David Thompson. David's restaurant nahm was the first Thai restaurant to get a Michelin star and he and his team serve authentic and delicious food based on Thai ingredients that he sources fresh each week direct from Bangkok's various markets. In the photo you can see the lotus shoot in the top left corner, the *sapodilla* looks like a wedge of brown papaya next to it (but tastes of Medjool dates and caramel) and the palm heart can be seen tucked in several places. There's also lightly pickled yellow beetroot, pomegranate seeds, julienned *jicama* and sliced, peeled prickly pears. The kaffir lime comes from my own tree here in London. The point of this explanation is really just to say that you want a mixture of many textures and flavours, from the sweet through to the crunchy and sour. Head to a friendly Asian greengrocer and ask for their help. Failing that, use a mixture of green papaya and mango, ripe papaya and mango, wedges of Medjool dates, pineapple slices, bean sprouts, apples and pears and whatever else takes your fancy. Mackerel works so well with all of these flavours as it is an oily fish and this goes well with sweet and sour; other good fish would be tuna, sardines and grey mullet.

For 4

Grilled mackerel on fruit & vegetables with pomegranate wasabi dressing

1 large golden beetroot
1 large juicy lemon, sliced into 8
45 ml (3 Tbsp) avocado oil
1-2 pomegranates
50 ml mirin
30 ml (2 Tbsp) lime juice, plus 2 whole limes
1-2 tsp wasabi paste
5 ml (1 tsp) toasted sesame oil
600-800 g assorted fresh fruit and vegetables as described on the left
4 mackerel, gutted, head can be left on if preferred
a handful of coriander

Peel the beetroot then slice quite thin on a mandolin. Place 500 ml water in a medium-sized pot with 1 teaspoon salt, the lemon and 1 Tablespoon of the avocado oil. Bring to the boil and simmer for 5 minutes, then add the slices of beetroot one at a time. Bring back to a rapid simmer and cook until they're ready – test one after 5 minutes, it should be tender but with a little bite. Take off the heat and leave to cool.

Make the dressing. Run a small knife around the outside of the pomegranates and pull them apart, avoiding cutting through the bitter white membrane. Pick out 2 Tablespoons of seeds then juice the remainder as you would an orange – you want at least 150 ml juice. Place this in a small pot with the mirin and ¼ teaspoon salt. Bring to the boil then reduce until you have a quarter. Leave to cool then mix in the lime juice and the wasabi, then the sesame oil and half the remaining avocado oil.

Prepare the fruit and vegetables. It's up to you how you slice them, but the only thing that's ultimately important is to peel the skin from those that need it, remove inedible seeds from others and cut things quite thin. Lay slices of the beetroot on the base of your plates then toss the fresh fruit and vegetables together with the pomegranate seeds and place this on top.

Brush the mackerel with the remaining avocado oil and season the stomach cavity and the skin with salt. Cook it over a moderate–high heat either on a skillet or heavy-based pan, or on a char-grill or barbecue. The fish is cooked when you can just pull the flesh away from the bone at the thickest part, about 2–3 minutes on each side.

To serve: Sit the fish on top of the salad, scatter with the coriander and then spoon the dressing on top or serve in a dish on the side.

Coriander

Fresh coriander (or cilantro as it's called in America) seems to split people on either side of the taste fence. I for one adore it, finding the flavour incredibly refreshing and vibrant. I love the way it enlivens dishes from Thai coconut curries through to roasted baby beetroot tossed with olive oil and lemon juice. However, after years of cooking for restaurant customers, I realise there are many of you out there who just don't have the same response – many likening it to soapy parsley. On the other hand, coriander seeds seem to please most people, and I've yet to be asked by a customer if I could avoid adding coriander seeds to any of my dishes. The seeds have a lovely citrus aroma and flavour and, as such, Europeans have added them to rye bread, hearty sausages and the likes for many years.

Coriander is thought to have originated in South-West Asia and Mediterranean North Africa, although the exact birthplace of this wonderful herb has never been pinpointed. Coriander seeds were found in the tomb of Tutankhamun; it has been grown in Greece and Turkey seemingly forever; and the seeds have emerged from Bronze Age sites in Eastern Europe. The Romans are thought to have introduced coriander into Britain when they ruled the land, but it's interesting that whilst the seeds have happily been used in Europe's many cuisines, the leaves, stem and roots are all but ignored. What is glaringly obvious from a Fusion point of view is that this herb, so closely associated with Thai, Vietnamese and Mexican cuisines, did not actually originate in any of these regions.

Trade routes, yet again, can be credited with the spread of coriander seeds and, therefore, the plant itself around the world. Thai curry pastes frequently have coriander seeds in them, as do many Indian spice mixes, where coriander is called *dhania*. In Belgium, there are beers brewed with the addition of the seeds, and in South Africa the traditional *Boerewors* sausage wouldn't be such without the flavour from the seeds. In Mexico, the leaves are added to many of that country's delicious salsa and sauces, and in Portugal, which seems to be the only European stronghold of the herb, it can be found extensively in dishes. The Chinese have a liking for the leaves especially in the Guangdong region, and whilst I could easily find sugar-coated coriander seeds in Istanbul (eaten as a snack), it was hard to find fresh coriander when I first started going to Turkey back in 1999.

Indians have a love affair with coriander in all its forms. I've eaten many a watery but tasty vegetable curry strewn with the leaves and topped with fried curry leaves and mustard seeds. I've seen coriander seeds toasted in a heavy pan before being smashed and added to a lentil soup (*dahl*) in both India and Nepal, and the smell of these toasting seeds is really lovely.

I also like to use the seeds in desserts – especially in baked foods like shortbread and focaccia. Infuse a spoonful of lightly toasted seeds in elderflower syrup for 24 hours before churning it to make a fantastic summer sorbet. Warm some crushed seeds in cream to add a wee twist to a traditional Italian panna cotta. The leaves are great when used as a herb sprinkled on everything from a cold beef salad through to a fish stew enlivened with saffron and shredded ginger. Remember too that the root of coriander is packed full of flavour, so if you're able to buy it with the root on make sure you simply bash it a little and add to soups and stews towards the end of cooking to impart some extra flavour, or chop it finely then pound it with some chilli, sugar, garlic and lime juice to make a wonderful Thai-inspired dressing.

Spain, renowned for its traditional cuisine, has over the last decade been recognised as the centre of a new culinary endeavour, galvanising many kitchens throughout Europe.

It is Spain people cite when they wish to pinpoint 21st century culinary innovation, experimentation and other-worldly dining experiences. People celebrate foaming liquids, hot gels set with seaweed extracts, pipettes of smoked this and bizarrely flavoured that. They eulogise pearls of pea purée and melon 'caviar' held together with yet more seaweed and other chemicals that cause the mixture to stay runny in the centre. They excitedly extol egg yolks that taste of asparagus and a soup made from algae-covered rocks dredged up from the bottom of the ocean, partnered with tuna spine fluid (all of which I've experienced). France, of course, long maintained the role of culinary world leader and for good reason. For hundreds of years they worked single-mindedly at improving their traditional dishes: sauces more refined, smoother purées, flakier pastries and less icy sorbets. *Sous vide* cooking (cooking in 'plastic bags' at low temperatures) become *de-rigueur* in kitchens all around the world (although I have to admit to having a huge dislike for all the plastic waste it produces). France set the standard for restaurant meals for hundreds of years, so it must be galling for them to

see Spain taking this mantle from them. It is towards the various Michelin-starred, award-winning restaurants from Jerez in the south to Barcelona and Roses in the north-east, Madrid in the centre and Galicia in the north-west that young chefs head. Paris has given way to St Sebastian of all places – and it's easy to see why.

Spanish chefs have been having fun and letting their hair down. They have been creating new techniques; discovering and blending new flavours and older textures. They have been exploring the world's store cupboard and have made some very interesting discoveries. Every year there is a Summit Conference (for want of a better description) of the great and the good from the world's stellar chefs. I attended it in 2005. It is called Madrid Fusion (the second word instantly appeals to me) and it is a forum where chefs who have 'made it', get to talk and teach techniques to those aspiring to do the same. It is part-hosted by Ferran Adria, of El Bulli fame. The year I went, Ferran spoke of how we must look towards the flavours of Asia if our cuisine is to move forward. As some of you may have picked up by now, reading this book, that's what I've been doing quietly for years anyway, so it was with huge interest I heard him say this to the hundreds of delegates assembled in the conference hall. The three days I attended were long and dense with information, and to be honest, not everything during that time excited me, but those things that did were wonderful. The aforementioned rock-soup, for example, was completely outrageous. The young Spanish chef (whose name I just can't recall) made a stock using rocks from the sea-bed, then added shaved cuttlefish skeleton (just like the ones you give to birds to help sharpen their beaks) plus seaweed, of course. He then poached the marrow from the spine of a huge tuna and served this in the broth. It was quite simply the most fascinating thing I'd ever seen made and it blew me away. One of Australia's culinary treasures, chef Tetsuya Wakuda, originally from Japan, also gave a fantastic demonstration, cooking everything himself, and tasting it as he went along (which, to be frank, wasn't the norm, with several chefs getting their assistants to do all the work). Then another Japanese chef, Yuji Wakiya, came out and gave a demonstration of the food he had been cooking for over 25 years: Chinese. He also gave a wonderful demonstration, ably assisted by none other than his good friend Nobu Matsuhisa who is possibly one of the most well known chef/restaurateurs in the world.

However, alongside this contemporary culinary extravagance there is also a really wonderful heritage of Spanish artisan meat and cheese production, and a fishing industry that leads the world in tuna, salt cod (*baccalau*), anchovy and sardine canning and preservation. The Spanish climate ensures the harvesting of a huge array of fruit and vegetables that ripen to perfection. Its geography covers almost every topographical extreme known to man, from the intense heat in the south around Cadiz and Jerez (the home of sherry wines), to the mountains of the Picos de Europa and the bracing seas off the northern coast of Galicia. It also has fostered a cuisine that is probably my favourite in Europe. What I love about the food of Spain is its heartiness. It's deeply flavoursome, and it's hugely satisfying. It also incorporates a national treasure that is tasty, versatile and delicious. This is *cerdo negro* or *cerdo Iberico* – also known as the Black Foot pig or

pata negra. It is an ancient breed of pig that used to roam freely through the *dehesa*, the flat plains of the Iberian Peninsula where oak trees grow, munching on acorns, fattening up each autumn. However, the *dehesa* have slowly disappeared in many areas due to humankind taking over the land and they're now quite scarce. This has caused these rare pigs to become the most valuable pork in the world, and also the most sought after, rivalling the best prosciutto of Italy. They are also clever. In 2006, I helped open a tapas bar in Auckland and I named it Bellota. Here's what I wrote for our menu:

Bellota (pronounced bey-otta) is the Spanish word for acorn, and it's the acorn that plays an essential part in the creation of one of the world's most prized delicacies – *jamon Iberico de bellota* (literally Iberian ham of acorns). The Iberian pig used to live all over Spain, Portugal and many parts of the Mediterranean, but due to the decline in its natural habitat, the *dehesa* (oak forests), they are scarce and, needless to say, incredibly expensive. They're also very smart pigs. I was speaking to a herder in Spain a few years ago and he said he'd noticed he was losing a few of the beasts every week. He suspected they were being stolen as they are so valuable, so he set up watch at the only gates that they could escape from. He couldn't believe his eyes. He watched three piggies approach the cattle grid at the gates, and then one by one they got onto their bellies and simply rolled and rolled over the grid. They jumped up and headed for the hills. It's because of this that we have to charge you what seems daylight robbery for just a plate of this delicious delicacy. But trust me, you'd be paying a fortune in Spain as well.

In early February 2008, Michael and I headed off to Spain to take part in an ancient Spanish tradition – the *matanza*:

It's 5.30 a.m., cold and dark and I'm hurriedly snipping leaves from a surprisingly healthy three-year-old kaffir lime tree that also produces wrinkly kaffir limes. It's surprising because this particular plant lives inside our apartment on the dining table, all year long, on the top floor of an Edwardian block in West Hampstead far from its South-East Asian roots. My partner Michael and I are heading to Zaragoza, Spain, to take part in an event I've been anticipating for years: the *matanza*, an ancient Spanish gastronomic tradition. We will butcher a pig, make *chorizo* and *longaniza* – and introduce our Spanish friends to laksa, the Malaysian coconut soup. Hence the lime leaves . . .

We'll be joining our friend Fernando and his family, and a constantly changing group of their friends at this ritual, which still takes place all over Spain, in one form or another, between November and February. Nando used to be employed in the kitchen at The Providores, but these days he works in London as a graphic designer at two prestigious fashion houses. His family comes from an Aragon village with the strangely futuristic name of Escatron. It was once a thriving place, but sadly, it's now in decline as the youngsters move off to larger cities to start a life, whilst the older residents simply get older. Less than a kilometre from the village centre there's a power station; plonked near the river during Franco's time, it was recently updated with two huge new stacks and flashing red lights.

The *matanza* is an old tradition whereby a pig is slaughtered and then parts of it are preserved for future use or eaten fresh during indulgent feasting over the following days. Its blood is drained to make *morcilla* (mixed with rice or grains to produce blood sausage); the loins (*lomo*), shoulders (*paletta*) and legs (*jamon*) are mostly cured, and the remaining bits and pieces are either grilled for meals, or minced to produce *chorizo*, *longaniza* or *botifarra*. The head, snout, ears, knuckles and stomach are used to make a redolent stew called *callos* (pronounced kai-yoss), and the skin is deep-fried till crisply chewy and served as a snack.

So, before sunrise, a dozen of us assembled at the family home, which in reality is a small, one-storey town block, the outer walls made up on two sides by the narrow rooms of the house, another wall by a huge shed which formerly housed 3000 chickens but now finds itself home to a dozen Vespa scooters from the '50s onwards, and the fourth wall – simply a wall. The vast internal courtyard had a fire burning all weekend, to either fend off the winter chill, or to barbecue the various slabs of meat and sausages that we produced. Nando's diminutive Aunt Cari and her husband José were in charge of the butchery 'department',

whilst various cousins and Nando's mother Emerita controlled the *chorizo* stuffing, hanging and sustenance departments. Due to a recent EU ruling, we weren't able to kill our own pig and bleed it, and hence we couldn't make *morcilla*. To get over that disappointment I ate a plate of piping hot sugar-doused *torijas* (similar to French Toast) and sipped on the local red wine from a communal pouch. Thus warmed, Michael and I, along with Nando and his brothers Antonio and Javier, walked to the local butcher in the chill, early morning darkness to collect the pig, which had been cut in half lengthways down the spine. The brothers carried the two halves back home, draped over their shoulders like two barbaric bagpipes.

The carcass was hung from two hooks in the courtyard and then swiftly and expertly portioned into the major limbs and joints by Uncle José. I was assigned the role of de-boning the legs and shoulders (I'd taken my own knives) alongside an ex-butcher friend of the family. It was decided that we wouldn't salt and cure them to make *jamon* or *paletta*, so we cut them into smaller bits. I was also given the task of taking the rind off the belly (to be deep-fried) and then slicing the meat into pieces small enough to go through the hand mincer. Most of the fat was removed from the meat and minced separately. All of this mincing took a varied crew quite a few hours to complete, as it's hard work, and I think you'd be surprised at how much meat there is on a single pig. As the sun rose the number of helping hands increased. At one point I looked up from my butcher's block and we were 24-strong in the courtyard, employed in various roles from fire-stokers and meat mincers through to mince mixers and cider pourers. All under the ever-watchful eyes of Mother and Aunty. The delicious still cider had arrived with a couple from San Sebastian who poured small amounts of it from a height into glasses, causing it to effervesce.

Once the animal had finally been reduced to mere bones and pieces of meat, most of the former were mixed with the *callos* ingredients (Aunty having cleavered the head in half after chopping the snout off) and placed in a huge cauldron of water on the interior open fire where they simmered for several hours before having freshly ground almonds added (shelled that morning by Nando's girlfriend Montse) to produce a rich, chewy, gelatinous stew. I have to confess that *callos* verges on being texturally challenging – but it's ultimately quite fabulous. The ribs were chopped into small pieces and put aside for the following day's rice dish, and the sausage skins (the intestines) were rinsed.

While we chopped, sliced and minced outside, the team inside were making two types of 'sausage' – *chorizo* and *longaniza*. They mixed lean beef mince, in varying proportions, with the minced pork and fat, then either seasoned it with *pimenton* (smoked paprika) and dried garlic for the *chorizo*, or with cinnamon and cloves for the *longaniza*. I ingratiated myself onto the sausage-tying table, where I learnt to seal the newly formed 50-cm long sausages at both ends with a sneaky little twist of string. Having proved expert with this chore (sealing 20 sausages), Michael and I then took control of the 50-year-old manual sausage-stuffing machine. We filled its hollow tube with the sausage mix, then wound its handle to force the meat through a nozzle, which we'd wrapped with an intestine. As the mixture was forced out, it filled the intestine and, before you knew it, you had a fresh *chorizo* in your hand. These were tied, then hung from a rack in the house's second kitchen, previously the pig pen. In all, we made around 70 of each sausage.

Two kilograms of reserved belly fat were cut into small pieces for making *migas*, our lunchtime treat and another traditional Spanish dish. Aunty fried the fat in about 3 litres of olive oil in a three-legged pot striding the internal fireplace, added 40 cloves of peeled, halved garlic, and fried this until it turned brown, then added 4–5 kg of freshly made coarse breadcrumbs. This was cooked over the fire, stirred continuously and then moistened with a little water. The end result was like cous cous, but rich and slightly smoky. It was served with red and green grapes and was surprisingly delicious – and quite bizarre when you think about its ingredients. Can you imagine sitting down to fried, fatty, garlic breadcrumbs with grapes?

The fabulous, raucous dinner that night comprised salad, *chorizo*, butcher-made *morcilla* and *Jamon Serrano* followed by boozy espresso (*carajillo*). Breakfast on Sunday was

churros and thick hot chocolate, followed by an amazing rice dish, more like a risotto than *paella* (made from the pork rib pieces, rabbit, snails, wild mountain mushrooms, artichokes, potato and vegetables), which was cooked by Javier and a friend. They told me that in Spain all large feasts are traditionally cooked by the men, whilst at home, meals are prepared by the women. It was fantastic to be immersed in a culture where everyone seemed capable of cooking.

That same evening, Michael and I made our surprise laksa for everyone. Along with the West Hampstead lime leaves, we'd brought dehydrated coconut milk, lemongrass, ginger, green tea noodles and crispy shallots. Nando had bought *nam pla* (fish sauce), soy and sesame oil. This particular version contained no chilli, coriander, meat or fish. And definitely no pork. I mean, how much can one be expected to eat! The group loved it, and for many it was the first dish of its kind they'd ever experienced. Even Aunty was impressed which meant a lot to me as she'd been a powerhouse all weekend and I'd decided early on that she'd be my new role model!

Over the weekend, an ever-changing group of 80+ people had shared meals together, all at a hugely long table, and almost all based on the one pig we'd butchered ourselves. It was a fantastic cultural experience; an Olympian, Spanish repast and a tradition that I'm pleased to know isn't on the way out just yet.

It's because old traditions like the *matanza*, passed down over the generations, exist side by side with the extraordinary culinary experimentation taking place, that I love Spain so much. But I have to be honest, it is incredibly hard to get a green salad that doesn't contain pork in some shape or form, or even some simple steamed broccoli or beans, in restaurants around the country. That's all I ever miss in Spain – simple, steamed greens. But then, that's what people are cooking at home every day of the week. When they eat out, Spain wants its diners to have a true Experience. And that is what they have, in every sense of the word.

Peanuts

Firstly, peanuts are not actually a nut. They are a legume, just like a lentil, a bean or a pea. Out of their shell and toasted, of course, they more closely resemble a hazelnut than a broad bean, but they are definitely not nuts. The fruits of the plant mature underground (hence the American name ground-nut) not on branches above the ground.

Peanuts are both demonised and adored in equal measure. Well, actually they are only disliked by a small number of people, and with good reason. Peanuts can cause anaphylactic shock in people allergic to them, and have caused deaths. What is surprising is that whilst some people in the Western world have grown allergic to them, it is almost unheard of in other countries in South-East Asia, China, Africa and India. A lot of research is currently being carried out to understand why this is. But it does pay to note, that if you are allergic to peanuts you may not necessarily be allergic to real nuts.

Peanuts seem an essential part of the Western diet, from eating a packet of them at a pub or on a train (in the old days you'd be offered them on flights but airlines have withdrawn them due to allergen concerns), through to peanut butter and jelly sandwiches and the lovely salted peanut candies in America. In Indonesia and Malaysia, satay sauce is one of the culinary highlights, and it would be impossible to think of Thai cuisine without the use of peanuts in various curry pastes or toasted and tossed through salads. However, like chillies and coriander, ingredients we closely associate with South-East Asian food, peanuts did not come from Asia. They came from South America, most likely from Peru. As with chillies and tomatoes, they made their way north and south through the Americas, wherever the climate allowed them to grow. It may seem odd that their arrival in North America, home of peanut butter, was by way of Africa. The Portuguese who had settled in Brazil had become fond of them and took them into Africa where they were grown and eaten extensively. From Africa they made their way back to North America. It was also the Portuguese that introduced them to China in the 1600s – currently the world's largest grower of this crop.

Whilst we most often eat them roasted, in some parts of the world boiled or steamed peanuts are more the norm. I can remember eating banana-leaf cones of steamed nuts throughout Indonesia when I was travelling there in 1985. When I travelled to the Guangdong region of China to film a TV show in 2005, I was surprised at how often they appeared in dishes from the region, most often boiled. In India, the second-largest growing nation, I barely recall them, but that's likely because they are grown more for their oil than for the actual peanut itself. Peanut oil is a wonderful oil to cook with as it has an almost neutral flavour and a high burning point (which means you can cook over a high heat successfully), but in the restaurants I've run I avoid using it due to the possible effect it might have on a customer allergic to peanuts.

I love the savoury flavour of peanuts, and like to boil them for 12 minutes before draining and cooling them, then frying in peanut oil until pale golden. This is my preferred toasting method – although you can, of course, also simply toast them in the oven. Also, we sometimes boil them with sugar and chillies for 20 minutes before draining them and tossing them whilst still a little damp and warm in caster sugar and leaving them to dry completely. Deep-fried they become the perfect sweet and savoury snack, or toss them through a salad of green mango, toasted coconut, avocado, smoked eel and lime juice and you are onto a winner. Lightly toast them then purée in a food processor with a little tahini to make a wonderful peanut butter. Or toast in the oven, finely grind them and add to a plain ice cream base and leave to infuse overnight. Next day strain out and churn – and serve with a berry compote and biscotti – better in my mind than peanut butter and jelly sandwiches!

four.
brunch

I created this stuffed savoury version of French toast in 2007 when I was wondering what to do with some leftover smoked mackerel in the fridge at home. It's fantastic, I have to say. The combination of hot smoked eggy fish and bread – absolutely lovely. For the fish, you can use any smoked moist fish such as British mackerel, New Zealand kahawai or hot smoked salmon. Here I team it with a simple salad but it's also great served with grilled bacon, or some avocado mashed up with a little chilli sauce.

For 4

Smoked fish & tomato French toast with horseradish, radish & watercress salad

200 g smoked fish – all skin and bones removed
8 slices of 2-day-old white bread (I used a baguette)
1 small red onion, peeled and thinly sliced
4 tomatoes, thickly sliced
3 eggs
100 ml cream
50 g butter or 45 ml (3 Tbsp) vegetable oil to cook with
10 g (1 Tbsp) freshly grated horseradish (although commercially made creamed horseradish works really well)
15 ml (1 Tbsp) lemon juice
50 ml crème fraîche
a handful of watercress, washed and drained
12 radishes, sliced

Preheat oven to 120 °C. Use your fingers to pull the fish flesh apart and loosen it up into a shredded mixture. Spread it over four slices of the bread and lay the sliced onion and tomatoes on top. Sit the remaining bread firmly on top (as if you're making a sandwich) and press down for a few seconds each to help hold it together. Whisk the eggs with the cream and a pinch of salt, then one by one dip the sandwiches in it to coat them on both sides, removing them onto a tray as you go. Pour any excess egg mixture over them as they need to be quite eggy to be really delicious. Heat a pan up (ideally one large enough to take at least two sandwiches at once) and when it's moderately hot add either the butter or oil. Once that's hot and sizzling add two sandwiches and cook them over a moderate heat until the eggy bread has turned dark golden. Gently flip them over and cook on the other side until dark golden, then remove and place on an oven tray and put in the oven to keep warm. Cook the next two sandwiches the same way and place these in the oven and cook for 3–4 minutes to ensure they're warmed all the way through.

Once they're in the oven make the dressing by mixing the horseradish with the lemon juice and crème fraîche.

To serve: Take the French toast from the oven and place on warmed plates. Toss the watercress with the radishes and the dressing and stack on top, then eat immediately.

Banana & pecan French toast with vanilla verjus syrup & lardons

This is the sweet version of French toast, or eggy bread as the British like to call it, and fair enough as that's exactly what it is. In French it's *pain perdu*, or lost bread – due to it using up stale bread that might otherwise be thrown out. You'll see there's also a savoury smoked fish French toast in this chapter too. We've had this version on the breakfast menu at The Providores almost since the day we opened our doors in August 2001 and I hate to think how many we have sold since then. If you don't eat pork then serve it as it is, unadorned apart from the delicious vanilla verjus. This syrup will keep in the fridge for a month or more and the combination of sour verjus, sweet sugar and aromatic vanilla is unbeatable. Try it drizzled over breakfast pancakes or even roast stone fruit and ice cream – it's fabulous. If you can't find verjus there really aren't too many alternatives, although you could use a mixture of sour apple juice and lemon juice.

For 2, although the syrup will make more than you need

1 large ripe banana

4 slices white sandwich bread, 1–2 days old, slightly stale

12 toasted pecan nuts

1 egg

50 ml cream

50 ml milk

2 tsp sesame seeds (optional)

50 g butter

20 ml (1 Tbsp + 1 tsp) vegetable oil

100 g thickly sliced bacon lardons (slice rashers of bacon into lardons, or simply use sliced bacon instead)

Vanilla verjus syrup

150 ml verjus

100 g caster sugar

½ vanilla bean, split lengthways and seeds scraped out

Make the vanilla verjus syrup first. Place everything, including the vanilla bean, in a small pan and bring to the boil then rapidly simmer to reduce by a quarter to a syrupy consistency. Scrape the sides of the pot down as it cooks to ensure the vanilla seeds don't dry out. Leave to cool and store in the fridge but serve at room temperature.

Preheat oven to 180 °C. Mash the banana with a fork, but keep it a little chunky. Spread this over two slices of bread and scatter the pecans on top. Put the other slices on top, as if you're making a sandwich, and press them firmly together. Beat the egg quite briskly with the cream, milk and sesame seeds and then coat the sandwiches in this (it might be easier to do it one at a time). You want the bread to absorb all the eggy mixture, so keep turning them in it.

Place a frying-pan that's large enough to hold both sandwiches at once over a moderate–high heat. Add the butter and cook until it stops sizzling then add the oil. Place the sandwiches in, drizzling over any eggy mix that hasn't been absorbed and cook until golden. Carefully flip over, making sure the filling doesn't come out, and cook on the other side until golden. Transfer to an oven tray lined with baking parchment and warm through for 3 minutes. Wipe excess fat from the pan, leaving a few teaspoons in, then add the lardons and cook over a moderate–high heat until they crisp up.

To serve: Cut the French toast in half. Place on warmed plates and scatter with the lardons then drizzle with the vanilla verjus syrup.

As I've already written, I backpacked through South-East Asia and other regions back in the late '80s for a year. In Thailand, I teamed up with an Australian, Stephen Smith, who remains a good friend to this day. While we were hitching along the Mekong River, on the Thai side but near the Laos capital of Vientiane, I came across the most delicious coconut-filled croissants. Now this may seem a somewhat odd thing to find on sale in Thailand, but bear in mind that the French had administered Laos for many years, and one of the many things they introduced to the country was baking and patisserie, even if only for the ex-pat community based there. What had obviously happened is that a baker from Laos had given the classic French breakfast snack a twist by introducing the locally abundant coconut as a stuffing. At some point that idea had crossed the Mekong into Thailand. Fusion cuisine at its simplest and most delicious. If you can't find pandan extract don't worry, just add a few drops of vanilla extract instead.

For 4

Pandan & coconut-stuffed croissants

4 croissants, 1-2 days old
80 g butter, softened but not melted
40 g white sugar
1 egg
2-4 drops pandan extract (or ⅛ tsp vanilla extract)
2 teaspoons flour, sifted
120 g desiccated coconut

Preheat oven to 170 °C. Lay the croissants on a board and, using a serrated knife, cut them from one side almost through to the other – make sure you keep both halves intact though. Place the butter and sugar in a bowl and beat with a wooden spoon until light and creamy. Beat in the egg and pandan extract and then stir in the flour and a pinch of salt, then the coconut. Open up the croissants and spread the mixture onto them as though you were buttering them. Place on a baking tray lined with baking parchment and bake for 12–15 minutes, at which point the filling should just be beginning to colour. Lovely eaten straight from the oven, they're also delicious eaten cold.

Sweetcorn, five-spice & date fritters with tomato & avocado

Growing up in New Zealand it seemed that there were a few classic dishes in our nation's repertoire – but that everyone had their own twist on them. Pumpkin soup was one, and corn fritters another. I recall versions of the former seeming racy if they had curry powder in them, or if they were made with cream and topped with grated cheese – that seemed very posh. However, the latter, the corn fritters, were pretty much all made from the same few ingredients: a can of sweetcorn, flour, egg and a little milk. Packed full of corn, they were absolutely delicious when grilled, thick-sliced bacon was laid across the top. Back in 1970, my father, Bruce, was most impressed with his garden (our family always grew lots of vegetables) and told my (soon to be) stepmum, Rose, how proud he was of his corn and pumpkin patch. Rose replied that back in London they fed corn to chickens and pumpkins to pigs – people didn't eat them! That made me realise that the use, or not, of particular ingredients in a nation's diet is often based on nonsense and lack of experience.

For 4–6 (8–12 fritters)

100 g flour

50 g wholemeal flour

50 g polenta

1 Tbsp sugar

1 tsp baking powder

½ tsp baking soda

1 tsp five-spice

2 eggs

330 ml buttermilk (or use a runny unflavoured yoghurt)

50 ml extra virgin avocado oil, plus more for cooking the fritters (or use a light olive oil for cooking)

1 corn cob (or 150 g canned corn kernels, drained)

12 Medjool dates, pitted and cut into 8

1 large avocado

2-3 tomatoes

30 ml (2 Tbsp) lemon juice

a handful of rocket or salad greens

Sieve the flours, polenta, sugar, baking powder, baking soda and five-spice with ½ teaspoon fine salt. Beat the eggs with the buttermilk and 30 ml of the avocado oil in a bowl, then tip the dry mixture in and stir it briskly to form a thick batter.

Peel the husk from the corn cob and lay it flat on a chopping board. Using a serrated knife, cut the kernels from it and add these to the fritter mix along with the chopped dates. Mix it all together and leave for 15 minutes.

Halve the avocado, remove the stone and scoop the flesh from the skin using a large spoon. Cut into chunks and mix with the tomato, the remaining 20 ml avocado oil and the lemon juice, then season with salt and pepper and put to one side.

Heat up a wide frying-pan and drizzle a few teaspoons of avocado oil into it then give the fritter mix a stir and dollop spoonfuls of the mixture into the pan and cook over a moderate heat until coloured. Carefully flip over and cook on the other side, until they're cooked in the centre – it'll take around 3–5 minutes all up, depending how large you make them. Once cooked, take from the pan and stack on a platter. Once they're all cooked (they can be eaten hot or at room temperature) divide amongst your plates.

To serve: Toss the avocado salad with the salad leaves and place on top of the fritters.

Feta & Manchego omelette with spinach, chorizo & sumac

This is my idea of brunch heaven. Spicy, oily, eggy – what could be better? As I've mentioned previously in the book, you want to make sure you buy cooking chorizo for this dish, the type that is made to be cooked, not to be sliced. I had some Manchego in my fridge at home, as I usually do, but if you don't have any then you can substitute it with pecorino, Zamorano or Parmesan – just choose a lovely firm cheese. Sumac may seem like an odd breakfast garnish here, but it's the astringency it offers to the dish which makes it a perfect breakfast spice – it's a real pick-me-up.

For 2

1 red onion, peeled and sliced
½ red chilli, sliced (more or less, to taste)
10 ml (2 tsp) olive oil
150 g cooking chorizo, sliced
4 eggs
50 g feta, cubed
2 Tbsp grated Manchego cheese
10 ml (2 tsp) extra virgin olive oil
50 g steamed or sautéed spinach, shredded
a handful of coriander, shredded stalks and leaves
2 tsp sumac

Fry the onion and chilli in half the olive oil until the onion begins to caramelise. Add the sliced chorizo and continue to sauté, the fat will render from the chorizo and help the onion cook. Keep warm at the back of the stove.

Use a fork to lightly beat the eggs with the cheeses, the extra virgin olive oil and 20 ml cold water then season with a little salt and pepper. You want the eggs to be streaky, not a one-coloured mass.

Heat up two 15–20-cm non-stick frying-pans (or cook these one at a time) and drizzle the remaining oil into them once they're hot. Quickly pour the egg mixture into them and shake the pans for a few seconds to distribute the eggs. Scatter the cooked spinach on top, then place the chorizo mixture down the centre. Sprinkle the coriander on and when the egg looks like it's almost cooked take the pan off the heat.

To serve: Using a spatula flip one side of the omelette over itself, then carefully roll it out of the pan onto a warm plate, sprinkle with sumac and eat it while it's hot.

Roast butternut with poached eggs & chilli butter

This dish is a bit of a hybrid really, the combination of a brunch dish at The Providores that we call Turkish eggs, and spicy roast butternut squash, or pumpkin, that I had left in my fridge. Turkish eggs have been a huge hit at the restaurant, and I first came across them in 1999 when I went to Istanbul for the first time. There they are called *Çılbır* and are often referred to as prostitute's eggs. Much like the more famous *sugo alla puttanesca* (prostitute's sauce) from Italy which is used on pasta dishes, the legend behind the name is up for dispute. However, the version I prefer is simply that it's quick to rustle up between clients and it's a hearty simple meal. Allepo chillies, named after the northern Syrian town, are what you ideally need for this, but you can use mild chilli flakes instead, or even chopped fresh red chillies. Aleppo chilli flakes are quite oily in texture and have very few seeds in them. In Turkey, they add raw chopped garlic to the whipped yoghurt but we don't at the restaurant – it can come as a bit of a surprise to our breakfasting customers. If you can't be bothered roasting the butternut squash then don't panic, it's great without it, but I would recommend some toasted crusty bread. When poaching eggs the trick is to use a deep pot of rapidly simmering water, just off centre on the stove. Never add salt to poaching water, but do add a generous amount of white vinegar (60 ml vinegar per litre of water).

For 2

200 g peeled butternut squash (or pumpkin), seeds removed
50 ml extra virgin olive oil
1 heaped tsp chilli flakes
100 g strained plain yoghurt (Turkish or Greek yoghurt)
1 clove garlic, peeled and finely chopped
40 g butter
a little torn coriander and/or flat parsley leaves
4 eggs
white vinegar

Preheat oven to 200 °C. Cut the butternut into chunks, toss with a little of the olive oil, a good pinch of the chilli flakes and some flaky salt. Lay on a baking tray lined with baking parchment and roast until cooked – around 15 minutes. Keep warm.

Beat the yoghurt with the garlic for 10 seconds, then beat in 4 teaspoons of the olive oil and beat until emulsified. Leave at room temperature.

Place the butter in a small pan and cook over a moderate heat until it turns a golden nut-brown colour. Add the remaining chilli flakes and leave them to sizzle for 10 seconds, then take off the heat and stir in the remaining olive oil and the herbs. Keep warm.

Poach your eggs in simmering acidulated water as described on the left.

To serve: Divide the butternut amongst warmed plates and spoon on half the yoghurt. Sit two poached eggs on top then dollop on the remaining yoghurt and spoon over the chilli butter. Eat these while they're really hot.

Black rice, quinoa, miso & banana porridge

250 g black rice
a few gratings of nutmeg
100 g quinoa
2-3 bananas, peeled and sliced 1 cm thick
60 g palm sugar, chopped or grated (or use maple syrup, runny honey or demerara sugar)
2 tsp shiro miso
300 ml coconut milk

This porridge, for want of a better word, is really a culmination of many things I've eaten and cooked over the years, including the first black rice pudding I ate in Bali made from black glutinous rice cooked with pandan, coconut milk, palm sugar and water. At The Providores restaurant we've had Michael's brown rice, miso and apple porridge on the menu since day one, and at a hippie café in New Zealand many years ago I was served a rather bland (and to be honest – really awful) quinoa porridge that would perhaps have been better if someone had added some sweetener to it. So I guess this is a combination of all three. The flavour of the black rice and coconut is enhanced by the addition of banana (a typical New Zealand addition to porridge), and the miso and quinoa (the super-grain) give one a sense of well-being and that's quite a good way to start the day, if you ask me. If you can't get hold of black rice, then brown rice will work at a pinch, but don't confuse wild rice with black rice. The former is actually native to North America and when it's cooked remains quite firm, whereas what you really want in a porridge is a slightly softer texture. If you don't have any quinoa to hand then just omit it – but you may feel less virtuous!

For 6–8

Rinse the rice for a minute under gently running warm water. Place in a pot with the nutmeg, 500 ml water and a pinch of salt and bring to the boil, then cook over a rapid simmer with a lid on until it's almost cooked, around 15–25 minutes.

While that's cooking, put the quinoa into a fine sieve and rinse under hot running water for 20 seconds – this takes some of the bitterness from the grain. Bring a litre of water to the boil, add the quinoa and boil until cooked and the grains begin to uncurl – anywhere from 8 to 15 minutes, depending on the freshness of the quinoa. You'll need to taste some – it should have a pleasant nutty bite to it. Drain back into the sieve while the rice is cooking.

Once the rice is almost cooked (it should have a little bite to it), stir in the bananas and sugar. Stir the miso into half the coconut milk to prevent lumps forming, then stir into the rice and bring back to the boil. Turn the heat down and keep cooking over a rapid simmer with the lid off until it's cooked, stirring frequently. Add the quinoa and taste for sweetness, adding more sugar if needed.

To serve: Ladle into bowls, pouring on the remaining coconut milk as you do so.

Manuka honey-roasted granola with vanilla-poached figs & vanilla yoghurt

Granola was invented in the USA and technically it differs from the Swiss breakfast cereal mixture, muesli, in that it is sweetened, baked and therefore crunchy. It's something you'll find in cafés all over New Zealand and Australia and we've been serving it at The Providores in London for 8 years with regulars popping in for a portion to help start a healthy day. You can spruce it up by adding toasted nuts and dried fruit once it's been baked and cooled, and you can add a few sprinkles of subtle spices – ground cloves and grated nutmeg work well. I offer a few garnish ideas below as well: the vanilla poached figs really make it special, and the vanilla yoghurt is so simple it's not really a recipe. The figs are also great mixed into a fresh fruit salad, or spooned over sliced roast pork or duck.

For 10–12

500 g organic jumbo oats
100 g pumpkin seeds
50 g sunflower seeds
4 Tbsp sesame seeds
50 g desiccated coconut (although I used freshly grated coconut which I toasted separately)
150 g Manuka honey (or any good honey)
100 ml extra virgin rapeseed oil, or extra virgin olive oil

Preheat oven to 160 °C. In a large bowl, mix the first five ingredients. Place the honey and oil in a small pan and bring to a simmer, stirring often, until the honey has become quite runny. Pour it over the oat mixture and toss it all together – although be careful as it will be quite hot. Line two baking trays, ideally with sides, with baking parchment and spread the mixture over these. Bake for 20–30 minutes, stirring often, until the oats are golden. If you undercook it, it will remain a little moist and not keep so well. What you need to achieve is a crumbly dry mixture, but one that isn't too dark. Remove from the oven, leave it to cool completely then store in an airtight container.

Vanilla-poached figs

12 dried figs, stalks cut off, cut in half lengthways
30 ml (2 Tbsp) verjus (or lemon juice)
½ vanilla bean, split lengthways
60 g sugar
1 star anise (or 2 cloves, 3 crushed allspice, ½ cinnamon quill or 2 crushed green cardamom)

Place everything in a small pot and pour on 200 ml water. Bring to the boil, then turn to a simmer and cook to reduce the syrup by half, gently stirring occasionally. Leave to cool in the liquid, then store in the fridge, in their liquid, for up to 10 days.

Vanilla yoghurt

200 ml thick Greek-style plain yoghurt
30 ml (2 Tbsp) manuka honey
½ tsp vanilla extract

Mix everything together with a small whisk.

Saffron

Saffron is a remarkable spice in many ways, and the highest quality is incredibly expensive – near enough the same price per gram as gold. In fact, in the early 1800s, it was the same price as gold on the Philadelphia commodities exchange market. It's also incredibly back-breaking to harvest, it can't be done with machinery, and the crocus flowers from which it comes must be harvested on the same day that they open, or else they wilt. Due to this labour-intensive process, the production has usually been limited to areas where labour is considered inexpensive, but also where the climate is just right. The plants need a reasonable amount of rain when planted, but then very little once they sprout, and definitely none once they flower. Iran, Crete, Turkey, Morocco, Spain, Kashmir, Italy and parts of America are all great places to grow it, but harvest costs can vary enormously in these countries and perhaps not surprisingly the bulk of the world's crop comes from Iran – more than 90 per cent. The saffron in the photo is actually from Cromwell in New Zealand. Until relatively recently saffron hadn't been grown in New Zealand, but now there are around 40 growers producing it in the Canterbury and Otago areas alone. I have to say that the best is of the highest quality of any I have tasted. In Britain, it was the Essex town of Saffron Walden that was once the centre of saffron production in the UK, but as I write I'm unaware of any being grown on a commercial scale.

It's thought that the saffron crocus we know today was actually created in Crete during the Bronze Age through selective breeding to take advantage of the elongated stigmas (the orange-red part) that were noticeable on some plants. As to how it got to move around the world is debatable, but what is certain is that it has always had slightly mystical and medicinal properties attributed to it, partly through its scarcity – saffron-dyed robes have been the preferred attire of Buddhist monks (although they've often been dyed with turmeric or artificial dyes), it's thought to be anti-carcinogenic, it was used to fight the Black Death, it was decoratively woven into fabrics thousands of years ago – and it's also great in food! Which is what most of the world does with it, after all.

As an apprentice chef in Melbourne we were told by our lecturers to only ever use it sparingly although we never got to use it as the college couldn't afford to buy it for us to play with. I can remember buying some Spanish saffron once to use in a simple risotto. I decided I'd be frivolous with it and put in lots to give my risotto a dark golden colour. What a mistake that was. What I'd been unaware of was that saffron is also incredibly strong in flavour. An almost bitter grassy flavour could best describe it, when used too generously. The next time I came across it in any great quantity was when I rented a room on a house-boat on the Jhelum River in Kashmir, away from popular Dal Lake in Srinagar. Here I was served one stamen in my sweet morning tea of cinnamon and cardamom – and it was heavenly. Heading into the market I saw vast numbers of sealed packets of it for sale and was impressed by the whole scene. The boat family told me that too much can cause nose bleeds – I have no idea if this is true but it was definitely believed by the locals.

I like to use saffron as the Scandinavians and Cornish do in bread baking, and use it sparingly in desserts such as creamy panna cotta or ice creams. It makes a lovely sorbet when left to soak in a sugar syrup, then churned with puréed ripe peaches or nectarines. In stews it adds a lovely background flavour when used in conjunction with cassia and star anise. Place two dozen stamens in a bottle of vodka with a vanilla bean to colour and flavour it for exotic cocktails, or simply soak it in a little white wine and add it to a risotto flavoured with sautéed bone marrow and plenty of Parmigiano-Reggiano. Delicious.

As I wrote in my introduction to this book, one of my seminal food experiences was eating fresh silken tofu, served in a bowl of iced water, at a Japanese restaurant in Melbourne when I was 19 years old.

For many years I've been an avid purchaser of Japanese produce as well as a regular at Japanese restaurants. I've always felt that there's an extraordinary adult clarity and purity to Japanese food, more evident than in other cuisines. Whilst a green coconut curry from Thailand, for example, may be a riot of sweet, sour and spicy flavours (although still combined with an underlying richness), the food of Japan has always seemed to me to be slightly austere. Serious. Delicious, yet a refined cuisine rather than a playful one.

So it was with enormous excitement that Michael and I headed to Tokyo and Kyoto in April 2008 to celebrate my 45th birthday, and our 20th anniversary - which just happened to be on the same day. I felt I was finally heading to my culinary spiritual home, the country that had inspired me for decades, the country whose cuisine had informed so much of what I do. Luckily for me I had help planning our visit in the form of my friend Akiko, who had cooked with me at The Sugar Club restaurant

in London back in the late '90s. Akiko was now living in Tokyo, married to Yoshi Takazawa, and they owned a remarkable restaurant called Aronia de Takazawa - a restaurant with just two tables! Akiko and I had been emailing for months and she had quite a few suggestions as to what Michael and I should do whilst in Japan.

Growing up in New Zealand I was aware that my birthday fell around the start of the Kyoto cherry blossom season, but it seemed that as I'd got older, and the world's weather patterns had changed, we might miss the blossoms altogether due to global warming. The word on the street was that the blossoms were opening much earlier this year. Akiko and Yoshi decided that they'd take us to Kyoto, to visit their favourite restaurant in Japan, and help us find any remaining blossoms. What a fantastic idea that turned out to be.

We took the Shinkansen (bullet train) from Tokyo and sped West to Kyoto, which proved to be one of the loveliest cities I've spent time in. Thus began our feasting on some of the most inspirational food I've ever had the pleasure to experience. We arrived at our hotel then immediately headed to Narita restaurant which specialised in *tsukemono sushi* which Yoshi and Akiko were keen to try, having heard about it back home in Tokyo. *Tsukemono* (pickled vegetables) are a Kyoto speciality, and they come in a huge range of types, textures and flavours. Whilst in Kyoto we managed to try around 20 different examples - from aubergines, with the flavour and texture of firm blue cheese, to daikon, redolent of washed rind cheese with the crispness of an apple, to crunchy radishes and cucumbers that tasted much as you'd expect. These pickles were subsequently served with pretty much every meal we had, and we developed a real liking for them from the first bite.

We left the restaurant and headed to Wakuden tea house around the corner, which Akiko assured us served one of the best *matcha* teas in all of Japan. *Matcha* (also spelt maacha) is a finely powdered green tea, which is the centrepiece of the Japanese tea ceremony, although in recent years you may have spotted it appearing in anything from panna cotta, ice cream and even jellies. It was served in a wide shallow bowl, which I found surprising as I thought it would come in small ceramic tea cups, which is how I'd experienced Japanese green tea previously. Yoshi ordered several Japanese desserts that were local specialities, one of which was bizarrely delicious. It would best be described as brown flour-coated jelly. It was, in fact, a type of mountain root starch, cooked into a chewable but soft paste, cut into uneven chunks which were then dusted in a powder called *kinako* which is made from dark-toasted soy beans mixed with sugar.

We then headed to the food market, which is much like a covered street that stretches for many blocks, lined with cafés and restaurants alongside stores with the most beautiful displays of foodstuffs, cookware, ceramics and even knives. What struck me most forcibly was the extraordinary variety of plant shoots, tendrils, roots and seaweed on display. There are few ingredients that I feel are completely new to me, that I haven't either heard or read about. But here in the marketplace was stall after stall of new, and familiar, edible treasures. One, for

example, specialised in *kombu* seaweed - the mainstay of *dashi* broth, and an ingredient I always add to pulses, especially chickpeas, when I'm preparing them to speed up the cooking process and to add mineral nutrients. They sold beautiful squares of the stuff; long shards of *kombu*, *kombu* cooked in *mirin* with *sansho* pepper berries, so many different types of *kombu*, with prices ranging from fair to expensive according to their quality and provenance. Here there were also fresh, salted and pickled *sansho* pepper berries, shredded red seaweed and green seaweed. I was reminded yet again of the utter diversity of the world's cuisines and that what might seem strange to one culture is commonplace to another.

Stalls selling baby abalone, strange horny shellfish, even stranger looking fish and dried *bonito* shaved to order (the other mainstay of *dashi* broth) competed for space with others proffering pieces of squid and octopus (you could buy just one tentacle). Vegetable stalls sold fresh bamboo shoots - of which we ate a lot in the coming days, and which bore absolutely no comparison to the canned or frozen matter we're more used to in England. There were also fern fronds, seedling shoots, and what I think were the tips of large tree branches, picked before they could begin to turn woody. Soy sauce (both wheat-free *tamari* and the more common *shoyu*), *miso* of various shades and robustness, *mirin*, *sake* for cooking and drinking - I had found food paradise in a Japanese marketplace. I bought a beautiful knife at one shop and was told, politely but firmly, that it was only to be used for breaking down chickens. Absolutely nothing else!

That evening we walked across town in the cool April air to a tiny restaurant owned by a wonderful chef friend of Yoshi's, Mr Kawamoto. With only six seats at the bar, and just two low tables capable of seating perhaps another eight guests, this was our introduction to locally sourced and produced food, using purely what was in season. Cherry blossom time coincides with the start of the bamboo shoot season (a delicious treat), as well as with the availability of fresh *sansho* pepper berries and *kinome* leaves. *Sansho* pepper and Sichuan pepper are actually the same ingredient, but you're more likely to be familiar with it under its latter guise - its Chinese name. It's used to astounding effect in the cuisine of Sichuan, as well as in Nepalese and Sumatran cuisines. Both the *sansho* berries and the young leaves (*kinome*) herald the start of spring, and hence it's likely that if you're in Japan in April you'll often be served bamboo shoots with *kinome*. The berries and the leaves are quite bizarre as the effect they have on the tongue is one of a numbing tingle, and the flavour is best described as a citrus pepper. New Zealanders will know this numbing sensation from eating indigenous *kawa kawa* leaves, but it is quite unusual for most other cuisines.

It was also at this meal that we ate sashimi from a living fish. A first. I know it sounds awful, and I'm sure the fish wasn't too happy either, but apparently it is only a skilled chef who can manage this while the protein is still breathing. Needless to say, our host and fellow guests were ecstatic. Less dramatically, a ceramic bowl filled with soy milk sat on a charcoal-fired brazier on our table. Every few minutes Akiko would skim the skin off the top and we'd take turns eating the skin, which is called *yuba*. This was a brilliant example of the subtlety of Japanese cuisine. Bamboo shoots braised in seaweed sauce followed, garnished with *kinome* leaves, along with sushi made from fermented one-year rice and mackerel. It was an inspiring meal and set the tone for the rest of our time in Japan.

Next day, our day of celebration, we headed off to the Ryoan-ji garden, famous for its Zen stone garden. We walked amongst the planted gardens and the amazing twisted cherry blossom trees, took time to drink in the quiet of the garden itself (admittedly hard to do when you have 100 people sitting either side of you), then headed off to have the best meal of my life at Yoshi and Akiko's favourite restaurant, owned and run by Hisao Nakahigashi and his wife, who oversees the restaurant. Again, this was a tiny place, with seating for about a dozen at the bar, directly facing the culinary action taking place behind it, with a tatami room on the first floor for larger groups. Here on the ground floor, Mr Nakahigashi and his team quietly produce a daily changing no-choice *kaiseke* meal (many courses that follow a particular pattern) featuring produce he's mostly sourced himself that morning from Kyoto's environs. He'll have foraged

for herbs, shoots, weeds and bulbs from the land, visited fishermen who catch river fish for him and sourced baby squid and other ocean fish from long-time reliable suppliers. I have to say he's the sort of chef one could easily turn into a hero – quietly but expertly producing the most wonderful food, using only what's at hand. A highlight of the meal could be best described as a broth with sliced bamboo shoots and seaweed, served in a pottery vessel with a spout, heated over a gas flame. It was served with salted sea cucumber ovary which looked like a small carrot, and some fresh *kinome* leaves. The chewy, salty sea cucumber was truly delicious, the broth subtle, the bamboo crunchy, and the *kinome* leaves numbing the tongue in a pleasant way. Another dish featured paper-thin slices of carp, straight from the local river, served with the weeds and flowers of the plants growing alongside the river – marvellous. As it can take up to five months to get a table at Mr Nakahigashi's restaurant, you'd best plan a long way ahead if you want to eat there. You'd also be advised to bring along someone who can speak Japanese if you want to know what you're being served, as none of the staff spoke English, and it was fascinating finding out all the details of the meal.

And so it went on, one amazing meal after another. Warm fresh tofu was served to us as part of a *kaiseki* breakfast when we stayed in the amazing Hiiragiya Ryokan (Inn) in Kyoto. The tofu was presented in a wooden container filled with hot water heated by a lump of charcoal, and I have never had a breakfast like it in my life. Taro was served alongside tofu sheets filled with rice, a rolled egg omelette was presented in *dashi* broth with fresh *kinome* leaves, and grilled river fish came with *tamari* and pickled ginger.

The pick of our remaining meals in Tokyo would have to include the incredibly simple but delicious chilled *sobagaki* (buckwheat curd served with *tamari*, *wasabi* and spring onions) prepared by chef Karibe at Takeyabu restaurant in Roppongi Hills. At Mutsukari restaurant in Ginza we ate the *omakase* (chef's choice) menu which included a brilliant dish of simmered bamboo shoot, webfoot octopus, *wakame* and butterbur topped with *sansho* pepper. At Sadaharu Aoki's patisserie in the Midtown shopping centre (he's based permanently in

Paris but luckily has a few stores in his home-town) we ate three delicious cakes which included his take on Gaston Lenôtre's 'Opera' – but this time with the addition of *matcha* tea. At Chocolate House Mon Loire we bought blue cheese chocolates that were simply superb. At Nabura in Roppongi we ate the best selection of sushi of my life, all prepared in front of us by chef Masaru Furusawa. However, the highlight was a sea urchin that had been emptied of itself, filled with a light and soft jelly that hinted at *dashi*, topped with the sea urchin roe and freshly grated *wasabi* – absolutely stunning.

And just to put the icing on the cake, as it were, we ate at Akiko and Yoshi's restaurant one quiet Sunday morning. Yoshi was centre stage in the dining room, cooking from a 'stove' on a slightly raised platform about 2 metres from where we sat. There were around eight courses in total, which we found fascinating. Yoshi has taken some of the concepts from the molecular gastronomy school of cooking, using liquid nitrogen to freeze oils and purées; foaming ingredients and utilising seaweed-based powders in the construction of some of his dishes, such as his bitter digestive-like jellies served on a beautiful glass slipper, to play with his guests' concept of what constitutes a meal in the 21st century. However, he's introduced these ideas into a personal cuisine that is entirely delicious – where a certain playfulness doesn't hide the quality of his food. His vegetable mosaic terrine is a thing of beauty. With more than a dozen different vegetables gently held together in a jelly, then wrapped with a red cabbage border, the terrine is two mouthfuls of crunchy texture, strong fresh flavours and gorgeous visuals. His Candleholder is a clever play on two ingredients that were made for each other, yet would seem to be a modern Fusion classic – foie gras and mango. The foie gras is presented much like a crème brûlée, but sitting inverted atop a 'candle' made from mango salsa. A delicious thin slice or two of fig bread is placed on the side. As for his beef dish, in which he combines rice crackers, seaweed, dehydrated soy sauce powder and several other Japanese ingredients – it's just marvellous.

Whilst Japanese cuisine is clearly based on a classical repertoire, utilising seasonal ingredients cooked simply, often presented incredibly beautifully, there is a sense of experimentation and Fusion afoot. Blue cheese chocolates, green-tea French pâtisserie, mango served with foie gras. Combinations that are new, using ingredients not always indigenous to Japan's numerous islands. These are not crazy things dreamt up by a group of maverick cooks, these are dishes that are being created by some of Japan's top chefs. When I read many years ago that olives were being grown in Japan, I have to say, it made me wonder if olive sushi would begin to appear on the country's menus – and if it did, would it be labelled absurd Fusion sushi, or simply contemporary Japanese cuisine?

Tomatoes

Tomatoes are the most versatile of all berries, falling under the classification of fruits, rather than vegetables – although we tend to think of them as the latter due to the fact that they're used in savoury dishes (although you must try my tomato and celery dessert on page 248). Tomatoes come in thousands of varieties, with colours ranging from white through to orange-striped, green and the more familiar red. Size-wise they can be tiny pea-tomatoes through to huge beef-steak varieties, but the one defining characteristic is that they should always be a pleasurable balance of acidity and ripened sweetness. Unfortunately, due to our huge worldwide demand for them 12 months of the year, many tomatoes we eat are bland, watery, almost floury and tasteless. The truth is, the best tomatoes are grown in the sun during the summer months. Because we want to eat them in the depths of winter, tomatoes have unwittingly, but frequently, been used in the food miles debate, an erroneous argument that claims that the further food has to travel the worse it will be for the global environment. In an early British January, the best thing you could do to help the planet would be either to avoid eating fresh tomatoes at all, or use ones that have been shipped in from warmer regions like Spain – the cost to the environment of heating local glasshouses 24 hours a day far outweighs the fuel and related environmental costs used to ship them in from non-heated countries.

However, I'm sure the first tomato plants, from the Andes in South America, had no idea that they would be the centre of environmental debate, or one of the key ingredients of so many dishes, from Spain's *gazpacho* and *pan con tomate*, Italy's *panzanella* salad and numerous tomato-based pasta sauces, India's green tomato *sabji*, America's tomato ketchup to Britain's baked beans. Tomatoes were originally yellow cherry-sized fruits that grew wild but their smallish fruit weren't exactly abundant and it wasn't until AD 700 that the Aztecs and Incas began to farm them. Tomatoes spread slowly up into Mexico and then to North America and in the 16th century they arrived in Europe, although it's not exactly clear how: either on Spanish trading ships from the Caribbean; or via Jesuit priests who brought them to Italy from Mexico. Whatever the route, we should all be grateful that they did and that they were finally eaten. Initially they were thought to be poisonous due to being from the nightshade family and so they were grown purely ornamentally, much like their cousin the potato. In fact, when I think of some of my favourite vegetables they all come from this family – tomatoes, potatoes, chillies and aubergines. Tobacco, another cousin, is thankfully not something I crave. When they arrived in Britain the English called them tomatoes as the Aztec word for them is *tomatl*. The Italians originally called them *pomi d'oro*, the Germans *Goldapfel* (both meaning golden apple) and the French *pommes d'amour* (love apples).

I am a huge fan of the tomato. As a child Dad gave all us kids our own garden patch and tomatoes and beans were always the summer favourites. We'd eat them raw in salads or sliced in white bread sandwiches, grilled on the barbecue, or made into tomato sauce that my stepmum Rose would bottle for winter months. These days I love them on toasted sourdough with lots of extra virgin olive oil, goat's cheese and avocado, or packed between stale white bread alongside mackerel and made into French toast, or chopped and added to roasting chunks of line-caught cod with saffron and white wine. They're great added to chutneys and the green unripe tomatoes are just as good as the film says – sliced 1-centimetre thick, coated in flour, beaten egg and breadcrumbs and fried till golden. Yum.

five.
tea
trolley

Sweet muffins

240 g flour
120 g caster sugar
1½ tsp baking powder
¼ tsp baking soda
a good pinch of fine salt
2 eggs
40 ml (2 Tbsp + 2 tsp) vegetable oil (try using virgin
  rapeseed oil or a little walnut oil mixed into sunflower oil)
180 ml buttermilk (or runny unflavoured yoghurt)

Preheat oven to 190 °C.

Sieve the dry ingredients. Lightly whisk the eggs, oil and buttermilk together then mix this into the dry ingredients – don't mix it too much, just bring it together. Add flavourings then dollop mixture into your moulds and bake at 190 °C until a skewer inserted comes out clean – 18–24 minutes.

Muffins come in many shapes and sizes, from the huge airy (and mostly bland) American versions, through to lovely, intensely flavoured dense muffins at cafés all over New Zealand. Muffins are easy to make, just ensure you have good-sized muffin tins, or paper cases that will sit in a muffin tray, or do as I've done and experiment with different-shaped tins like the small loaf tins I found in New York a few years back. If baking them in a tin then make sure you butter it generously and dust with flour before placing the tin in the fridge – the cold butter will make their removal easier once cooked. Following are two recipes, each with two variations – one for sweet muffins, and the other for savoury ones. Flavour combinations are endless, but these suggestions will lead you in the right direction. Bake muffins at 190 °C.

Both will make 6–10 muffins depending on the size of your tins

Banana, white chocolate & poppy seeds

Add 1 sliced banana, 100 g chopped white chocolate, 2 Tablespoons poppy seeds and 1 teaspoon grated lemon zest to the mixture. Spoon into your muffin tins, poke some extra sliced banana into each and sprinkle with a little extra sugar.

Plum, currant & coconut

Add 3–4 ripe plums, cut into large chunks, along with 100 g currants and 2 Tablespoons desiccated coconut to the mixture. Spoon into your muffin tins and sprinkle with a little extra desiccated coconut.

Savoury muffins

240 g flour
30 g caster sugar
1¼ tsp baking powder
½ tsp baking soda
¼ tsp fine salt
2 eggs
50 ml extra virgin olive oil
180 ml buttermilk (or runny unflavoured yoghurt)

Preheat oven to 190 °C.

Sieve the dry ingredients. Lightly whisk the eggs, oil and buttermilk together then mix this into the dry ingredients – don't mix it too much, just bring it together. Add flavourings then dollop mixture into your moulds and bake at 190 °C until a skewer inserted comes out clean – 18–24 minutes.

Spinach, feta & smoked paprika

Add 1 teaspoon sweet smoked paprika to the dry ingredients when sifting them. Then add 150 g diced feta and 100 g shredded, blanched and refreshed spinach to the mixture.

Tomato, sweetcorn, sumac & pepita

Remove the kernels from 1 corn cob. Quarter 2 tomatoes and discard the seeds, then cut into chunks. Toast 80 g pepitas (pumpkin seeds). Mix 2 teaspoons sumac into the dry ingredients when sifting them, then add the corn, tomatoes and pepitas to the mix before baking.

There's nothing better than offering your guests some handmade chocolates at the end of a meal, or with their afternoon tea. There are now countless boutique chocolate shops all over the world, and I make it my business to visit them, all in the name of hard work, of course. It's tough eating one's way around the world. The rule of thumb for chocolates is that the higher the cocoa butter content the chocolate has, then the higher quality it SHOULD be. However, there are 30 per cent cocoa chocolates out there that are far superior to some 70 per cent ones – so it pays to do a little research. Also, a higher percentage chocolate will be less sweet, unless sugar has been added. There are now some 100 per cent chocolates available, and unfortunately most are lacking in flavour. Much like a great whiskey to which you add a little filtered water to release its flavour spectrum, a little cream (or substitute) often brings out a far richer chocolate personality. One hundred per cent cocoa chocolates are great, however, when grated and added to gamey meat stews in the last stages of cooking. When making your chocolates bear in mind that the more chocolate you have in the mixture the firmer the finished product will be. The more cream, butter, coconut milk, etc. you add, the softer the finished chocolates will be. Chocolates should never be eaten straight from the fridge, as they'll be too firm and have less flavour when cold. However, unless you have a lovely temperature-controlled room, it's best to keep them in the fridge until you want to eat them, then simply leave to come to room temperature for at least an hour before serving.

All of these recipes will make around 15–20 chocolates depending how large you roll them

Chocolates

Pomegranate, coconut & lime

80 g unsweetened coconut milk or coconut cream

½ tsp finely grated lime zest

150 g 40-60% chocolate, roughly chopped or grated

1 Tbsp pomegranate molasses

80 g white chocolate for coating the chocolates

a handful of fresh pomegranate seeds to garnish

Place the coconut milk and lime zest in a small pan and slowly bring almost to the boil. Add the chocolate and pomegranate molasses together and mix it in until the chocolate melts. Leave to cool, then place in the fridge to firm up. Roll into log shapes using your hands. Place on a baking tray lined with plastic wrap and put back in the fridge to firm up. Using a fork or your fingers, drop the chilled logs into the melted white chocolate and coat them evenly, then lay them back on the tray. Poke one or two pomegranate seeds onto the top then put back in the fridge and leave to harden. Eat within five days.

Salted basil

150 g 60-70% chocolate, roughly chopped or grated, plus
 another 80 g to coat them
a handful of best-quality basil leaves
⅛ tsp fleur de sel salt (or other high-quality sea salt), plus
 a little extra to garnish
100 ml double cream from the fridge

Melt the chocolate. Pound the basil leaves with the salt using a pestle
and mortar then gently stir the cream in. Mix in half the melted
chocolate to combine, then stir in the remaining chocolate. Leave to
cool then place in the fridge to firm up. Roll into balls using your
hands. Place on a baking tray lined with plastic wrap and put back
in the fridge to firm up. Using a fork or your fingers, drop the chilled
balls into the remaining melted chocolate and coat them evenly, then
lay them back on the tray, sprinkling on a little extra sea salt. Put
back in the fridge and leave to harden. Eat within three days.

Blue cheese

140 ml double cream
50 g blue cheese, crumbled or chopped (these are best
 made with a strong blue like Stilton, Roquefort or Picos
 de Europa)
150 g 70% chocolate, roughly chopped or grated
¼ cup cocoa powder

Bring the cream almost to the boil in a small pan then add the cheese
and stir it until it melts into the cream. Add the chocolate and stir to
combine. Leave to cool, then place in the fridge to firm up. Roll into
balls using your hands. Place on a baking tray lined with plastic wrap
and put back in the fridge to firm up slightly. Take from the fridge
and roll in the cocoa, then, using a fork, also dipped into the cocoa,
press it down to flatten the chocolates slightly. Put back in the fridge
and leave to harden. Eat within five days.

Scones are a typical New Zealand and Australian café offering, as well as something, historically, that most households used to rustle up for visitors with a moment's notice. Sadly, this has been on the decline over the past 5–10 years; which is a shame, purely from a stomach-led point of view. In Britain, the home of scones, they're too often in a bad state. As a child I used to dream about coming to London to have a freshly baked scone served with clotted cream and jam, and a cup of Earl Grey tea. I can tell you, that as someone who always eats a scone when on offer, they are too often from the school of 'sad, dry and mass-produced', especially when served at cafés in various historic properties all around Britain. For something requiring such little effort there really is no excuse for a bad scone. Nevertheless, my childhood Sundays were marked by someone at home, often my father Bruce, making a batch of scones – flavoured with either Cheddar cheese and cayenne pepper or dried dates.

The basic recipe is the same for all of the following three versions, as are the cooking times. You can cut scones into any shape you want, but make sure you keep them at least 2 cm thick – any thinner and they just look a little sad and don't rise as well. Don't overwork the dough, as too much kneading toughens it, so if you're cutting out rounds just very gently bring the off-cuts together and press them back into one mass – don't knead the dough at all.

All recipes will make 8 scones, more if you make them smaller

Scones

80 g butter
240 g flour
1 Tbsp baking powder
1 Tbsp sugar
a good pinch of fine salt (more for savoury scones)
180 ml buttermilk (or runny unflavoured yoghurt)

Preheat oven to 200 °C.

Using either a food processor or your fingers, rub the butter into the flour to resemble breadcrumbs. Mix in the baking powder, sugar and salt. Mix in the buttermilk and gently knead until it just comes together. Tip onto a lightly floured board, dust with flour and roll, or press with your hands, to give you a slab at least 2 cm thick. Cut out, using a knife or pastry cutters, and transfer onto a baking tray lined with parchment. Bake for 12 minutes. Leave to cool on the baking tray for a few minutes before moving to a cake rack to cool, or eat while still oven-warm. Once cooled, they can be stored in an airtight container for a maximum of two days, in which case warm in the oven for 5 minutes to refresh them before serving.

Medjool date

Remove the stones from eight Medjool dates and cut each date into six. Mix into the dough when you add the buttermilk. Brush the scones with a little extra buttermilk before baking.

Cheddar & smoked paprika

Add ½–1 teaspoon sweet smoked paprika (or cayenne pepper or paprika) to the dry ingredients, then mix in 70 g coarsely grated Cheddar when you add the buttermilk.

Blueberry & garam masala

Add ¾ teaspoon garam masala to the dry ingredients, then mix in 150 g blueberries when you add the buttermilk. Brush the tops with melted butter before baking.

Pistachio & orange blossom shortbread

These shortbread would, I hope, make my Grandma Molly happy. I've based them on her old recipe, adding both orange blossom water and pistachios to them, but this gives them a lovely, dainty edge. Try making them with another nut, or even coconut, or add rose water instead of the orange blossom.

Makes 24–30

125 g butter, at room temperature
100 g sugar (I like to use unrefined caster sugar)
1 egg yolk
30 ml (2 Tbsp) orange blossom water
80 g ground pistachios
200 g flour
1 tsp baking powder
a pinch of salt

Preheat oven to 180 °C.

Cream the butter and sugar briefly, avoiding whipping too much air into it. Beat in the egg until absorbed, then mix in the orange blossom water and the pistachios. Sieve the flour, baking powder and salt and mix this in. Form together into a mass, wrap in plastic wrap and flatten slightly then place in the fridge and leave for an hour. Take from the fridge and divide into two. Roll out between two sheets of baking parchment until ½ cm thick. Cut into whatever shapes you want and place on a baking tray lined with parchment. Prick with a fork and sprinkle with a little extra sugar then bake until just beginning to go golden, around 12–18 minutes. Take from the oven and leave to cool on the baking trays for 10 minutes, then transfer to a cake rack to completely cool. Store in an airtight container for up to a week.

In late 2007 we ate the most delicious meal at the home of Ulker and Mehmet Yasin, friends of Tarik and Savas's in Istanbul. The baklava they served had been delivered that day from the town of Gaziantep. This town, in south-eastern Anatolia, is thought to be one of the oldest continually inhabited cities in the world. And their speciality is baklava. We were served three different types, all made with the greenest pistachios imaginable. The filo pastry used in them was soft and subtle. The nuts were like fine breadcrumbs, and they were neither overly sticky or sweet. They were a revelation. However, I have no idea how they were made. The baklava I make is somewhat sweeter, as Turkish baklava has no honey in it, and my shop-bought filo pastry more crunchy – but mine are delicious too! Years ago my sister Tracey and her partner Roesheen had a biscuit company in Byron Bay, Australia, and they specialised in making biscuits and slices using indigenous Australian ingredients (bush foods) such as macadamias, wattleseed, etc. So it's for their son, Kai, that I created this recipe. Lemon myrtle, indigenous to Australia's sub-tropical rainforests, has a flavour very similar to lemon verbena, so use that or finely grated unwaxed lemon zest if you can't locate any. Use a mild honey.

Makes 20–40, depending how large you cut them

Spiced lemon myrtle & macadamia baklava

300 g macadamia nuts
1 Tbsp dried ground lemon myrtle
60 g unrefined caster sugar
3 Tbsp poppy seeds
a generous pinch of saffron
8 cloves, ground
1 x 400-g packet filo pastry
250 g butter, melted

Honey syrup

160 g runny honey
120 g unrefined caster sugar
30 ml (2 Tbsp) lemon juice
4 cloves
50 ml orange blossom water

Preheat oven to 150 °C. Line a deep-sided 22-cm square, or 18 x 25-cm baking tin with non-stick baking parchment and brush it with a little butter.

Place the nuts, lemon myrtle, sugar, poppy seeds, saffron and ground cloves into a food processor and grind until you have crumbs, not too fine, but definitely not coarse.

Cut the filo sheets to approximately the same size as your baking tin. Lay six sheets of filo snugly into the baking tin, brushing each sheet with butter as you stack them up and pressing them in firmly. Scatter one-third of the nut mixture on top then lay five sheets of filo on top, again brushing each sheet with butter as you lay them in. Add another third of the nuts, then five buttered sheets of filo. Then the last third of the nuts and finally six buttered sheets of filo. Make sure you press the pastry down firmly as you layer it up. Bake for 60 minutes in the centre of the oven.

While it's cooking make your syrup by gently boiling the honey, sugar, lemon juice and cloves with 250 ml water until it resembles a thin syrup, around 6–8 minutes. Turn the heat off but keep it warm.

Once the baklava is cooked, bring the syrup back to the boil, stir in the orange blossom water and immediately pour it over the pastry (it'll bubble a bit), then leave it to cool down, pressing a sheet of baking parchment on top after 15 minutes to help keep it flat. Leave to cool, preferably overnight, then invert onto a chopping board and cut with a sharp serrated knife for best results. Store in an airtight container in a cool place for up to a week.

Chocolate & orange Anzac biscuits

Anzac biscuits are a firm favourite amongst New Zealanders and Australians alike. They are named to honour the soldiers in the First World War who were part of the Australian and New Zealand Army Corps. It's hard to imagine the hardship that families endured in New Zealand and Australia during the First World War and the years following, and so, although these don't have eggs in them (they would have been dried and sent off to aid the war effort and feed our citizens far away), they do have luxurious, imported, foreign coconut in them which I find really interesting. In many ways they're like a sweet oatcake with a twist. I've made them even more twisted by adding orange zest and sesame seeds and then piping chocolate on top – which gives a luxurious touch, if not completely inauthentic. I have to say that I hope you notice my piping designs. I drew New Zealand and Australia (with a cake sugar bauble representing Stewart Island and Tasmania) and the crescent and star from the Turkish flag (with a bauble representing the star). All three countries have had a huge impact on my own life and they also became inextricably linked at the battle of Gallipoli (*Gelibolu* in Turkish) during the First World War. To this day Anzac Day involves a pilgrimage for many young Antipodeans who are keen to see where their ancestors fought, many losing their lives.

Makes 20–24

75 g flour
70 g unrefined caster sugar
70 g desiccated coconut
70 g rolled oats
15 g toasted sesame seeds
50 g butter
40 g golden syrup
2 tsp finely grated orange zest
½ tsp baking soda
chocolate for decoration – around 150 g

Preheat oven to 175 °C.

Sieve the flour, sugar and a pinch of fine salt into a bowl and stir in the coconut, rolled oats and sesame seeds. Place the butter, golden syrup and orange zest into a small pot and slowly heat it until the butter has melted. Mix the baking soda with 2 Tablespoons of very hot water then mix it into the butter and stir this into the dry ingredients. Mix the dough with your hands, then shape it into a log shape about 20 cm long (I made mine rectangular), and wrap it tightly in plastic wrap, then leave it to cool down. After an hour or so, unwrap the dough and slice it into 20–24 biscuits. Lay these on a baking tray lined with parchment and bake for 12–14 minutes, turning the tray around halfway through. The biscuits will turn golden quite quickly after about 10 minutes, so keep an eye on them. Leave them to cool on the tray for 5 minutes, then transfer to a cake rack and leave them to cool completely.

You can either melt the chocolate and dip them into it, or pipe patterns on them as I did (and now you know why I'm not a graphic artist).

Fig, date & almond friands

Although I've been to France countless times, I don't think I've ever seen a friand on sale there. Yet the first time I tasted one, back in the mid-'80s in New Zealand, I was told they were a cake to be found all over France! Clearly I had been frequenting the wrong cafés and shops. Friands of varying flavours and persuasions can be found sitting on counters in many New Zealand and Australian cafés alongside an eclectic selection of muffins, biscuits, lamingtons and fairy-cakes. Research has shown that they're traditionally only flavoured with the almonds they contain. They're very similar to *financiers* (something you definitely see in France) although these seem to be made using *beurre noisette* (cooked nut-brown butter). Whatever their origin, and whatever their future, they are a lovely firm but buttery cake that deserves its place on the tea trolley. I've flavoured mine with dried figs and Medjool dates – which gives them a lovely texture – the fig seeds are wonderful.

Makes 8–12 depending on the size of your tins

160 g butter
120 g whole blanched almonds
60 g plain flour, plus a little extra for preparing the baking tins
200 g caster sugar
70 g dried figs, stems removed, cut into small chunks
40 g Medjool dates, pitted and chopped
4 egg whites
pinch of salt

Preheat oven to 190 °C.

In a small pan, melt 20 g of the butter over a moderate heat until it turns pale nut-brown in colour. Leave it to cool for a few minutes, then use this to generously butter your friand or muffin tins. Place the tins in the fridge to go cold then dust lightly with a little extra flour and again place in the fridge until you need them. You can avoid this step by baking your friands in paper muffin cases – in which case you will only need 140 g of butter.

Place the remaining butter in the pan and melt it without it getting too hot.

Place the almonds, the flour and 140 g of the sugar in a food processor and blitz to a not-too-fine crumb. Tip this mixture into a medium-sized bowl and make a well in the centre. Pour the butter into the centre and work it all together, then stir in the chopped figs and dates.

Whisk the egg whites with the remaining 60 g sugar and the salt to form soft peaks. Quickly mix one-third of this into the almond mixture, then fold the remaining two-thirds in. Spoon the mixture into the prepared moulds and bake for 25–30 minutes, until a skewer inserted comes out barely moist and they've turned golden. Leave to cool for 10 minutes before gently tapping out and cooling on a cake rack.

These are best eaten straight away, but they keep really well in an airtight container for 2 days.

I'm a big fan of shortbread – my Gran, Molly Gordon, was the world's best shortbread baker as far as I'm concerned. The only negative thing I can say about this wonderful traditional biscuit is that I find the very pale ones (although traditionally they should have no colour) lacking in . . . well . . . colour. I prefer them to have a tint of golden brown to them as I find the flavour more appealing. But then, as you'll see in the following recipe, I make them even more rebellious by adding lime zest, pine nuts and cloves as well. What was I thinking? Trust me, they may be simply a flavoured shortbread, but this combination is great. I've been making biscuits and chocolates flavoured with lime and cloves for years and it's still one of my favourite combinations.

For 20

Lime, clove & pine nut shortbread

200 g butter, at room temperature

90 g unrefined caster sugar, plus extra for dredging the shortbread

200 g plain flour

130 g cornflour

2 good pinches of salt

8 cloves, pounded (¼ tsp)

50 g pine nuts, pounded

finely grated zest of 1 lime

Preheat oven to 160 °C.

Beat the butter and sugar together until pale. Sift in the flour, cornflour, salt and cloves, then add the pine nuts and lime zest. Using your fingers, gently bring the mixture together – you don't want to work it too hard.

Lay a large sheet of non-stick baking parchment on your bench and place the dough on top, off centre. Fold the other side of the parchment over it then roll out to around 1 cm thick – which will give you a sheet of dough around 20 x 30 cm. Transfer the sheet onto a flat baking tray and using a blunt knife, cut out 20 fingers, or whatever shape you'd like. Place the baking tray in the fridge or freezer for 20 minutes to firm up.

Take the tray out of the fridge, then carefully pull the fingers apart (run a blunt knife between the shortbread and the baking sheet to lift them up) as they spread during baking. Prick them all over with a fork and sprinkle with a little extra sugar.

Bake for 20 minutes or more, until pale golden, then take from the oven and let them cool on the tray for 10 minutes, before transferring to a cake rack to completely cool down. Transfer to an airtight container. They'll keep for a week.

Brazil nut & goji berry Sydney special

According to my paternal grandmother, Molly, the wheat-free crunchy and slightly crumbly slice that I based this on was Dad's favourite as a young man. I have to say I don't remember it from my childhood Wanganui days (and nor does Dad, interestingly) but I found the recipe that inspired this in a handwritten book my mother has of recipes she'd collected from family, friends and magazines, stretching back years. Why it's associated with Sydney is anyone's guess – we have no relative called Sydney and Dad didn't go to Australia until I was 16 years old. I also like the fact that this slice seems so incredibly virtuous. Goji berries, as I wrote about earlier, are considered by some to be a super-food. Brazil nuts are grown in the Amazon, so by using them regularly you're helping keep the Amazon forested. And finally – it's wheat-free – which seems to be more and more in demand. So, ignoring the amount of sugar and butter in this, eating it should make you feel like you're doing your bit to help the world.

Makes 12–20 pieces, depending how large you cut them

150 g butter
170 g light Muscovado or brown sugar
30 g goji berries, or try it made with dried cranberries or sultanas
170 g oatmeal or rolled oats
80 g desiccated coconut
70 g chopped Brazil nuts
a pinch of salt

Preheat oven to 160 °C.

Line a 25-cm square baking tin with non-stick baking parchment.

Melt the butter in a pot over a moderate–low heat. Stir in the sugar and goji berries and keep stirring, turning the heat up slightly, until the sugar has melted into the butter – rather like a fatty caramel. Mix in the remaining ingredients then gently press the mixture into the tin. Bake in the centre of the oven for 20–25 minutes until dark golden in colour, turning the tin around halfway through. Leave to cool for 5 minutes, then cut into portions while still in the tin using a bread and butter knife. Leave it to cool down in the tin then carefully remove and place on a cake rack for 10 minutes. Store in an airtight container for up to a week.

Basil

Basil – for me it conjures up a deliciously light and aromatic pesto tossed with pasta and potatoes that I ate with our friends Stephen and Marina in a Ligurian seaside restaurant in Cinque Terre on Italy's west coast around 12 years ago. It also takes me back eight years to a light tomato and fish broth Michael and I ate in Nice, southern France, that had a spoonful of *pistou* added as it was served. In Thailand, I've enjoyed holy basil scattered over coconut curries at the end of their cooking, and I've loved the piles of mint and basil served almost as a salad in Vietnamese restaurants over the years. However, this herb, which is indispensable in many cuisines and also significant in European folklore and in religious belief from India through to Serbia, China and South-East Asia, actually originated in the warm, tropical parts of Central Asia, Iran and India, where it's been cultivated for thousands of years. Central Asia and Liguria may be worlds apart culturally, and several thousand miles away from each other geographically, but as with so many of our foodstuffs these days, we take for granted that often they have entered our kitchens through much travel, cultivation and history.

Basil is one of my favourite herbs. At home in London in warm months I always have a tub of the small Greek variety (as in the photo) growing on my kitchen windowsill – as much for the aroma as the edible possibilities. The first time I went to Greece, to Mykonos, they had tubs of the stuff growing on almost every terrace and balcony as it's supposed to keep flies away. I didn't see any flies, so maybe it works. It certainly acts like a 24/7 aromatherapy infusion, giving my kitchen a lovely, holiday feel to it. I remember when I first saw purple basil, or Opal basil as it was called then, back in Australia when I was 19. It seemed so bizarre that this herb which I always thought was the most beautiful of greens, could also come in this rather strange colour. It wasn't as light and delicate as the more usual green variety, and had a much more menthol and clove character to it, but I found it was great shredded in pork and chilli salads, and also stirred through fish

and chicken stews. Travelling through South-East Asia, especially Thailand, I discovered many more varieties, used in all sorts of diffent ways: Thai basil leaves deep-fried until translucent and crisp then scattered over a salad of grated coconut, green papaya, peanuts and small shrimps; holy basil tossed with abandon into stir-fries.

Arriving in Europe I began to see quite a different way of using it in the kitchen. It's rare that I've seen basil used in spicy dishes, the flavour considered too subtle to douse with chilli, but then chilli gets little use in Europe, apart from regions of southern Italy and Spain – what a lost opportunity, I think.

Cobus, who was the inaugural head chef at my Auckland restaurant dine by Peter Gordon, introduced us to Falooda seeds which he said were used in cold drinks back in his native South Africa. We still use them today in savoury dressings and sweet dessert syrups in the restaurant and it was great to finally realise what these little black seeds were. I'd noticed in South-East Asia and India that in the various iced drinks, and strange desserts like Malaysia's *bubur cha cha* and *es kacang*, there were often little frog-egg-like things floating around that I could never seem to find out the provenance of. It turns out there are several varieties of basil whose seed has the ability to swell up in a clear, slightly mucous-like way, with a pitch black centre, when water is poured over them.

I find fresh green basil is great when used in desserts such as my pomegranate panna cotta on page 236, as well as tossed through strawberries, sliced poached stone fruit or fresh white peaches. In savoury dishes, you'll find the delicate European varieties are best left uncooked, but the basils of Thailand and India seem to handle cooking a bit better. Play with them, they're a great family to have in your kitchen.

Istanbul, Friday afternoon: the office at Changa restaurant, Taksim Square.

As I write this, I sit observing Changa restaurant's two owners Tarik and Savaş, my good friends, locked into their computers, concentrated as ever, looking after business, anticipating the arrival of the funky Friday night DJ. Meanwhile Zekiye, their wonderful manager, is organising the waiters, bar staff and chefs – and sorting out the new seed sprouter they'll soon be using to grow their own cresses. The two restaurant dogs, Changa and Abajur, street strays from Istanbul and Bodrum respectfully, are at my feet hoping I'll let them have some of the *mantı* that I'm eating for lunch. *Mantı* are little pasta parcels containing minced beef that resemble a Chinese dim sum as much as a ravioli, although they come in a variety of shapes and sizes. They're boiled and served smothered with a thin yoghurt sauce containing huge amounts of raw garlic plus masses of melted butter, warmed up with an infusion of *kirmizi biber* (chilli flakes). Dried, rubbed mint and sumac, traditionally sprinkled over the top, gives them an even more delicious aroma and sharpness. Before the *mantı* we ate a tasty Armenian mackerel *dolma* with salad – *dolma* meaning stuffed. The mackerel had been boned but kept whole (minus the head) and then filled with a mixture of rice, pine nuts, dried currants, dill, dried mint, black pepper, olive oil and a hint of cinnamon before being baked in the oven.

Both the *mantı* and the mackerel dish are great examples of the cuisine in this part of the world. In its simplest form, it is pure and uncluttered, but with a juxtaposition of textures and flavours that would seem out of place in another country. I can't, for example, picture an Italian kitchen smothering ravioli with runny yoghurt and butter, or the French serving mackerel with cinnamon, but here they're both traditional recipes. That's why I love Turkish cuisine and that of Turkey's neighbouring countries, as much as I do. Historically, the Ottomans and therefore the Turks have played with sweet, fruity and savoury flavours alongside myriad spices usually used for desserts in a way that just isn't part of other European kitchens.

As for the *mantı* themselves, Tarik and I bought them from the owner of a tiny little pastry shop a few minutes walk from his home. His range of products is really quite small. One of his specialities is a pastry called *yufka* that he makes by hand, rolling a wheat-based dough into large, paper-thin rounds before cooking them on top of a convex black metal plate used for various versions of *börek*. Perhaps the most unusual product he sold though was a pasta called *erişte*, which is made from wheat flour grown in Konya, mixed with milk, water, eggs and salt before being rolled out and then cut into 4-mm thick, flat, narrow noodles about 4 cm long which he bakes and dries in the oven for storage. This baking gives it a wonderful subtle, smoky flavour and a firm texture once it's finally prepared in the customer's kitchen. Unlike regular pasta it's not boiled in masses of water but rather simmered the way one cooks risotto rice. (I bought a kilo to take back to London and I'm really looking forward to creating a new dish with it. At the moment I'm thinking of tossing it with shredded smoked mackerel, wilted spinach, crisp fried garlic and crumbled feta.)

Just when I think our lunch is over, Zekiye presents me with a plate of the most delicious *şekerleme* ('candied' fruits), consisting of tomatoes, a green walnut and a smallish aubergine, all of which have been preserved in a light sugar syrup. The tomatoes have a firm, crunchy, juicy texture, and are sweet, sour and really flavoursome. The walnut in appearance is much like a pickled walnut you'd find in a European kitchen, but as it has also been preserved in a similar sugar syrup, rather than a vinegar brine, it has none of the sourness I would have expected. The aubergine is like a semi-firm peach in texture – with a walnut (a ubiquitous food in Turkey) stuffed into the end of it. Zekiye tells me the fruit is washed in a lime solution before preserving it which is what gives it such an interesting texture. I made a note to myself to look into this use of lime (the chemical, not the citrus fruit). I've eaten many syrup fruits in my time in Turkey but I have to admit, these would have to be some of the best. And to top off this unique fruit plate, Savaş has just given me a preserved orange rind that his mother, Neriman, makes for the restaurant. The staff at Changa and Müzedechanga eat oranges for weeks on end before the skins are shipped to her home in Ankara where she transforms them, with the help of her husband, Ziya, into these lovely preserves. They are then sent back to Istanbul – currently in pride of place on a mosaic cake that Savaş's sister, Serpil, makes.

One of my favourite dishes at Changa was originally created by Tarik's mother, Günsel. It's in the form of a pie, although fresh anchovies serve as the 'pastry', and the filling is a rice pilaf flavoured with sultanas, pine nuts, a little curry powder and lots of fresh herbs, especially *Arap saçı* (Arab's hair), better known as fennel fronds. This is a dish that Günsel created for her husband Rifat and herself many years ago. Tarik says the fact that his mum adds curry powder to it is, in itself, her own unwitting homage to Fusion cuisine. It really is a family affair here at Changa

and Müzedechanga and that's probably one of the reasons why both restaurants are so successful.

I actually first met Tarik and Savaş on 19 August 1999. I well remember the date as it was just two days after a massive earthquake had struck Turkey, killing over 30,000 people across the country. Tarik had emailed me in mid-1999 asking if I'd be interested in becoming a consultant chef to their soon to open restaurant, Changa. After many emails and phone calls over the months preceding our first visit, Michael and I headed off to Istanbul, wondering if it were wise to arrive at such a dreadful time for the country. The guys assured us it would be a welcome emotional break. I have to say that neither Michael nor I were that clued up on Turkey or Istanbul, and as our flight touched down at Atatürk airport it became apparent that a major humanitarian crisis was unfolding as the terminals were housing many Red Cross, United Nations and other aid/charity aeroplanes and trucks. Over the next few days we came to realise what Turkish hospitality was all about as Tarik and Savaş's friends treated us to numerous treats prefaced by 'you simply have to try this . . .'. Burçak, a wonderful woman who now lives in Sydney, became joint tour leader with the guys, and between them they made sure we got to see the best places in town. We ate the freshest and most delicious baklava, börek and breads around the Grand Bazaar, and had lovely fresh mint tea at the funky Fez café inside the market. Around the Egyptian Bazaar, or the Spice Bazaar as it's also known, we bought a sharp, salty feta-type cheese called *Tulum Peyniri*, which is left to cure inside the skin of a goat or sheep. The Turks are fanatical about fish and whenever there's a chance of dangling a fishing rod or line in the Bosphorus, or any other of Istanbul's waterways, you'll find men (I'm yet to see a woman fishing) hanging out, gossiping and hopefully catching their dinner. Take a walk at sunset over the Galata bridge that crosses the Golden Horn and you'll find it teeming with such fishermen, as well as mobile carts selling *poğaça* pastries and sesame-covered *simit* that resemble bagels.

Fish definitely have their own seasons in Turkey. As I write this story, it's the end of February, and turbot has only just come into its own. Mackerel are plentiful, and so are anchovies, however; Changa have been asked to cater an event in June and it seems the only fish available then will be sea bass or bream. Turkey has a brilliant piece of legislation that states that no fish can be caught in the months of April to September which means that during the breeding season they get the chance to repopulate. They'd need a two-year break to really get back to the levels of the past, but the fact that a nation is so passionate about fish that it willingly supports this measure is a testament to what can be done worldwide to keep the oceans' harvest at sustainable levels.

I've just had a walk along İstiklal the main shopping street that runs from Taksim Square down towards the Pera Palace Hotel where Agatha Christie wrote *Murder on the Orient Express.* The much-celebrated transcontinental train used to finish its European run at the Golden Horn, just across the water. What struck me most on this walk is that although there are many fast food outlets along the street, the food they sell is by no means 'fast food' as we in the West know it. One shop was selling mounds of minced lamb topped with tomatoes and what looked like mozzarella cheese, although in actuality, this will be a traditional Turkish cheese called *kaşar*. Alongside it was a stew of braised baby okra, and in another compartment green beans that had slowly cooked in olive oil with tomatoes and onions. They looked delicious. On Taksim Square itself there are a collection of *döner kebap* cafés, 'döner' meaning to spin, and 'kebap' denoting anything grilled, although the word kebab seems to have taken its place in modern parlance. Although in reality, they are fast food outlets, they also offer freshly squeezed orange or pomegranate juice which they've been selling for years, well before pomegranate juice became the must-have drink of the Western world's health-conscious. In this neighbourhood, you'll also find many shops, restaurants and cafés selling a vast array of cakes and sweets. Pistachio or walnut baklava is probably one of the most familiar of these outside of Turkey, but the dessert that I find most fascinating is *tavuk goğüsü*, a dessert made by slowly cooking chicken breast meat in milk, then finely shredding and thickening it and baking it in a flat deep-sided dish like a flan. Who but the Ottomans would have thought of turning chicken into a dessert?

Their empire was truly vast, and lasted from 1299–1923, a reign of 624 years! Because of the far-flung reach of the Ottoman empire, which stretched across South-Eastern Europe, the Middle East and North Africa, Istanbul became an incredibly important trading port, and a cultural centre with few equals. Ottoman cuisine, at its zenith in the kitchens of the Topkapi Palace, was incredibly creative and playful with many savoury dishes containing spices, nuts and fruit as the norm. Rice and grains were brought in from many Ottoman-controlled lands as well as India and the Far East. Saffron and sumac, cinnamon and cloves, pine nuts and pistachios, dates, tamarind, figs and green almonds all featured heavily in the recipes of the court, and inevitably these culinary ideas, and tastes, filtered into the proletariat diet and its kitchens.

Dining out in modern Istanbul is a real treat for visitors, and the local population alike, as many culinary influences from outside the city (regional Turkish and international) have made themselves felt in recent years. For example, in Rumeli Kavağı you'll find lots of old-fashioned fish restaurants sitting side by side. The fare on offer in all of them is tasty but fairly similar as you'll pretty much be served salad, bread and whatever fish has been caught that day. In comparison, there's a wonderful Antipodean-style café in Bebek called Mangerie that you should visit, where you can sit on the terrace and have a lovely salad, toasted sandwich or a slice of chocolate brownie with a great cappuccino and enjoy the view over the Bosphorus. Towards the airport, you'll find a totally different dining experience at Beyti, a restaurant named unsurprisingly after a Mr Beyti who invented a type of lamb kebap. We ate there a few years ago and I have to say it was a meat fest like none other I've ever experienced. The food was really delicious, but it just didn't stop coming – probably mostly a reflection of Tarik and Savaş's generous but excessive ordering. On our first-ever visit to the city, and a couple of time since, we've taken a boat across the Bosphorus to Kanlıca to eat sea bass baked in salt at Körfez, a trip well worth taking, especially on a balmy summer's evening as you glide between the Asian and European sides of the city on a water taxi. In Ortaköy, where our friends Ahmet and Engin run Hazal, a fabulous kilim and carpet shop, housed in an old harem, you'll find one of the very first House Cafés. These days it's part of a chain that is rapidly expanding. House Cafés serve contemporary food, great coffees and juices, simply presented in gorgeously designed surroundings. The Tünel House Café is part-owned by Seyhan Özdemir who is half of the award-winning architectural design duo called Autoban, the company who designed Tarik and Savaş's second restaurant Müzedechanga, helping them to win Best New Restaurant in the 2007 *Wallpaper* magazine awards.

At Müzedechanga the food is a blend of contemporary Turkish and Mediterranean. Sipping Doluca's Safir, a delicious Turkish wine, on the huge terrace in summer, looking over the Bosphorus towards Asia is an amazing experience. The fact that the restaurant sits atop a world-class art museum, the Sakıp Sabancı Museum, makes it even more special – and recently a concert hall has been added to the property. Changa restaurant itself, where I'm writing this story, is located just off Taksim Square in the centre of town in one of only a few surviving Art Nouveau buildings. It was falling into decay before Tarik and Savaş found it and convinced Tarik's brother Tayfun and his wife Suzan to buy it. They renovated it so that now a three-storey modern glass atrium forms the bulk of the dining area, with an artwork by internationally acclaimed artist Canan Tolon covering the rear wall. From here diners can look down into the kitchen through its circular glass ceiling. Initially, I'd been asked by Tarik and Savaş to create a menu much like the one I was cooking at The Sugar Club in London at the time, but after visiting Istanbul I was blown away by the produce available in Turkey, produce I had never experienced before. In 1999 it was almost impossible to buy lemongrass, kaffir lime leaves, *nam pla* (Thai fish sauce), tapioca and even fresh ginger in Turkey, some of my staple ingredients at the time. On the other hand, they had a brilliant fish culture, plenty of spices and herbs and more purslane and samphire than you could think of things to do with. So the menu has evolved over the years into a combination of the best of Turkish and Asian ingredients, with a heavy focus on Japan, as well as hints from Mediterranean Europe.

All in all I have to say that Istanbul is truly the most wonderful melting pot of cultures, religions, languages, foods, design and life experiences. In Ortaköy there is a mosque, a synagogue and a Christian church all just a few blocks from each other. Today, in the pastry shop, we bumped into a woman in her sixties who Tarik said was Jewish. The reason he knew this was that her accent still had traces of Spanish from the time her ancestors, the Sephardic Jews, fled Spain during the Inquisition in 1492, and were then warmly welcomed into the Ottoman Empire. Today I walked past a Christian bookshop selling replicas of Jesus in the manger, crosses and many imprints of the Bible. There are beautiful mosques all over the city that are always in your sight. Their minarets rise above most other buildings, and the call to prayer can be heard around the city like a calming and peaceful tune at different times of the day. Turkey is most definitely a Muslim country, although secular in its politics. However, as numerous peoples with their differing religious beliefs and festivals have been absorbed into the Turkish fabric, so too have their foods and cuisines been assimilated over the centuries during Ottoman times and before. Turkey straddles Asia and Europe in a literal and a spiritual sense, and for this reason alone it is a really important part of the world. This is also why Istanbul is my favourite city in the world. And, purely selfishly, I am so glad Tarik and Savaş asked me to come visit them all those years ago, as my life has definitely been enriched by them and their homeland.

Tamarind

The tamarind tree is a personal favourite of mine as it helped me a great deal when I was hitch-hiking around western Thailand back in 1986. Hitch-hiking wasn't really the preferred method of transport for most travellers and tourists, and the border area with Burma (or Myanmar as it's now called) was often just a kilometre or less away. When I think back it's amazing I wasn't given more grief by the local police and military, but I think they were often just amused by my Western way of trying to save bus fares when I must have appeared very rich in the locals' eyes – even if I did often look like a smelly hippie! Anyway . . . back to the tamarind. The tree is magnificent – huge, spreading branches, often a majestic height, and frequently found planted along the side of the road as a wonderful sun-block for the locals. The fruit, resembling brown broad bean pods, would simply fall to the road when they were ripe and ready. Some days I'd sit for three or four hours under their shade, wondering if I'd get a ride, and I found that by sucking on the pulp from the inside of the tamarind I was kept refreshed – their sour and astringent flavour keeping my mouth salivating. One day, after about five hours in the incredible heat, I was amazed to see an elephant hurtling towards me from far away along the scorching road. I was transfixed until it got quite close and I realised it was actually on the back of a small pick-up truck – the haze coming off the road had kept that hidden from my tired brain. It whizzed by, I didn't get a ride that day, and I headed back to whatever town I was trying to leave and no doubt ate a Pad Thai or stir-fried rice flavoured with tamarind amongst other things.

Tamarind had always been associated with India in my mind but, when I arrived in India several months after leaving Thailand, I found out it was native to tropical areas of Africa such as Madagascar (the animal TV programme lover in me knew that some types of lemur liked to eat it). I'd even heard it referred to as an Indian date when I'd eaten at a Persian restaurant while living in Melbourne, and I've realised since that this is due to the fact that it must have entered the cuisines of Persia and other Arabic regions via trade routes between them and India. The tamarind pod is a brown, hard case that, when broken open, contains some really hard, large brown seeds enveloped in a sticky brown paste, which in turn has some coarse thick fibres wrapped around it. The bit you eat is the pulp, and this can be best extracted either by mushing the pulp between your fingers in a bowl of tepid water then pushing through a sieve, or if you buy a compacted block of tamarind, which is easier to source, you can cut it up with a big knife, then simmer in water until it breaks apart, and again push through a sieve. I bought the tamarind pods in the photo from China Town in London and it was a type I wasn't too familiar with. The pods were quite juvenile and lacked the dense sticky paste, but they had a great astringency – which is the wonderful attribute they offer to many cuisines, including Mexico, the Philippines, India, Sri Lanka, Jamaica, Puerto Rico, Vietnam, Egypt, Thailand and so many more.

In India, I discovered tamarind used in all sorts of dishes and chutneys, but it was also recommended to me as a good way to help with a stomach upset I had – and it seemed to work, drunk as a tea, simply muddled into hot water and left to cool. Often when I'm giving a cookery demo in England I will ask if anyone regularly uses or eats tamarind. The 'white faces' in the audience generally say no. I then hold up a bottle of 'The Original & Genuine Lea & Perrins Worcestershire Sauce' and ask who eats this regularly and suddenly almost the whole room has its hands up. I then tell people that it actually contains tamarind as one of its key ingredients. The reason I do this is to try to get people to realise that while some of the ingredients I use may seem weird and alien, they have a history well before I began using them in my contemporary cooking style. Try whipping a Tablespoon of the pulp into a batch of chantilly cream and dollop it on a warm pear and almond tart, or mix some into an ice-cream base before churning it. Add a few Tablespoons to a red-meat stew to give it another depth of flavour, or whisk some into your next salad dressing, cutting back on the vinegar or lemon juice. It's a fantastic addition to your repertoire and one you'll find hard to put down.

six.
desserts
& puddings

Pomegranate panna cotta with pear & basil jelly

6 leaves gelatine

320 ml chilled pressed pear juice (if you can only get watery pear juice then you'll need to add an extra half sheet of gelatine)

10 g basil leaves – the leaves from 6 leafy stalks

90 g sugar

400 ml cream

300 ml milk

30 ml (2 Tbsp) grenadine

40 ml (2 Tbsp + 2 tsp) pomegranate molasses

pomegranate seeds to garnish

Pomegranates originated in the Middle East, somewhere in Persia, between Pakistan, Afghanistan and Iran. They are a fruit mentioned in all the main religions originating from the region, and remnants have been found which date back thousands of years. Funnily enough, even though they're incredibly exotic and don't grow in the UK, my partner Michael remembers eating them in south London as a wee boy back in the 1950s. So, it might be fair to say they've been part of the British diet for a while. They're surely one of the most beautiful fruit, but you need to make sure you pick the seeds properly or they can have a bitter taste. The best way to prepare them is to wear gloves and an apron. Cut the fruit around the outside with a small sharp knife, avoiding cutting in too deep as the white pithy flesh is bitter. Pull the two halves apart and then 'tear' each half in two, folding them back on themselves, as though turning them inside out, and pick the seeds out. The pomegranate molasses I tend to use in my cooking comes from Lebanon, but I also use Jordanian and Turkish varieties that work really well. Some are quite bitter so taste it first – you may need to add a little more sugar to the recipe. Serve this with a crunchy biscuit like biscotti or a nutty *tuile*.

For 8

First make the jelly. You'll need eight jelly moulds able to hold around 200 ml each. Soak two leaves gelatine in icy cold water. Heat 50 ml of the pear juice almost to boiling point, drain the gelatine and mix it into the hot liquid until dissolved. Mix in the remaining juice and put to the side. Leave the juice to cool to room temperature. Using a pestle and mortar, pound the basil leaves with 30 g of the sugar until you've made a paste then mix this into the cooled pear juice. Pour 3 Tablespoons into each jelly mould. Place on a tray and leave to set in the fridge for at least 2 hours.

Once the jelly has set, make the panna cotta. Bring the cream, milk and remaining sugar almost to the boil. Take off the heat, pour into a metal bowl (ideally) and stir in the grenadine. Soak the remaining 4 leaves gelatine in icy cold water for a few minutes, then drain and add to the now pink cream, mixing them in until completely dissolved. Sit the bowl in an ice bath to help it cool down quicker, although this isn't essential. After a few minutes mix in the pomegranate molasses. You'll notice the mixture thickens a little when you add this, which is fine. Once the mixture has cooled to body temperature, or cooler, you can carefully ladle it on top of the jelly. If you add it while it's still hot, you won't get a clean line between the jelly and the panna cotta. Place in the fridge to firm up, then cover with plastic wrap and leave to set fully, preferably overnight.

To serve: Either dip the moulds very briefly in hot water, or carefully run hot water over their upturned moulds. Shake them a little from side to side, then invert over a plate and tip out. Garnish with pomegranate seeds.

Baked raspberry custard with strawberry, mint & orange blossom salad

In 1990, not long after I first arrived in London, I was cooking at a restaurant called First Floor on Portobello Road in Notting Hill. It was a very cool restaurant filled with A-list celebrities and their hangers-on, and it was a lot of fun. This was also the time that every restaurant in London seemed to be serving prune and Armagnac tart, or lemon tart. In fact, it was said that you could tell how good a chef was by the quality of their lemon tart. That seemed absurd to me, as lemon tart was something only Western chefs were cooking. I'd have thought flavour balance would have been a better test, but there you go. Anyway, I had a go at the lemon tart, too, and I think I did pretty well. However, one day we received a wrong order, way too many berries, and so I tried to use them up before they went off. They were just on the point of being overripe, so I puréed them to make sorbets, jellies and then I tried using them instead of lemon juice in a tart. Then, years later, I adjusted the tart filling I'd created to make this recipe – much like a baked custard. The key to its success is that the berries have to be perfectly ripe – or else the custards taste a bit too creamy and bland. You can also bake them in soufflé-type dishes, instead of ramekins, in which case increase the berries by 50 g for extra flavour. There are many grades of orange blossom water – my current favourite comes from the Sidon region in Southern Lebanon, made from a specific bitter orange species.

For 8

150 g raspberries
10 ml (2 tsp) lime or lemon juice
70 g caster sugar
260 ml whole eggs (5 medium eggs)
280 ml cream
¼ tsp vanilla extract (or ⅛ vanilla bean, split and scraped)
15-20 strawberries
6 mint leaves
1 Tbsp icing sugar
10 ml (2 tsp) orange blossom water

Preheat oven to 160 °C. Position the oven rack just below the centre of the oven. Lay a kitchen cloth or thin tea towel on the bottom of a deep-sided roasting dish, ideally with handles to help move it, and sit 8 x 150 ml metal ramekins on top. This is your bain marie.

Purée the raspberries with the lime juice and half the caster sugar in a blender, then add the eggs and whizz for 10 seconds.

Bring the cream, vanilla and remaining sugar to a simmer then gently whisk it into the berry mixture. Pass through a fine sieve to remove the seeds then pour into the ramekins.

Place the bain marie in the oven and pour in enough boiling water to come two-thirds of the way up the outside of the ramekins. Place an inverted oven tray on top of the ramekins (this keeps the fierce heat off the top) and shut the door. They'll take 45–60 minutes to cook. To test, poke a thin skewer or toothpick into the centre of one. It should come out clean although the mixture will be a little moist, so some mixture will stick to it. Carefully take the bain marie from the oven and leave it to cool for 10 minutes then remove the ramekins and leave them to cool completely. Cover tightly with plastic wrap and place in the fridge to firm up, at least 6 hours.

To unmould the custards run a thin, narrow knife around the inside of the ramekin, then holding one in your hand, firmly shake it out into your other hand. Slide off your hand onto a plate, then unmould the rest.

To serve: Hull the strawberries and slice thinly, or julienne them as I did. Shred the mint and toss with the strawberries, icing sugar and the orange blossom water then sprinkle this over the custards.

Plum tapioca with apricot-stone baked apricots

4 plums, halved and their stones removed
¼ vanilla bean, split open
80 g white sugar
50 g (4 Tbsp) tapioca
4 large apricots (or 8 smaller ones)

In this book you'll realise that I really do like tapioca – from the glistening soy pearls in my salmon sashimi tapa, through to my coconut tapioca on page 252. I first conceived of actually using apricot kernels for their flavour when I discovered that the famous Italian liqueur and biscuits, from the town of Saronno, are both flavoured from the kernels. Prior to this I'd always thrown the kernels away, thinking them useless. In Turkey, I've also eaten roasted apricot kernels and they're so delicious it's hard to put them down, a combination of bitterness and sweetness – which is always a good thing. I also tried switching the fruit around in this dish, flavouring the tapioca with stewed apricots and the chopped kernels, and serving it with roast plums, but I decided that although it was pretty good, this was a better taste and a far prettier photo.

For 4–6

Cut the plums into chunks and place in a pan with the vanilla, 60 g of the sugar and 250 ml water. Bring to the boil, then turn to a simmer and cook for 10 minutes. Mash them, or purée with a stick blender.

While the plums are cooking you'll need to cook the tapioca. Bring a litre of water to the boil and add the tapioca, stirring it to keep it separated. Boil for 10 minutes, then add a cup of cold water and bring back to the boil. Turn the heat to a gentle boil and cook for another 5 minutes, before adding another cup of cold water. Keep it boiling until most of the tapioca pearls have become translucent – although some will remain white in the centre. Drain into a fine sieve (they're quite small when first cooked so don't use a colander!) and refresh under gently running cold water for 20 seconds. Drain them again and mix into the puréed plum compote. Leave to cool then place covered in the fridge and leave for at least 6 hours, stirring occasionally. The tapioca will absorb the plum compote liquid and swell up into beautiful balls just like in the photo.

Turn the oven to 180 °C. Cut the apricots in half lengthways and lay them cut-side facing up on a baking sheet lined with baking parchment. Remove the stones and wrap half of them in a tea towel or kitchen cloth. Using either a hammer or a pestle, gently but firmly hit them to crack them open. Remove the white inner kernel from the shell, then chop it roughly and mix with the remaining 20 g of sugar and sprinkle it over the apricots. Bake for 12–20 minutes, depending on the size and ripeness of the fruit. They're cooked when they're a little soft when squeezed.

To serve: Simply spoon some of the plum tapioca into a bowl and sit one or two apricot halves on top.

Spiced berry, maple syrup & vanilla risotto

This is so incredibly easy to make but also incredibly delicious. It's also equally tasty when served cold on a hot summer's day, when berries are at their best, but if you're making it to serve chilled then reduce the butter to just 20 g. It's great served with extra berries scattered on top and a dollop of crème fraîche isn't bad either. I have to say that when I first made this I was a bit surprised I hadn't done it before. Whenever I'd cooked rice as a pudding I'd always baked it in a dish with plenty of milk, butter, cream and cinnamon and not much else. I have cooked rice pudding in a pot, but always used Bali's black rice as my starting point. The rice and quinoa porridge on page 188 is a version of that. However, this recipe was the first time I used white rice cooked in a pot as a dessert. This is also really good made with very ripe diced peaches and nectarines, stirred through about 5 minutes before the rice is cooked.

For 6

200 g (1 cup) risotto or paella rice
60 g unsalted butter
½ vanilla bean, split lengthways
4 green cardamom, crushed lightly with the side of a knife
4-cm stick cinnamon
2 cloves
100 g mascarpone
80 ml maple syrup
2 Tbsp icing sugar
120 g raspberries
120 g strawberries, hulled and halved
120 g blueberries

Rinse the rice for 10 seconds in a sieve under warm running water. Place in a medium-sized pot and add 600 ml water, the butter, vanilla and spices. Bring to the boil then simmer for 15 minutes with a tight-fitting lid on. Check to see if the rice is cooked, and when it's almost ready mix in the mascarpone, maple syrup and sugar, then gently stir in the berries. Put the lid back on, take off the heat and leave for 5 minutes in a warm place. Gently stir it again and it's ready.

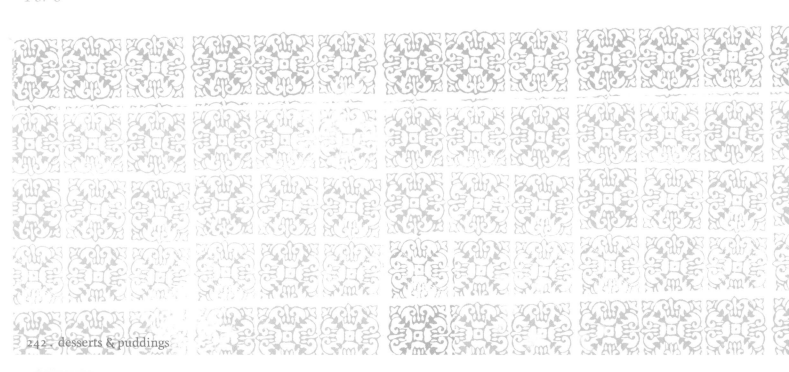

Raspberry white chocolate mousse with black pepper & strawberries

This mousse is incredibly light, rich and refreshing all at the same time – which is down to the fact that the fruit is quite a large component of the recipe. The gelatine allows it to set a little, and the white chocolate gives it a bit more body. Served with strawberries and black pepper it's fantastic.

For 8–12

350 g raspberries
⅛ tsp vanilla extract
15 ml (1 Tbsp) lemon juice
2 leaves gelatine
160 g white chocolate, grated or chopped
300 ml double cream
20 g icing sugar
strawberries and cracked black pepper to garnish

Purée the raspberries and vanilla with the lemon juice and pass through a fine sieve.

Soak the gelatine in icy cold water for 4 minutes to soften it. Remove from the water and gently squeeze out any excess water then place in a clean bowl. Pour on 60 ml (4 Tablespoons) boiling water and stir to dissolve it thoroughly, then gradually stir in the berry purée until thoroughly mixed.

Melt the chocolate with 80 ml of the cream over a double boiler or in the microwave.

Lightly whip the remaining 220 ml cream with the sugar to form soft peaks then stir a quarter of this into the melted chocolate. Tip the chocolate mixture back into the whipped cream and fold it in. Add the berry purée, then fold this through making sure there are no lumps or streaks of purée. You can either pour this into a tub, to be quenelled later (as I did) or pour it into glasses or ramekins – whatever you'd prefer. Leave to cool, then cover and place in the fridge to set for at least 6 hours.

To serve: Serve the mousse with sliced strawberries sprinkled with a little black pepper.

Strawberry ice cream with chillied cherry compote

The reason I love this ice cream so much is that in reality the dairy/custard part of the mixture makes up only half the final mix. This means that although the berry flavour is carried by the fat in the cream, it doesn't mask it. It tastes fresh, fruity and very moreish. It's best made from strawberries that have become a little overripe, or too mushy to serve, which will give a heightened flavour.

Makes around 2 litres – enough for 12 people or more

500 g strawberries, hulled and thinly sliced
30 ml (2 Tbsp) runny honey
180 g caster sugar
300 ml cream
200 ml milk
4 egg yolks

Place the strawberries in a pan with the honey and 80 g of the sugar. Bring to a rapid simmer, cook for 3 minutes then cool in a bowl over iced water.

Make a custard by bringing the cream and milk to a simmer. Whisk the yolks with the remaining 100 g sugar, then carefully whisk in half the hot cream. Pour it back into the still simmering cream mixture and turn the heat up to moderate. Cook until the custard coats the back of a spoon, stirring constantly and making sure it doesn't boil. Strain through a fine sieve into a clean bowl and allow to cool down to body temperature. Stir in the cooled strawberry mixture then cover and place in the fridge for a few hours to chill down. Churn in an ice-cream machine or pour into a freezer-proof dish and freeze for an hour. Use a fork to break up the ice crystals as they form every hour, and keep freezing it, until you can stir no more.

To serve: Depending how hard the ice cream is, take it from the freezer 30 minutes before you're going to serve it and leave it to 'temper' in the fridge before scooping and serving with the following compote.

Chillied cherry compote

This compote works on so many levels, from the sweetness and sourness (of the sugar and verjus) through to the unexpected hit of chilli and the plump cherries. It is great with the strawberry ice cream and also with the raspberry white chocolate mousse. It will keep in the fridge for 6 days if kept in a sealed jar.

For 10–12

150 ml verjuice (or 80 ml lemon juice and 80 ml apple juice)
50 ml water
100 g caster sugar
2 cloves
1 tsp grated ginger
½ red chilli, finely chopped (more or less to taste)
300 g cherries, pitted and halved

Place everything except the cherries into a pot, bring to a rapid simmer and cook for 5 minutes. Add the cherries and continue to simmer for 5 minutes with a lid on, stirring several times. Take from the heat and leave to cool.

Poached tomato petals, celery & apple sorbet & tomato ginger syrup

This recipe may look daunting, with so many components, but in actuality it's not really that hard. Ideally you'll need an ice-cream machine, but you can make a sorbet in the same way as I describe making ice cream on page 245. The sorbet is my take on a 100 per cent celery sorbet that my head chef, Miles Kirby, created with another chef, Hamish Brown, at The Providores a few years back. For this dessert, I wanted the celery to be prominent, but not too overpowering, so I added a few other things. You can make this vegan by excluding the egg whites, but they do add a lightness to the final sorbet. The tomato ginger syrup came about when I was making tomato chilli jam a few years back (that recipe appeared in my first book *The Sugar Club Cookbook* back in 1996). And as for the poached tomato petals, I've been serving variations on this theme for many years, treating the tomato as one would a fruit – which in fact it is.

For 8

Celery apple sorbet

This will keep for 10 days in the freezer and makes almost a litre which is more than you'll need. However, it's incredibly refreshing and makes a great mid-afternoon snack, so you may as well make a full recipe. The best way to get the juice is though a juice extractor (as you would carrot juice) but you can also purée the chopped vegetables and fruit individually, but less successfully, in a bar blender.

180 g caster sugar

15 g glucose syrup (or use a pale runny honey)

200 ml celery juice (you'll need around 500 g celery stalks)

100 ml apple juice, I prefer to use Granny Smiths (you'll need 2–3 apples)

10 ml (2 tsp) ginger juice - you can finely grate 50 g ginger and squeeze the juice out

40 g egg whites (optional)

First make a stock syrup by bringing 150 g of the sugar to the boil with the glucose and 150 ml water. Simmer it for 3 minutes then strain into a clean bowl and leave to cool before chilling in the fridge for an hour. Mix the celery, apple and ginger juice into the syrup. Beat the egg whites to a soft peak with the remaining sugar and whisk the juice into this. Churn according to your machine's instructions and store in the freezer.

Poached tomato petals

The key here is to use ripe tomatoes, but not so ripe that they turn to mush when poached. Underripe tomatoes will taste awful and have a floury texture, so it might be best to avoid making this in winter from hot-house fruit.

200 g caster sugar

⅛ vanilla bean, split lengthways

1 thumb of ginger, peeled and thinly sliced

250 ml verjus (or use 80 ml rice vinegar, 50 ml lemon juice and extra water)

⅛ red chilli, sliced (more or less, to taste – but it's a brilliant addition)

¼ tsp fresh thyme leaves

5 ripe tomatoes

Bring everything except the tomatoes to the boil in a wide pan with 120 ml water and boil for 4 minutes. While it's cooking cut each tomato into quarters, then cut out the seeds and the membranes with a knife, reserving them. Add the petals (quarters) to the boiling syrup, gently stirring as you do so, turn the heat off and then leave them to go cold. Peel their skins off using your fingers (reserve the skin), place the petals into a container and strain over just enough syrup to cover them. Keep in the fridge for up to 4 days.

Tomato ginger syrup

This syrup is also lovely drizzled over fried eggs and goat's cheese on toast, and on grilled pork chops.

Place the reserved skins back into the syrup. Chop the seeds and membranes quite fine with a knife and add this too. Bring back to the boil then simmer for 10–15 minutes until the syrup has thickened and become glossy. Pass through a fine sieve into a clean bowl. This will keep covered in the fridge for 3 weeks.

Thai-flavoured poached peaches with cashew caramel mascarpone

As I was writing this book I realised I use chilli in quite a few of my desserts. It's the combination of fruity sweetness and the bite of chilli that appeals to me. You can opt not to use it and the dessert will still be lovely, but it will be missing that special something. The cashew caramel mascarpone is really good and is also lovely served with a steamed pudding or a wedge of fig and walnut tart (see page 256). It was in India that I first overdosed on cashew nuts. Although a native of Brazil, it must have been the Portuguese traders who settled in Goa who introduced them. They'd always been a really expensive delicacy when I was growing up in New Zealand, but in India, and in Goa in particular, they were reasonably priced, fresh and delicious. There was also a not-so-nice liqueur made from them, or their fruit, so perhaps it was actually that that I had too much of. To this day, however, I can never stop at just a handful of them – I usually eat them until there are none left, which isn't a good look.

For 6

6 ripe peaches
2 thumbs of ginger, peeled and thinly sliced
1 stalk lemongrass, discard 2 outer layers, thinly sliced
½ red chilli, sliced
2 kaffir lime leaves
30 ml (2 Tbsp) lime juice
150 ml runny honey
200 g sugar
80 g cashew nuts, toasted
150 g mascarpone
100 ml double cream or whipping cream

Using a small, sharp knife, score an X 3 cm long into one end of the peaches, barely cutting into the flesh – this will help you peel it later. Place the ginger, lemongrass, chilli, lime leaves, lime juice, honey and 150 g of the sugar into a pot wide enough to hold all the peaches in one layer – don't crowd them. Add 2 litres of water. Bring to the boil then simmer for 10 minutes. Gently drop the peaches in off a slotted spoon and bring back to a rapid simmer. Place a cartouche (see page 147) on top of the peaches and poach until cooked – you should be able to poke a toothpick into the centre easily. From time to time, give them a tumble to help them cook evenly. Once they're cooked, turn the heat off, carefully take them out of the liquid and plunge into a bowl of icy water. Leave for a few minutes then peel the skin from them and return to the still hot liquid and leave to cool in it. Once cooled they can be kept covered in the fridge for 5–6 days, so long as they float in their liquid.

Reserve a dozen cashews and split them in half, then roughly chop the remainder. Place the remaining 50 g of sugar in a heavy-based pan and place over a moderate heat. Cook until it melts and then turns golden brown. You can stir it gently once it begins to melt, but go gently or it can caramelise. If nothing is happening to the sugar turn the heat up until it does. Stir in the chopped nuts then tip onto a baking tray lined with non-stick paper, spread it out, being careful not to burn yourself with the hot caramel, and leave it to go cold. Carefully pour a litre of hot water into the pot and leave it to simmer for a few minutes – this helps when it comes time to clean it. Once the cashew caramel has cooled and set, break it up by bashing with a rolling pin or similar and mix into the mascarpone. Then mix in the cream and stir briskly to incorporate it all.

To serve: Place the reserved cashews into your serving dishes, add a peach and some of the poaching liquor and serve the cashew mascarpone on the side. I also like to serve extra runny cream as well.

Coconut tapioca with avocado, mango & yuzu sorbet, passion-fruit mango salsa & sesame praline

Avocado, mango & yuzu sorbet

This recipe contains, admittedly, a lot of steps. However, the finished dessert is sensational and has been on the menu at my restaurants in Auckland and London and our guests are always really amazed by it. The sorbet actually started out as a salsa to serve on top of poached brill, but it was way too mushy, so I decided to blend it up and churn it to see what would happen. A few tweaks here and there and it became a sorbet. The *yuzu* juice I use is salted – the salt helping extract the juice from the fruit. The salt is an unexpected twist for most people but it also makes it quite moreish. You can use grapefruit or lime juice instead if you can't find yuzu. Glucose is added to the sorbet syrup to prevent ice crystals forming, and if you can't find that then simply add 2 Tablespoons runny honey instead and another 20 g of white sugar. The mango and avocado should be fully ripe and blemish-free for this to taste spectacular.

For 12

120 g white sugar

50 g glucose syrup

1 avocado

1 mango

1 thumb of ginger, peeled and thinly sliced against the grain

40 ml (2 Tbsp + 2 tsp) salted yuzu juice

Place the sugar and glucose into a pot with 180 ml water and slowly bring to the boil, stirring to dissolve the sugar. Boil for 1 minute then leave it to cool down completely.

Cut the avocado in half and remove the stone, then scoop out the flesh and place in a bar blender. Peel the mango, cut the flesh away from the stone and place it in the blender. Add the ginger to the blender along with the yuzu juice. Pour in the sugar syrup and blend it all together really well. Pass through a sieve into a clean bowl then churn in an ice-cream maker and freeze.

Coconut tapioca

50 g tapioca

40 g caster sugar

250 ml coconut cream or coconut milk

Cook the tapioca the same way as you do for the plum tapioca on page 240. Once cooked and drained, place in a bowl. Bring the sugar to the boil with 80 ml water and boil for 1 minute, then add the coconut cream and bring back to the boil. Pour this over the tapioca and mix it in well. Leave to cool down, then cover and place in the fridge and leave for at least 6 hours, stirring occasionally. The tapioca will swell up and thicken the coconut cream.

Sesame praline

3 Tbsp caster sugar
1 tsp toasted sesame seeds

Line a baking tray with non-stick baking parchment or a silicon pastry mat. Place the sugar in a small dry frying-pan (a non-stick omelette pan works really well) over moderate–high heat. Keep a close eye on it and eventually the sugar will begin to melt. At this point it's okay to stir it gently to make sure it begins to melt evenly. Once it becomes a caramel colour, stir in the sesame seeds. Take off the heat, then very carefully make shapes on the baking sheet pouring the hot caramel off a spoon. Leave the shapes to cool, then store between sheets of non-stick paper in an airtight container.

Passion-fruit mango salsa

2 ripe passion-fruit
½ ripe mango - use the gorgeous Alphonso mangos when they're in season
4 mint leaves, shredded

Make this no more than an hour beforehand to keep it fresh. Cut the passion-fruit in half and scoop out the seeds. Peel the mango and cut the flesh off in two 'cheek' shapes. Cut into small dice, then mix with the passion-fruit and the shredded mint.

To serve: Use either a lovely bowl or a martini glass. Place the mango salsa in the bottom, spoon on the coconut tapioca then scoop the sorbet on and garnish with a sesame praline.

The combination of figs and walnuts always makes me think of Turkey, as it produces some of the finest of both ingredients. On one of my first visits to Turkey we headed to a town called Gümüslük at the tip of the Bodrum Peninsula. Gümüslük is a fishing village which has been frequented by artists for years, but these days it has become something of a tourist mecca, which is always a shame but inevitable. However, the fish restaurants that line the small foreshore serve some of the best fish in the region and at one of these restaurants they also served a wonderful dessert of grilled walnuts and halva. It was literally sesame halva crumbled over walnut halves, sprinkled with a little sugar and water and then grilled. The walnuts were superb and the whole dish was inspiring. Back in Istanbul we bought the sweetest juiciest figs ever, and ate them with a walnut paste and *kaymak* – a rich buffalo-milk-type clotted cream – and my favourite ever dairy product.

This will make 1 tart, large enough for 8 good portions

Fig & walnut tart with tamarind & maple syrup ice cream

120 g butter, softened to room temperature

120 g unrefined caster sugar, plus 1 tsp extra

2 eggs

2 Tbsp flour

2 tsp ground ginger

pinch of salt

10 ml (2 tsp) vanilla extract

170 g lightly toasted walnut halves

1 lined 24-26-cm fluted, loose-bottomed tart shell, not blind baked, see page 257

6 figs (they must be really ripe)

Preheat oven to 180 °C. Cream the butter and sugar in a bowl using a wooden spoon, or blitz them together in a food processor. Beat in the eggs, one at a time – the mixture may look like it has curdled, but don't worry, it'll come together. Sieve the flour, ginger and salt and stir this in. Mix in the vanilla. Reserve 12 walnut halves, finely chop the remainder and mix these in, then tip the filling into the uncooked tart shell and press it flat. Cut the figs in half lengthways and press them into the mixture then tuck the reserved walnut halves, which you've broken into two, in as well. Sprinkle the reserved sugar over the fig cavities.

Place the tart on a baking tray and bake in the lower centre of the oven for 50 minutes. The tart is ready when the rim of the pastry has turned the colour in the photograph. If for some reason your tart filling or fruit looks like it's burning, then place a sheet of foil, the same size as the tart, on top.

Take from the oven and leave to cool on a cake rack before removing from the tin.

To serve: Cut a wedge of tart and sit it on a plate with a scoop of ice cream on top. The tart can be eaten warm or at room temperature.

Sweet shortcrust pastry

150 g unsalted butter, taken from the fridge 20 minutes beforehand and cut into 1-cm cubes
¼ tsp fine salt
90 g icing sugar, sifted
30 g finely ground almonds or walnuts or hazelnuts
1 egg
250 g white flour, sifted

Place the butter and salt in the mixing bowl of a food mixer and, using the paddle mixer, beat on medium speed until soft and smooth.

Turn the speed to low then mix in the icing sugar. Once incorporated, mix in the ground nuts, then the egg and lastly the flour. The instant the mixture resembles a dough, albeit a loose one, stop mixing. Tip it onto a clean bench and gently bring it together into one mass. Roll into a ball, press flat, divide into two and wrap tightly in plastic wrap. Place in the fridge and leave it to rest for at least 3 hours before rolling out on a lightly floured bench to line your tart shell. Chill the lined tart shell for an hour in the fridge before baking.

To bake blind: Make a cartouche (see page 147) and press this into the chilled pastry shell, then fill to two-thirds with rice, dried pulses or baking beans. Place on a baking tray and bake at 180 °C until the pastry rim turns golden. Take out of the oven and carefully pull the cartouche and its contents out. Patch any tears with extra dough. Put the empty shell back into the oven and bake until it's golden all over.

I prefer to use loose-bottomed tins as they make it easier to remove the cooked tart when finished. Simply sit the tart base on a soup plate and lower the rim to the bench, then slide the tart off the tart base onto a serving plate or board. The dough will keep for 6 days in the fridge.

This will make enough pastry for 2 x 24-cm tart tins

Tamarind & maple syrup ice cream

350 ml double cream
350 ml milk
½ vanilla bean, split lengthways then cut into 6
7 egg yolks
120 ml maple syrup
80-100 g tamarind paste (to taste)

Place the cream, milk and vanilla in a pan and slowly bring to just below boiling point. Put a lid on and leave to infuse for 30 minutes. Whisk the egg yolks and maple syrup together until foamy. Bring the cream back to almost boiling, then slowly pour it onto the yolks, whisking continuously. Pour back into the pan and cook over moderate heat, stirring continuously until it forms a custard. Strain through a fine sieve into a clean bowl and when tepid whisk in the tamarind paste. Leave to cool, then chill in the fridge for a few hours. Churn according to your ice-cream machine instructions.

You will need an ice-cream machine to make this the creamiest, but, failing that, freeze it in a shallow tray, breaking it up as it freezes with a fork. When it's frozen solid, chop it up then whizz it briefly in a food processor until fluffy and freeze it again. If you simply can't make this ice cream, then beat 200 g mascarpone with 50 ml maple syrup, 30 g tamarind paste and 100 ml double cream to form soft peaks and use this instead.

For 1 litre – enough for 2 tarts

Pear, chocolate, hazelnut & wattleseed tarts with wattleseed custard

Wattleseed powder comes from Australia and it has a taste similar to coffee. In fact, in the townships of Northern New South Wales you can buy what most espresso fanatics would consider the biggest insult to the coffee bean – wattleccinos. These are cappuccinos made with soy milk and wattleseed – I think they're great, albeit quite hippie at heart. Commercially, wattleseed is made by roasting and grinding the edible seeds of the acacia tree. Acacias are to be found around the world in temperate climates, but around three-quarters of them are native to Australia. If you can't find the powder then these tarts are also really tasty when made with ground coffee beans instead.

For 8 individual tarts

4 pears, peeled and halved lengthways
½ juicy lemon, sliced into 6
50 g sugar
1 heaped Tbsp ground wattleseed (slightly less if using coffee)
500 g puff pastry
5 egg yolks
80 g chocolate (40-75% cocoa butter), melted
30 g roasted skinless hazelnuts, roughly chopped
250 ml cream
2 Tbsp butter, melted

Preheat oven to 220 °C. Remove seeds from pears using a melon baller or teaspoon and place pears in a pot with the sliced lemon and sugar. Cover with just enough water to immerse the pears. Place a cartouche (see page 147) on top and bring to a boil. Turn to a rapid simmer until the pears are cooked (20 minutes). To test them poke a skewer into one – it should go through easily. Once they're cooked add two-thirds of the wattleseed to the poaching liquid and then leave them to cool.

While the pears are cooking, roll the pastry out into a rectangle 40 x 24 cm. This should be enough for eight pear halves unless your pears are really large, in which case roll it bigger. Beat one egg yolk and brush on the pastry, then place in the fridge until the pears are ready.

Mix the chocolate with the hazelnuts and half the remaining wattle-seed and put to one side. Once cool, take pears out of the syrup, draining any syrup from them, then lay them, cut-side up, on a tray. Fill cavities with the chocolate mixture. Place in the fridge for 20 minutes.

Strain the syrup then reduce it to 150 ml. Add the cream and remaining wattle-seed and bring to a simmer. Whisk the remaining egg yolks then pour on the hot cream, whisking continuously, then return to the pan and cook out to a custard. The lemon in the syrup will thicken the cream quite quickly and it may look like it's going to split, but it won't. Once it's cooked, pass through a sieve into a clean bowl and sit a cartouche on top to prevent a skin forming.

Take the pears and the pastry from the fridge and sit the pears evenly over the pastry, 4 x 2, cut-side facing down. Cut around the pears leaving a 1.5-cm border. Fold the borders in towards the pears to form a ridge then place on a baking tray lined with parchment. Brush the pears and the pastry with the melted butter then bake in the top half of the oven until the pastry is golden (20–25 minutes).

To serve: Place a warm tart on your plates and spoon the custard around it. This is also delicious served with lightly whipped cream to which you've added a little icing sugar and vanilla extract.

Fruit crumbles are a truly great British dessert. In fact, in recent years they are perhaps the only British dish that French foodies have truly taken to with gusto, a previously unspoken loathing of British cuisine being the prevailing opinion of most of our neighbours across the channel. There's something really comforting about a crumble straight from the oven on a cold day, but equally they can be really delicious eaten cold on a hot day – so long as the crumble part is suitably crunchy. In America, they eat cobbler –I have had many in my time, my preferred one being made with blackberries. Cobblers vary in styles though, from a very crumbly topping through to a pie crust made using buttermilk. And these can also be served hot or cold. The common theme in crumbles seems to be a need to combine tart fruit with the sweet crumbly topping, so apples, rhubarb and gooseberries seem obvious choices. However, in this version, it's the sweet-sourness of pineapple and poached quince that works its magic.

For 8–10

Spiced quince & pineapple oat crumble

2 large quince, around 700-800 g in total
250 g white sugar or mild runny honey
6 cardamom, squashed slightly
½ tsp freshly ground black pepper
2-3 cinnamon or cassia quills
1 medium-sized pineapple
250 g flour
100 g pale demerara sugar
⅛ tsp fine salt
230 g butter, chilled, cut into 1-cm dice
80 g rolled oats

Peel the quince, cut into quarters and remove the seeds with either a melon baller or a small knife. Cut the quarters into 2-cm chunks and place in a pot with the white sugar, cardamom, black pepper and cinnamon. Pour on enough hot water to cover the quince by 3 cm, put a cartouche (see page 147) on top and bring to the boil, then turn to a rapid simmer and cook for 30 minutes. Top and tail the pineapple and cut the skin off. Cut lengthways into quarters then cut out the core and discard. Cut the flesh into 1-cm dice and stir into the quince, put the cartouche back in place, bring to the boil again, then turn to a simmer and cook for another 15 minutes. Take the cartouche off and cook until the syrup has reduced by half, stirring occasionally.

While the fruit is cooking, make the topping. You can rub it all together by hand or use a food processor. Blitz the flour, the demerara sugar and the salt in a food processor for 10 seconds. Keeping the machine running, add 200 g of the butter until it resembles breadcrumbs. Tip into a bowl and mix in the oats.

Turn the oven to 180 °C. Ladle the cooked fruit out into a 2–3 litre ceramic, or non-reactive, roasting dish or pie tin with half the cooking syrup. There will still be quite a lot of syrup left in the pot but you don't want all of it in the dish as it will be too soggy – this can be served warmed up in a jug when you serve the crumble.

Scatter the crumble topping over the fruit and gently level it out with a fork, but don't press it flat. Dot the top with the reserved butter then bake until golden and bubbling – around 40–50 minutes. It makes sense to place the dish on a tray to catch any of the juices that may bubble out as it cooks.

To serve: Simply scoop it out of the dish, drizzle on some extra syrup and serve with cream, ice cream, custard or whatever takes your fancy.

Soy

I am a huge fan of the soy bean's various guises, from the delicate subtlety of freshly made silken tofu, through to the rich saltiness of miso and the crunch and freshness of *edamame* (fresh soy beans). I drink soy milk more than I do regular cow's milk, and I get annoyed with myself if I've run out of tamari (a wheat-free soy sauce, generally made by smaller producers) at home as I think it really does add a wonderful edge to food, especially stews and braises – fermented soy products are credited with being high in the Japanese fifth flavour sensation they call *umami*. When I was growing up the only soy product we knowingly ate was Chinese soy sauce, usually very dark, salty and quite bitter. However, what my family didn't know, as food labelling laws were quite different then, is that soy is used in many processed foods, just like maize and corn, and so we were probably eating it unwittingly in ice cream and margarine, amongst other things, and it's likely that the soap we bathed with may have contained it as soy bean-based oils are prolific in food and commercial usage throughout the Western world.

When I moved to Australia, I really got stuck into soy in a big way. I discovered a love for the flavour and sensation of fermented soy products such as miso, soy sauce (whether it be dark Chinese, rich Japanese *shoyu* or wheat-free *tamari* from Japan) and *tempeh*. I found that soy milk was a brilliant alternative to dairy milk, which had always caused my nose to run, and this meant I could drink café lattes and flat whites and not feel blocked up afterwards. I developed a lasting appreciation for tofu after sampling some freshly made tofu at a wonderful Japanese restaurant and I tried to enjoy the delights of *natto* (a Japanese fermented soy product which looks like lumpy slime). Finally, in 2008, I ate some in Japan with my friends Akiko and Yoshi and I enjoyed it. The one product I've had equal difficulty with is TVP (textured vegetable protein) but I think this is a visual problem based on seeing it formed

into the shape of lamb chops and sausages over 25 years ago. I have no issue with people who choose not to eat meat, but I just can't get my head around a vegetarian or vegan wanting to eat a meat-free product made in the image of a cutlet.

Soy beans originated in central China around 5000 years ago and have been used not just for the production of food and oil. It was discovered early on that if other arable crops were rotated with soy beans (and other legumes), the soil appeared to become enlivened. This is due to the legume family being able to 'fix' nitrogen in the soil. As time moved on, numerous foods were created from the seeds, which grow inside the hairy pods. As the plant moved through Southern and Eastern Asia into Korea, Vietnam and Japan, and into India, Thailand and Burma, soy, soy milk, tofu, *tempeh*, fermented bean curd, salted black beans, fermented yellow beans and so much more came to enter various cuisines. In America (where much of the world's crop is grown) and Europe, soy beans are used in far more subtle ways – mainly for their oil, and the remaining husks and pith are used as stock-feed.

Soy beans are also incredibly nutritious, containing decent amounts of all the essential amino acids required by humans and they provide a great alternative to meat-based protein, which is great for the developing world. They have, however, also come under a lot of criticism. The majority of soy beans grown in the United States are genetically modified, and as such they, and their by-products, cannot be imported into Europe. Also, they are being used in the production of bio fuels, and as such their extensive growth in Brazil is being partly blamed on deforesting the Amazon.

I'll keep eating them though, in all their various unmodified forms, as I think they are one of the wonder-foods of a modern pantry.

At the end of 2009 I will have lived in London for more than 20 years.

By then, I'll be 46 years old. That's quite a chunk of my life to have lived in one city. I truly love this amazingly diverse and bustling metropolis, its parks and open spaces; its extraordinary cultural life; its diversity and potential – and the underground tube system (I think I'm its biggest fan). It really is a privilege to be able to live and work here. Obviously many people, from all around the world, feel similarly. With a population of over 7½ million, London is the largest city in the European Union and provides a home to almost every race and culture existing on the planet.

From a culinary viewpoint, London has just about every ingredient one could ever need, although obviously the more exotic produce has to be imported. Britain's climate isn't conducive to growing produce like mangos and avocadoes, olive trees and rice, coffee and cocoa. But, as weather patterns slowly change, and budding entrepreneurs begin to look at possible new enterprises, it's fascinating to see what is now being harvested right here in England. In Cornwall they are now growing the shrub *Camellia sinensis* and producing fantastic teas at the Tregothnan estate – run by the same family since 1335 – the current incumbent, the Honourable Evelyn Boscawen, and head gardener, Jonathon Jones, looking after the burgeoning tea plantation. It makes complete sense to me that the English, so keen on their tea, should now cultivate it on their own soil. It's only in the last decade that this has come to fruition but its success has been remarkable, with

Tregothnan tea now being exported to the very countries who formerly traded tea to England including China, Japan and India, as well as other countries fortunate enough to be able to import it. As if growing 'local' tea wasn't enough, we're also producing red and white still wines and award-winning sparkling wine (which makes even more sense, as the UK is one of the largest importers of French champagne). I have to say that to be able to drink a glass of world-class fizz or to sip on a cup of tea, both produced here in England, is fantastic.

Last weekend I went to Whitstable, a seaside town in north-east Kent famous for its oysters. Simon, the new man in my life, took me there, along with his wire-haired fox terrier, Harvey. I'd heard plenty about the town over the years from my fellow chefs and friends, many of whom had made the journey there to eat the famous molluscs and walk the pebbly beach which looks out towards the offshore wind farm and kite surfers. What I hadn't realised was that Whitstable had been inhabited for centuries – as far back as the Bronze Age and before. And as recorded in the Domesday Book of 1086, the record of the Great Survey of England commissioned by William the Conqueror, or William the First, it had originally been called Witenestaple. I knew that oysters had been harvested from the coast during Roman times, and legend has it that oysters were shipped from here to London to feed the Roman legions in what was then called Londinium. It was somehow inspiring to know that 2000 years previously, the Romans had been eating the ancestors of the very oysters Simon and I were consuming in 2009 and this fact made me appreciate London and its culinary history even more. The oysters of Old London were inexpensive due to the fact that they grew wild and simply needed harvesting, which is why you'll see them used as 'padding' in old recipes such as beef and oyster pie – the oysters were cheaper than the beef.

Of course, by now you've already discovered the kind of food I love to cook represented in this book. It's based on using ingredients from all around the world. It relies on trying to understand the nature of each of these ingredients then using them in conjunction with others from different sources. Recently, at The Providores, we held a lunch showcasing Spanish strawberries and raspberries, hosted by one of my favourite people Maria José Sevilla, Director of Foods and Wines from Spain at the Spanish Embassy. My brief was to explore the virtues of these berries, and it obviously made sense that I should use them not just for dessert but also for the savoury courses. First up, I made a 'gazpacho' by puréeing tomatoes and raspberries, to which I added lime and ginger juice and seasoning. I sieved out all the seeds and chilled the remaining liquid. Then I made a purée from toasted sourdough bread, olive oil and Greek yoghurt (I know, this isn't sounding good). Finally, I diced a peeled cucumber which I tossed with lemon juice and salt, sliced some spring onion tops into fine rings and toasted tiny croutons of homemade chilli focaccia we had left over in the bread basket. To serve it, I ladled the gazpacho into chilled bowls, dolloped in the bread purée and sprinkled the garnishes on top. The *pièce de résistance* was a good slug of dry *fino* (sherry) drizzled on at the last minute. The end result was brilliant, even if I say so myself! If you'd just eaten the gazpacho on its own, it would have been merely challenging, but the combination of the fruity, tart and slightly tangy soup, together with the earthy, yoghurty bread purée, the textures of the toppings, finished off with the slightly salty and dry *fino* worked a treat on the palate. Another course combined seared yellow-fin tuna sliced over candied beets, topped with a raspberry-infused rice-vinegar and horseradish dressing, served with cubes of chillied strawberry agar jellies. It,

too, was wonderfully playful, but more importantly, a dish which was seriously good to eat.

After my 20 years in London town, I can't help but look at what I create now and compare it with what I was cooking previously. When Michael and I arrived in 1989, fresh from New Zealand, the food I was cooking was in many ways 'stifled' – first at a Kensington restaurant called Launceston Place, then at Carla Tomasi's Friths in Soho. Not that it was inferior in any way, but as I had been running the kitchen at The Sugar Club in Wellington for two and a half years prior to that with total creative control, it was quite difficult to cook other people's food when their philosophy was poles apart from my own. I remember on my first day at Launceston Place one of the chefs asked me to fillet the turbot. I asked what turbot was (a fish we don't have in New Zealand) and he simply rolled his eyes, said he thought I'd been a head chef, and stated that obviously restaurants in New Zealand served dreadful food. I thought 'Oh my God. It's true what I've heard – British kitchens are full of arrogant, ignorant chefs.' Of course, both sides were wrong in several respects, but it was an interesting insight into what some people from a different food culture might think of my homeland, a country that I considered to be advanced and forward-thinking, albeit with a scarcity of ingredients. In my third week at Launceston Place, I put on a starter of lobster and soy consommé that I served with poached lobster eggs (previously attached to the body), pickled cucumber, wakame seaweed and chives. The head chef, Charlie, thought it was great, but the next week I resigned in order to find a kitchen where, for example, chefs didn't immediately view waiters as the enemy – too often the norm in London kitchens.

Friths was less hierarchical, and the food we cooked was more my style, although firmly rooted in the Italian kitchen with influences from North Africa – very exciting, but still I had to conform to Carla's principles. Next up was a stint at Wodka – a Polish restaurant which was actually just down the street from Launceston Place. Here my brief was to revamp the menu and make it more appealing to the lucrative 'ladies who lunch' crowd. After a few weeks there, putting on dishes like grilled vegetables with homemade spinach linguine, I realised that what the regulars really wanted was simple Polish food, so I left, happy to have picked up some great ideas from the friendly Polish chefs who worked there. Thus began my journey through many London kitchens, only working in those where I could have some say in the menu, and avoiding establishments where ginger, fish sauce and coconut milk might seem out of place. I also made a rule that I would never put up with angry chefs, abusive managers or kitchens where the food was dull. A woman I'd met at a party, Margot Clayton, was recruited to be head chef at a brand-new restaurant called First Floor on Portobello Road and she asked me to come and help. It was a brilliant time. The menu changed every day (something I'd never experienced before) and the staff, both in the kitchen and back and front of house, was an eclectic mix of both highly skilled restaurateurs and others with no experience at all: models, actors, musicians, ceramicists and everything else in between. At the same time, I started working for the Govett family who owned an estate in Wiltshire called Fosbury Manor. This was a wonderful period for me, as I'd work at First Floor four to five days a week (and then later at a gay, private members' club called Embargo – which was hilarious and frustrating in equal measure), then drive to Fosbury early afternoon on Fridays and cook for Penny Govett, her family and friends over the weekend. One highlight was cooking for the owners of the legendary Petrus Vineyard. That weekend Penny had told me to buy the best of the best produce from Harrods, and to cook a simple menu all weekend so that the wine wouldn't have to compete with my food. My friend Diana Stoll was over from New York, and as she'd trained to be a chef in Paris, I begged her to come and help – which was the best thing I could have done as she has a wonderful nose, palette and taste buds. At the Harrods meat counter I bought black-legged French chickens and gorgeous British beef rib-eye. I was, however, most proud when I asked the butcher for his best lamb and he told me it was from New Zealand!

My next major, long-term job was cooking at another private members' club, Mayfair's Green Street, for two and a half years in the early '90s. This was also a great job, but initially the clientele were not big eaters, my food simply being an adjunct to their evening's more eclectic pursuits. However, it was always exciting to stand in the bar at the end of the night and have Lucien Freud buy me a whisky. One afternoon I came upstairs to see Leigh Bowery painting Damien Hirst's genitals for an art project as he sat atop the bar. Damien's pickled sheep have never looked the same since. Jade Jagger held an exhibition of her daisy paintings, almost a hundred of them, and Brad Pitt and Antonio Banderas had dinner with their friends. Artists and rock stars and all of London's A-listers ate there and the time flew by in a wonderful haze, far from my Wanganui roots. But ultimately, I knew that I needed to work in a restaurant where the main draw for the customers was the quality and creativity of the kitchen.

During this period I helped my friends Margot (from First Floor days) and Fergus Henderson, now married, during the launch of their restaurant The French House which sat above the best pub in Soho. The restaurant remains, but they have both since moved on. They paid me for my time, but I used the money to buy much-needed equipment for their fledgling kitchen. Fergus had enjoyed eating my food during the Green Street days, but my slowly evolving cooking style was a total anathema to him and the style of cuisine he was likewise evolving in his own quiet way. St John, one of London's most lauded restaurants, is the culmination of his culinary philosophy, much in the same way as The Providores is the culmination of mine. The only time I ever saw Fergus look scared was when I told him, jokingly, that I'd use some coriander and coconut cream in a dish that I was going to serve in The French House. It was a fun period. There were two people working in the kitchen at the same time who have since become incredibly talented chefs in their own right, operating their own businesses, Anna Hansen (The Modern Pantry) and Skye Gyngell (Petersham Nurseries). At different times, both women came to work with me at Green Street and both have been part of my London culinary life.

The second incarnation of The Sugar Club, after Vivian Street in Wellington, New Zealand, opened on All Saints Road in Notting Hill in 1995. Ashley and Vivian chose the site because it was affordable – the road being one of the most heavily policed in Europe at the time. The three crack dens located within one block of the restaurant probably helped to keep the rent down. At last I was able to bring all the culinary ideas I'd been working on together in one kitchen, and focus solely on serving creative, tasty food. It opened with a bang, with food critics who'd eaten at Green Street keen to see what I'd do when I left the restrictive environment of the members' club. Foodies and celebrities (a great mix to spread the word and keep the tables full) flocked to us almost from the day we opened the door, and within months we had the likes of Calvin Klein and Ralph Lauren saying it was their favourite place to eat. In the year we opened, we won two prestigious food awards in the same week: *Time Out* magazine's Best Modern British restaurant, and an Eros award from *The Evening Standard* for Best Pacific Rim restaurant. I became confused and wondered what I was actually cooking. I thought it was simply my own personal style of food, which had been a very gradual evolution. I then read about a chef in America called Norman Van Aiken whose cuisine was described as Fusion and I decided to use that term. During the next two and a half years I wrote my first cookbook, created menus for Air New Zealand and wrote monthly articles for *New Zealand House & Garden* magazine. I appeared on numerous television shows, touted as a chef cooking a new style, 'Fusion Food', and found that, generally, I was as busy out of the kitchen as I was in it. The neighbourhood tidied up its act (although losing some of its gritty character along the way), and I decided that I needed to move on to something new over which I would have more control – and not just in the kitchen. However, Ash and Viv wanted to move the restaurant into the West End and asked me to help them, which I did, agreeing to stay just one year. It was a great experience, moving a brand that I'd helped build into a new venue, one much larger, and much more demanding. Again, we seemed to have the Midas touch – always full with happy customers and the critics loving us (with notable exceptions). My year sped by.

In 1994, before All Saints Road opened, my sister Tracey, who helped me cook some of the recipes in this book, was diagnosed with acute myeloid leukaemia. In order for her to find a donor for a bone-marrow transplant, one of the best ways to fight the disease, all of our family were tested and it turned out that I was a near-perfect match. So in 1995, after a year or so of planning, I headed off to Melbourne for the operation. Much happened for Tracey and her partner Roesheen, and for both families in the 10 weeks that I was there, but eventually I headed back to London and Tracey began her remarkable recovery. Three years later whilst I was cooking at the Soho Sugar Club, Karen Linfield who worked at the Hammersmith Hospital, wrote to me asking if I'd consider donating a cookbook for a charity. I contacted her and when I found out it was a charity working for leukaemia, I explained my own connection with the illness. That conversation was the start of a chain of events which ultimately brought me into contact with Hannah Lewis and Bettina Bradfield who were heading a charity committee (now called Leuka) involved in raising funds for Hammersmith Hospital – one of the world's leading oncology centres. Chris Corbin, then co-owner of the Ivy restaurant group (now co-owner of The Wolseley restaurant), came on board along with chefs Sally Clarke, Mark Edwards from Nobu and Mark Hix from the Ivy group, along with many others and between us we managed to bring my idea to fruition. 'Who's Cooking Dinner?' is an event where each attending chef cooks their own individual four-course dinner for 10 guests, served with their own chosen wines. So instead of guests attending a dinner where everyone eats exactly the same meal, ours feel they're attending a special dinner-party for just 10 people. For 10 years now, we've had 19–21 guest chefs working side by side in the one kitchen, something unheard of previously. I think this is probably the event I'm most proud of in my culinary career – especially as we have raised over £3,000,000 for the charity, all of which has been donated for the building and running of the Catherine Lewis Centre. I've also taken this event to New Zealand where it's called 'Dining For A Difference', working with Pru Etchevery and the team from SKYCITY. We held our second dinner in April 2009 and all monies raised went to the New Zealand Leukaemia and Blood Foundation.

The Providores and Tapa Room opened on Marylebone High Street in August 2001 and finally I was a co-owner and director of my own restaurant – something I'd worked long and hard at achieving. Fortuitously for Michael and me, a wonderful woman called Annie Smail came on board as an investor and partner. She and her husband, Derek, have proved to be not only wonderful supporters of the business but also great friends alongside us on The Providores' journey. At the same time we asked Tarik and Savaş from Istanbul if they'd consider coming in as investors and partners and they jumped at the opportunity too. Anna Hansen (of Green Street days) and Jeremy Leeming joined us as our hands-on business partners, with Anna and me running the kitchen together, and so began an adventure for all of us. The restaurant is really two quite distinct spaces. The ground floor café wine bar, the Tapa Room (named after the huge Rarotongan bark-paper 'tapa' cloth which hangs on the wall) is open all day, seven days a week from breakfast through to the ever-changing menu available from noon to late in the evening. The Providores situated on the first floor is only open for lunch (brunch on weekends) and dinner. It is much more focused on fine dining - albeit with the casual approach to fine dining that we like to experience ourselves. We have one of Europe's largest New Zealand wine lists, with over 80 bins, and we serve some of the best coffee in London (our regulars say it is the best!). Our staff are key to its success and we've been lucky to have had our manager, Scunthorpe's famous daughter, Sophie Uddin, working with us from our opening in 2001; our head chef Miles Kirby from Wellington, also with us almost from the start and sous chef Cristian Hossack from Marton (an even smaller town than my own Wanganui) for over five years. Our assistant manager Tracey Te Anini from Palmerston North and our bar manager Jessica Peden from Central Otago make up the rest of the management team that have helped keep us at the top of our game. Anna left the business in 2005 and runs her own restaurant The Modern Pantry in Clerkenwell these days, whilst Jeremy moved back to New Zealand in 2008 to focus on his first love, jewellery-making. So these days it's Michael and me, along with our fantastic team, with Annie, Tarik and Savaş in support mode, running the show.

And for me - what does the culinary world have in store? Well, fortunately, it just seems to keep evolving and getting better with new ideas, new ingredients and new inspiration. A new chef may arrive in our kitchen and before long they talk of a dish their family has always made which gets us all thinking. Or Miles comes back from Germany and introduces a new spiced duck dish that uses a kitchen favourite - mayonnaise! Cristian harvests and pickles green walnuts from the Grand Union Canal and creates a tasty new starter with them, while Martine Cadet, our pastry chef, revamps her delicious berry trifle with a twist! Our kitchen is founded on egalitarian ideals and I encourage everyone to suggest dishes for the ever-changing menus, and we never run out of inspiration.

But lately I've also been discovering the various foods to be found in London's East End with Simon and Harvey. Whether it be the famous bagels or Bangladeshi Cuisine on Brick Lane, Spanish tapas on Columbia Road, or Vietnamese noodles on Kingsland Road, the areas of Hackney, Shoreditch and Dalston have become a whole new area of discovery for me. On Broadway Market near London Fields we've bought plump fresh plaice, organic celeriac and beetroot, Spanish olives, London smoked salmon, English fudge and Turkish baklava. At Dalston market you can buy goat heads and plantain from the Caribbean traders, whilst absorbing the chaos of the market and marvelling at the fact that this is in fact England and not Kingston, Jamaica. This sunny Spring weekend we bought tubs of aromatic English herbs (as well as nasturtiums, tomatoes and sweet peas) from Columbia Road Flower Market (teeming with people on Sundays) to plant in the garden, then used them to flavour a huge rib-eye that we roasted on the bone, bought from The Ginger Pig butcher near Victoria Park. These areas are rich with the influences and history of the local Cockneys and other British folk, as well as Jewish, Huguenot, Bangladeshi, Vietnamese, Pakistani, Caribbean and migrants from many other cultures. People from so many walks of life and of varying ethnic ancestry, manage to live together - mostly in harmony - and all contribute to the patchwork of London's culinary life, whether it be the local grocer shops, the market stalls, restaurants or a mother or father cooking the family's special Friday night 'tea'. This culinary diversity gives a great insight into London's unique vibrancy and energy as a whole. It never lessens, it never runs out, and for this we are all the more richer.

Corn

First things first: corn and maize are the same plant – but I have to admit, it does get a bit confusing knowing which part is the ear, what is a cob or kernel and whether corn bears fruit. The ear and the cob are actually the same thing and the kernels, grains or fruit are also the same thing with differing names. This confusion is largely due to whether it's being grown in the USA, Europe or the Antipodes. My family grew a lot of corn in our garden in New Zealand as it was an easy vegetable to grow, so long as it was kept watered, and it grew so quickly that you could see it change from day to day, which impressed me as a kid.

As a kid I wasn't that keen on corn-on-the-cob, I have to say, I much preferred canned sweetcorn heated up and spooned on buttered toast. I found it almost dessert-like in its character and as I have a sweet tooth this appealed to me. The only way we ever cooked corn was to boil the cobs and rub salted butter over them, but I found them too tactile and fibrous, and too much hassle. Years later, travelling though India I discovered the joys of eating grilled corn. It was a revelation and it's how I prefer to cook fresh corn to this day.

During my early days of being a chef I was taught to make polenta the correct way by my Italian boss Adriana Rogalsky. We never used instant polenta, we always used a 'slow-cook' brand, and it would take about 40 minutes of slow stirring to cook it until it was ready. On one of the menus at Rogalskys, Adriana's husband Tony and I made a terrine of polenta that we mixed with poached kidneys, sweetbreads and livers. We let it cool down in the terrine and set, then we sliced and grilled it till crispy – it was a fantastic dish.

As a young apprentice I also became aware of the ingredients corn oil and corn syrup. These were hard to find and rarely used in New Zealand and Australia, but whenever you read an American cookbook, especially a dessert book, they would always be listed.

North America grows more corn than any other country these days and that's probably not so surprising, as corn as we know it originated just a little further south around Mexico and Central America, domesticated between 6000 and 9000 years ago. It seems that it was selectively bred and eventually its importance as a carbohydrate in the locals' diet was recognised by the various people living in that part of the world. It spread north into the USA and Canada and from there, as Europeans began discovering these parts of the world it made its way to Europe, then on to Asia, Africa and anywhere where the growing conditions were right. Like soy beans, corn is used in many different foods and also for bio-fuel production as well as being used in the production of plastic and fabrics. And like soy beans, the genetic modification of corn has given it something of a bad rap. However, one of the good things that corn is made into is bourbon whisky – after being fermented and distilled to produce grain alcohol. Masa flour, corn flour treated with lime, is used in the production of Mexican tortillas, and hominy grits, which taste rather like bland porridge or polenta, is something I still attempt to enjoy.

Last week I was in New York and ate one of my all-time favourite dishes at Café Habana on Prince Street in Nolita. They grill whole corn cobs then smother them with melted cheese, chilli powder and lime. It's always exactly the same - messy to eat, utterly delicious and very tactile. Try making grilled corn salsa by oiling the cobs and grilling them until they blacken a little. Then cut the kernels off, mix with lots of finely diced red onion, lime juice and coriander, add as much red chilli as you can bear and use it to smother over roast pork or grilled mackerel. This sweet and sour salsa is simply one of many tasty things to do with this wonderful cereal.

Glossary

Ajowan – sometimes called Indian cumin. Small, pale brown seeds with a thyme-like flavour.

Akudjura – this might best be called a native Australian 'bush tomato'. We buy in our akudjura dried and coarsely ground.

Amaranth – a salad green, although we often use one called 'red amaranth' which is red and green. The food of the Incas – an incredibly complete food, very nutritious.

Anchovy – a small fish, the main diet of Mediterranean-caught tuna. When the anchovies 'run' the fishermen know the tuna will follow. Anchovies are mostly salted and preserved, but you can also get lovely ones in olive oil. Italy, Spain and France are the best producers and Ortiz anchovies from Spain are considered the best of all.

Atari goma – goma is Japanese for sesame seed, and this is much like tahini – sesame seed paste. It can be made from either white or black sesame seeds.

Barley – the oldest cultivated cereal grain in Europe and the Middle East (it may actually even be the oldest, possibly pre-dating rice). Malt is made from it and it helps your body to break down cholesterol.

Berbere – a traditional Ethiopian spice mix used when cooking dried beans and lentils. The mix varies but a standard combination is sweet paprika, cinnamon, turmeric, ginger, coriander seed, nutmeg and cloves.

Black cardamom – despite its name and the fact that its flavour has similar characteristics to the green cardamom we are all familiar with, it is not a member of the cardamom family (known as false cardamom). Its flavour has a more medicinal quality and traditionally it is used only in savoury preparations.

Bok choy / pak choy / choy sum – choy or choi are very loose translations of 'cabbage' in Chinese although these greens can be eaten cooked or raw. They have juicy stems and soft leaves.

Borlotti beans – an Italian bean, usually bought dried much in the same way as butter beans. However, they have increasingly become available fresh, and they have a striped red skin once podded.

Buckwheat – a plant related to rhubarb and sorrel, it isn't actually a cereal, it is a seed. It is very hardy and can grow in cold areas with bad soil – so it has been used in parts of Japan and Eastern Europe where other crops can't survive. A staple in soba noodles (Japan) and blinis (Russia) and it produces buckwheat flour.

Candle nuts – also known as kemiri nuts, these are native to the Moluccas Islands, Malaysia and the Pacific. It's a hard oily nut which is mostly used in Malaysian and Indonesian cookery to thicken sauces and curries. Macadamias make a good substitute but they are sweeter than candle nuts.

Cassava – a root vegetable, grown in tropical climates, also known as yuca. Tapioca is made from this.

Cavolo nero – a Tuscan vegetable meaning black cabbage. Long dark green leaves with a chewy central 'spine' that is removed before cooking.

Celeriac – a root vegetable, round in shape, that can be eaten raw or cooked, and that has a nutty, celery-like flavour.

Chard / Swiss chard/ ruby chard – known in NZ and Australia as silverbeet. Chard is a type of 'green' vegetable, with a white stem and green leaves. However, ruby chard has a mixture of red and green colouring and is generally small-leaved and used in salads rather than cooking as a vegetable.

Chipotle – a type of smoked chilli. – wrinkly and moderately hot.

Chorizo – a spicy pork sausage from Spain, flavoured with pimenton (smoked paprika). There are two basic styles of chorizo – those that are cooked (perilla) and those that are sliced – much like a salami.

Curry leaf – these look like very small bay-leaves, they come from trees in Southern India and have a nutty taste.

Daikon – also called mooli or white radish. It has the taste of a regular radish, but can grow up to 60 cm long.

Den miso – miso that has been cooked with mirin, sugar and sake. Fairly sweet – but also earthy. Used as a marinade or in dressings.

Dukkah – an Egyptian nutty spice and seed blend – often used as a dip for bread that's been dipped in olive oil. Traditionally containing hazelnuts or chickpeas, sesame seeds, pepper, coriander seeds, cumin and salt.

Edamame – fresh soy beans. We serve them steamed in the pod and sprinkled with salt.

Enari / inari – we use this term for the deep-fried tofu pockets which are used in Japan to serve inarizushi in. The Japanese tend to call them aburage or atsuage.

Enoki – a type of mushroom, originating in Japan. Looks like a short thin white knitting needle with a cap on.

Feijoa – fruit native to South America, and also known as a pineapple guava due to its pineappley perfume and guava-like texture. Every New Zealander will have happy memories of eating these delicious, aromatic and perfumed fruit which grow prolifically throughout the country.

Fennel – sometimes called Florence fennel in Australia, this is the bulb of the fennel plant. It has a sweet anise flavour, is pale green white in colour and has a fine frond / feathery 'leaf'. Can be eaten raw or cooked.

Five-spice – a Chinese / Cantonese spice mixture made from ground star anise, fennel seeds, cloves, Sichuan pepper and cinnamon (or cassia bark). There are several versions but this is the most authentic. It's said to represent the five basic flavours of Chinese cuisine: sweet, sour, bitter, pungent and salty.

Galangal – related to ginger, this rhizome is native to Asia, possibly China down to SE Asia. The Chinese call it blue ginger, and it has a flavour like ginger and white pepper crossed. It was used in Europe in the 13th century in a dried form for medicinal purposes. We tend to cook with it, using the fresh root rather than the dried powder.

Green tea noodles – a wheat-based noodle using green tea for flavour and colour.

Gremolata – a mixture of chopped lemon zest, garlic and parsley. Usually served with the classic Italian dish of osso bucco (braised veal shin). We also use preserved lemon.

Guindilla chillies – pickled long green Spanish chilli, mild to hot.

Habanero chilli – a very hot chilli with a subtle caramel flavour. We make a chocolate ice cream with it.

Hapuku – a fish native to New Zealand – flaky, sweet and a little oily – very delicious.

Harissa – a fiery chilli paste from North Africa – Morocco, Algeria, Tunisia and Libya. It can be as simple as ground chillies, although it is also made with the addition of garlic, caraway, coriander, cumin and olive oil. There is also a variety made that is scented with rose petals. Moroccan cous cous is always served with a dish of harissa to the side.

Harusame noodles – harusame is a Japanese term meaning 'spring rain' due to their appearance. They are clear round noodles. They are wheat-free and made from various kinds of starch including mung bean, sweet potato, cornflour, soy bean and potato. The kind we use are made from potato.

Hijiki – a black seaweed harvested in the sea off Japan. Like all sea-weeds, it has a rich mineral taste.

Hokey pokey – like feijoas, any New Zealander will remember this flavoured ice cream from their childhood. Made by stirring honeycomb through vanilla ice cream. We make our honeycomb from golden syrup instead of honey.

Jamon – the Spanish word for ham.

Jerusalem artichokes – they are neither related to artichokes nor from Jerusalem. Native to colder northern America and Canada, they were the staple diet of the Indians of these parts. Related to the sunflower (the Italian for sunflower is girasole – which sort of sounds like Jerusalem), this is most likely where the name came from, as well as the fact they taste a little like artichoke hearts.

Jicama – also called yam bean in Chinese shops. This dirt-coloured skinned 'vegetable' has a crunchy texture and watery taste (if there is such a thing). A little sweet, great in 'slaws' and salad.

Jus – a reduced meat stock.

Kaffir lime – a wrinkly lime of little juice from South-East Asia. The lime leaf is the most commonly used part of the plant.

Kataifi pastry – a Greek pastry in origin (in Turkish it's kadaif) but used around the Aegean. This is a pastry that looks like very fine vermicelli, made from wheat. Mostly used in desserts, one of the best being a rolled-up pastry filled with pistachio nuts soaked in sugar honey syrup.

Kelp – a type of seaweed. Bull kelp is one of the fastest growing plants in the world and grows incredibly tall. Will only grow in unpolluted waters.

Kohlrabi – a vegetable that resembles an upside-down jellyfish. Can be eaten raw, but is usually cooked. It's related to the wild mustard plant and tastes a bit like broccoli stem.

Kombu seaweed – a member of the kelp family, kombu is a wide-leafed seaweed that is primarily used to make the most famous Japanese stock called dashi (which also has bonito flakes – a type of tuna – in it). Kombu is most popular in Okinawan cuisine, but is used all over Japan, as well as being an important ingredient in parts of China and Korea. We also use it when cooking our dried beans as it speeds up the cooking process as well as adding nutrients.

Kumara – a sweet potato native to New Zealand, but most likely originating in South America. It was taken to NZ by the

Polynesians from across the Pacific around 600 years ago. Initially these were very small tubers, but once the colonials arrived in NZ and began selective breeding, they became the fat sweet potatoes we are familiar with today. Very rich in taste with purple skins (although there are now varieties that have orange and golden-yellow flesh).

Labne / labneh – a staple of the Lebanese kitchen. Plain yoghurt is mixed with salt, then put into a calico bag and suspended – excess moisture drips off and the yoghurt becomes quite firm. It's then either rolled into balls and kept in olive oil, or used as a dip or spread for pita bread, etc.

Laksa – a term that derives from the original Persian word for noodle, laksha (meaning slippery). The soup itself originates in Malaysia and Indonesia, and is usually made with fat rice or wheat noodles and broth, with lots of bits floating in it. It is also made in Singapore from fine vermicelli noodles and coconut milk.

Lemon myrtle – a tree native to Northern New South Wales in Australia. It has a lovely lemon aroma, more like vervain / lemon verbena than lemon. The tree is a lovely evergreen.

Liquorice – a small leguminous plant whose thick roots and underground runners contain a very sweet compound called glycyrrhizin. In its pure form this is 50 times sweeter than ordinary sugar, but the plant also contains bitter substances which partly mask the sweet taste. Its name is a corruption of the original Greek name glycorrhiza, meaning sweet root, which is also an old English name. The root can be dried then chewed as a sweet meat, the extract can be used in savoury preparations, or combined with sugar, water, gelatin, and flour

to give the liquorice used for confectionary.

Macadamia nuts – native Australian nuts that many think actually come from Hawaii. Grown commercially in Hawaii and Australia – mainly Queensland and Northern New South Wales. They're very rich with an extremely hard shell.

Manchego – a firm pasteurised ewe's (sheep's) milk cheese from La Mancha. Probably the most famous of all Spanish cheeses – it's often compared to Italian Pecorino. It has a black-grey or buff-coloured rind with a cross-hatch pattern on the rind – which comes from the baskets these cheeses were traditionally made in.

Manouri cheese – Greek ewes-milk cheese, subtle taste, quite bland.

Manuka honey – a honey native to New Zealand. The bees feast on the pollen of the manuka – a native shrub/tree.

Mascarpone – a fresh Italian cheese made from cream similar to cream cheese, although not as sharp.

Millet – one of the oldest grains known, it was grown during the stone-age in what is now known as Switzerland, and in China over 2700 years ago. It's the worlds sixth most important grain and is a staple food in Africa, India, Japan, Russia, China and Egypt. It is also used as animal feed (often given to budgies) but is nutritional and tasty, with a slight nutty taste and grainy texture.

Miso – a paste made primarily from rice and soya beans, fermented for at least six months. There are many hundreds of varieties and types, some made with the addition of barley or wheat, some red, some dark brown, some sweet, etc.

Mizuna – a type of salad leaf, Asian in origin, slightly mustard tasting, spiky leaves.

Molasses – either a: the caramel component of sugar (caster sugar is bleached and has its molasses removed whereas Muscovado sugar is high in molasses) or b: a sweet rich syrup with a high sugar or fructose content – you can get date or pomegranate molasses.

Monte Enebro – a creamy pasteurised goat's milk cheese from Avila, Spain. It means 'juniper hill' (juniper is used to flavour gin).

Moromi miso – a lumpy, chunky dark miso made from a variety of grains (barley, soy, rice, etc.), but unlike smooth miso it isn't blended or puréed.

Nam jim – a spicy Thai sauce made from red chillies, garlic, fish sauce, coriander root, lime juice and palm sugar pounded together. Used as a dip or a dressing.

Nam phrik num – a dressing based on various salads and dressings found in Asia, this is made from puréed mango, chilli, ginger and other aromatics.

Nigella seeds – a small black seed, somewhat resembling a sesame seed, but thicker skinned. Used in the Middle East in baking and for adding a subtle savoury flavour to foods.

Okra – also known in the West as 'ladies' fingers' due to their pointed finger-like shape, is a ridged green pod with a gummy inside which is what gives okra its special character. It is native to Africa where it is also known as 'gumbo' hence the gumbos of Cajun and Creole cooking where they feature heavily. They are also used extensively in the Middle East. They are also delicious

dusted in spiced flour or battered and deep-fried.

Palm heart – also called heart of palm, palmito or swamp cabbage. It's harvested from the inner core and growing bud of certain palm trees. The outside woody bits are stripped away leaving the tender centre – which has a texture like cooked asparagus. It's expensive as the minute you harvest the palm heart you kill the tree and they take many years to grow. There is now a cultivated palm (Peach Palm) that has as many as 40 stems and so they can be harvested without killing the palm – which has also lowered the price. Grown commercially in Brazil, Ecuador, Costa Rica.

Pancetta – cured Italian or Spanish pork belly. Sliced and cooked like bacon but usually served in a more elegant way. Sometimes smoked, but usually not.

Pandan – the pandanus 'tree', from South East Asia and Northern Australia, has spiky leaves that impart a subtle green colour and distinctive taste used in both savoury and sweet preparations. Typically Thai in character. Known as the 'vanilla' of South-East Asia, not because of its flavour but because of the way and extent to which it is used.

Panizza – a firm set polenta-like mixture, made from cooking chickpea flour with water or stock then pouring into a tray or mould.

Panko – Japanese breadcrumbs. Tend to be larger and have a shredded appearance as opposed to the ground breadcrumbs used in the West.

Parmesan – the Italians call this hard cheese Parmigiano-Reggiano and they are the size of a huge car wheel (a cheaper version, but also delicious, is called Grana Padano). It's a cheese from the regions

of Parma and Reggio Emilia, Italy (Parma ham also comes from Parma too). Traditionally unpasteurised, it has a hint of pineapple to it and well-aged ones have an almost crystal crunch to them.

Pecorino – a cheese from Italy, made from ewe's milk.

Pimientos de Padron – small green peppers, slightly fiery and fresh tasting, deep-fried whole and sprinkled with salt. The best quality come from Gallicia, in Northern Spain.

Piquillo pepper – a red pepper, which is most commonly sold in the UK in a smoked form. It is smoked over beech or oak wood then peeled. Piquillo translates as 'peak' in Spanish due to the shape of the pepper.

Plantain – looks like a large banana, often cooked as a carbohydrate when unripe, but sweet when fully ripe. Never eaten raw.

Polenta – a 'meal' made by grinding dried corn or maize. Italian in origin, it is cooked into a porridge by whisking into boiling stock, water, and sometimes even milk. Usually served as a savoury item either as a thick paste, or left to cool, then sliced, grilled or fried.

Pomegranate – a fruit from the pomegranate tree, native to Iran. Moses even promised the Israelites that they would find pomegranates once they left the desert heading to the promised land – such was its esteem.

Pomegranate molasses – a thick dark syrup made by reducing pomegranate juice slowly over heat. Sharp, sweet and sour tasting, it usually comes from Iran, Turkey and Syria.

Ponzu – a soy-based dipping sauce

that is basically soy and either lemon juice or vinegar. However, you will sometimes find it made with bonito (dried shaved tuna).

Quince – a type of fruit, often called a relative of the pear (I don't think it can be more than a distant second cousin though). Quince always need to be cooked – they take about 90 minutes or more. They have a thick perfumed aroma, with a slightly grainy pear texture. Membrillo is made from quince that have been cooked with a lot of sugar.

Quinoa – (pronounced Keen-waa) a grain grown by the Aztecs and the Incas way back in the Andes. Small and nutty in taste. A member of the corn family and incredibly rich in protein.

Sago – see tapioca.

Samphire – there are two types: rock samphire (also known as sea or true samphire and it's rarer), and marsh samphire (also called glasswort) – they're often confused but actually aren't closely related. Rock samphire grows amongst the rocks and shingle of sea coasts and on cliffs, whilst the latter grows on marshland.

Shichimi togarashi – a very spicy Japanese condiment of chilli, seaweed flakes, sesame seeds and tangerine or orange peel.

Shiitake – a type of mushroom, quite woody / musty-tasting. Often these come dried.

Shimeji mushroom – also called hon-shimeji, these mushrooms come grouped in clumps, they have little caps on longish stalks. Subtle taste with chewy texture.

Shoyu – the most common of the soy sauces, and one that has been enriched with wheat.

Sichuan / Szechuan – these are

both correct ways of spelling the same province in China. It's an area famous for its pepper and spicy food. The pepper has a tongue-numbing effect, and comes from the prickly ash tree.

Skordalia – also spelled 'skorthalia'. It's a Greek sauce of pounded garlic, bread, almonds or walnuts and olive oil. Thickish and used as a dollop rather than a dressing.

Smoked paprika – also called pimenton. Mild to hot red chillies, smoke dried over wood to produce their distinctive taste and aroma.

Soy sauce – a condiment. Steamed soy beans and roasted crushed wheat are mixed with a starter culture and allowed to ferment. Salt is added and then further fermentation is allowed to take place. The end product is soy sauce.

Star anise – the dried small star-shaped fruits of the Illicium verum tree. Its flavour is similar to that of anise as they both share the same essential oil 'anethole'. It is cultivated almost entirely in southern China (which is where it is believed to have originated) as well as a few areas of South-East Asia.

Tahini – a paste made from ground sesame seeds, and occasionally a little oil. Used throughout the Middle East and Japan.

Tamari – a wheat-free soy sauce.

Tapioca – tapioca (and sago) look like fish eggs when cooked – little balls of transparent starch. For the British it represents nursery food and is made from the cassava plant, much in the same way that sago is made from the sago palm.

Tarator – there is some discussion surrounding this sauce. The Turkish and Middle Eastern version often resembles the skordalia of Greece, but it's always made with walnuts. However, it can be a dressing made from tahini, lemon juice and garlic. In Bulgaria, however, it refers to a chilled soup of cucumber, yoghurt, garlic and walnuts, which is in itself almost a version of tzatziki!

Tataki – this word, in Japanese, actually translates as 'pounded' but in modern cooking parlance it is used to denote fish or meat which has been seared in a hot pan, then either left to cook naturally, or plunged into iced water, to stop the flesh cooking any further.

Tomalley – this is the soft goo found in the body cavity of crabs, lobsters and crayfish, and is usually considered a luxury – although for many people it is simply awful. It can be eaten raw, although at the restaurant we cook it with brown crab meat, palm sugar and fish sauce to make a concentrated paste which tastes delicious – but strong. In crayfish the tomalley is green, in crabs it's a little more yellow.

Tomatillo – means 'little tomato'. Also known as husk tomato due to the fact that it has a papery layer on the outside. It's a member of the physalis family, is native to northern South America and was eaten by the Aztecs. It has a fresh, tart flavour which mellows a little when cooked.

Truffle – a tuber growing mainly in France and Italy, located through scent by specially trained pigs or dogs and then dug up carefully. The season is roughly September through to February, but they are weather-dependent. The best-quality white truffles can fetch up to £1,200 a kilogram. Truffles are very aromatic – some love them, some can't stand them.

Umeboshi – Japanese salted and dried 'plums' although they are in fact a type of apricot! They are called plums because of their colour and the fact that their flavour is tart like a plum.

Verjus – a concentrated sour grape juice, historically used by the Romans in cooking. Also, was often used as we now use lemons.

Wagyu beef – a Japanese breed of cattle, the most expensive beef to buy in the world. The only pure herds of wagyu are found in Japan – the Japanese government has banned the export of live cattle – although every wagyu in America and Australia is descended from the only four cattle ever sent abroad to the USA. These were then cross-bred with non-wagyu and whilst they're good, they're not as good as some of the NZ wagyu being produced. The NZ herds from Hawke's Bay are purer due to an intensive breeding programme that has recently been initiated.

Wakame – a seaweed that is quite thin and usually green. If you ever have a miso soup in a Japanese restaurant, it usually has flakes of this in it. Very subtle in flavour.

Wasabi – root from a plant that originally only grew in mountain streams in a small area of Japan, tasting of fierce horseradish.

Wasabi tobikko – tobikko is flying fish roe, very small and crunchy – this version is flavoured with wasabi.

Watercress – a salad green that grows in clean running water (usually in Hampshire if it's from the UK), peppery in taste.

Wattleseed – a native Australian seed from a variety of wattle tree, which is roasted to produce a coffee taste.

Yuzu – a hybrid citrus fruit that is extremely cold-resistant, hence it grows wild in Tibet and central China, but is cultivated in Japan. It isn't very juicy, so they are crushed whole with salt to extract the juice. They have the flavour of mandarin crossed with lime and grapefruit. They are now being grown experimentally at Seresin vineyard in New Zealand. Fingers crossed it's successful, as they're very expensive.

Zamorano – unpasteurised ewe's milk cheese from Zamora, Spain. If it were produced closer to Madrid it could be classified as a Manchego (from La Mancha). It is one of Spain's best hard cheeses. Quite hard, much like a young Parmesan or Manchego – slightly oily. It has a delicious lanolin type aroma and taste.

Zatar / zahtar – a Middle Eastern aromatic spice mixture. There are many variations but all contain toasted white sesame seeds, ground sumac, dried thyme and salt. Sprinkled on meats and vegetables and mixed with olive oil to make a dip for breads.

Recipe Index

I've thoroughly enjoyed every moment of writing this book and taking the travel photos, and there are a few people I'd like to acknowledge. Alison Brook commissioned it through Penguin Group (NZ), and I'd like to thank her along with my editor Andrea Coppock and my designer Athena Sommerfeld. My agent Fiona Lindsay has overseen it, and me, along with her colleague Mary Bekhait. This book is the seventh that photographer Jean Cazals and I have worked on together and he continues to impress me with his representation of my food. Sue Rowlands has sourced some gorgeous props and given the book a mood and a feel that I love. My restaurant teams at The Providores in London and dine in New Zealand have been incredibly supportive – especially Miles and Cristian in the kitchen in London for letting me take a lot of time off the roster. My sister Tracey came over to London to offer support and a helping hand and my family, as ever, have been brilliant. However, it's Michael McGrath who offered me lots of good advice, gave my stories the 'once-over' before sending them off to New Zealand for a final edit and offered his support whilst I worked on the book, and that kept me in check. Lastly, I'd like to dedicate this work to a special man in my life – he knows who he is – may we have countless meals and travels together ahead of us.

First published by Penguin Group (NZ) 2009

First published in the UK in 2009 by
Jacqui Small LLP,
7 Greenland Street
London NW1 0ND

Publisher Jacqui Small
Editorial Manager Kerenza Swift
Jacket designer Maggie Town

ISBN 978 1 906417 36 9

A catalogue record for this book is available from the British Library.

2011 2010
10 9 8 7 6 5 4 3 2

Printed in Singapore